Ed Giddens
Mt 5 '16

CHRIST FOR US
IN THE THEOLOGY
OF DIETRICH BONHOEFFER

JOHN A. PHILLIPS

CHRIST FOR US
IN THE THEOLOGY OF
DIETRICH BONHOEFFER

"What troubles me unceasingly is the ques-
tion of what Christianity—indeed, who
Christ really is for us today."
Letters and Papers from Prison

HARPER & ROW, PUBLISHERS

NEW YORK AND EVANSTON

This book was originally published in England under the title THE FORM OF CHRIST IN THE WORLD.

FIRST AMERICAN EDITION

LIBRARY OF CONGRESS CATALOG CARD NUMBER: 67-14934

Excerpts from the book —

"Three central theological ideas take shape following the Christological affirmation of 'the world come of age' which Bonhoeffer makes in his prison letters. Although several themes weave in and out of Bonhoeffer's letters beginning with the letter of 30th April 1944, his scattered thoughts may be collected and set in order beneath these three headings: 'this-worldly transcendence,' 'the non-religious interpretation of biblical concepts,' and 'sharing in the sufferings of God at the hands of a godless world.' These phrases are closely dependent upon one another,

with the third perhaps representing the final unification of Bonhoeffer's vision and incorporating a corrective to certain dangers to which the other two notions, taken by themselves, are susceptible. . . .

"[But] a systematization of his theological ideas would be the last thing Bonhoeffer would have wanted. His work is and must remain fragmentary — that is how he speaks and must speak to us, in 'fragments which must be fragments,' which afford us but a glimpse of 'the way in which the whole was planned and conceived,' and of what material he was

Pub. ed. $6.50

Special Club
Price $2.00

(Canadian and foreign price $2.20)

building with or should have used had he lived. To have known that his work provided us with such a glimpse and has thus made a lasting contribution to the renewal of theology and the disclosure of 'Christ for us today' would have gratified him deeply.

"Our task is to strike our tents and to go forth into the region which he sketched crudely but did not live to enter. If we should have the courage to do so, that too will be due in great measure to the life and work of this astonishing, disturbing, and comforting man."

Christ for Us in the Theology of Dietrich Bonhoeffer, by John A. Phillips, is a fascinating depth study of a remarkable man of our time who has been widely quoted and little understood. Dr. Phillips' book is a survey of the complete range of Bonhoeffer's theology—its beginnings, its development, and how it was changed by his responses to Nazi Germany.

Bonhoeffer's close friend and biographer, Dr. Eberhard Bethge, writes: "Phillips presents a sensitive and independent view of the sources and shows where the great thinker and activist came from, and where his achievements may lead."

And on this side of the Atlantic Dr. William Hamilton comments: "Dr. Phillips has managed to mix . . . a learned monograph, a lucid piece of writing, and some original theological reflections of his own. . . . To all of us, confident that our way of misusing Bonhoeffer is the only way, this careful study will prove to be necessary, disturbing, and helpful. . . . To say this is the best book on Bonhoeffer is to say not nearly enough."

Author John A. Phillips teaches in the Religion and Philosophy Department of Stephens College, Columbia, Missouri.

CONTENTS

CONTENTS

CONTENTS

To W.H. *and* R.G.S.
my Teachers

INTRODUCTION

We have grown up with the experience of our parents
and grandparents that a man could and had to plan,
fill out and give form to his own life; that there was a
purpose in life for which a man had to decide and
which he then must and could pursue with everything
in his power. But it has become our experience that we
are unable to plan even for the coming day, that what
we have built up may be destroyed overnight and that
our life in comparison to that of our parents has become
formless, even fragmentary. In spite of this I can only
say that I would not want to live in any time other
than our own, even if it treats our external well-being
so lightly.

Thoughts on the Baptism of D.W.R. 1944

Preface

Dietrich Bonhoeffer's fate as a theologian has been a singular one. No modern Christian thinker has had his name invoked more often to support the work of other men, while his own theology has been left much as he left it – fragmentary and enigmatic, unexplored and unchallenged. Bonhoeffer has had an astonishing effect upon a theological generation which has refused, at the same time, to examine carefully and critically, and in its own light and on its own terms the thinking that has stimulated them.

Bonhoeffer's discoveries had been known to the theological world some ten years when I first opened the *Letters and Papers from Prison*. I came to know first-hand and from seminary companions what a decisive impact his thoughts were having upon us. Yet no thorough analysis of Bonhoeffer's work had been accomplished or attempted up to that time. Now, twenty years after Bonhoeffer's death at the hands of a Nazi hangman, only two works claim to be definitive studies of Bonhoeffer's theology – both, like the present work, student dissertations. But even these have not fulfilled the pressing need for a thorough, interpretative study: John D. Godsey's *The Theology of Dietrich Bonhoeffer* presents a descriptive, journalistic, and for the most part uncritical treatment of the subject, and Hanfried Müller's stimulating and important *Von der Kirche zur Welt* is biased in its conception and misleading in its conclusions because its author chose a peculiar ideological vantage point from which to view Bonhoeffer, and saw pretty much what he wanted to see.

To be sure, there has been over the last fifteen years a steady flow of stimulating and important short examinations of one aspect or another of Bonhoeffer's thought. But these have only served to whet the appetite for a comprehensive examination which might investigate his theology in its entirety and dis-

PREFACE

close the fundamental motifs which would help us to unravel the remaining mystery of the prison letters. We have reached that point now where it is impossible to explore the fascinating region of the prison letters – no longer, thanks to many hands, quite the *terra incognita* it once was – without a serviceable map of Bonhoeffer's earlier theological journeys. It is hoped that the present work will provide such a map or, at the very least, initiate the conversation that will enable us to construct it.

Without the encouragement, understanding, patience, despair, wisdom, good humour and friendship of two men who shared greatly in this undertaking I would not have begun and certainly would never have carried it through to completion. The initial stimulus came from Professor William Hamilton of Colgate Rochester Divinity School, and the dissertation was prepared with the constant assistance of Professor Ronald Gregor Smith of the University of Glasgow. They and many others helped in the revision of the dissertation for publication – I would like especially to acknowledge the help of Eberhard Bethge, Bonhoeffer's close friend and editor. My own hand is of course responsible for any violence which might have been done to Bonhoeffer's thought as well as for the familiar rough edges of a student paper.

For the major financial assistance which made it possible for me to undertake doctoral studies in the Faculty of Divinity of the University of Glasgow, at the University of Hamburg, and in Berlin, I am grateful to the theological committees of the World Council of Churches, the British Council of Churches, and the Evangelische Kirche in Deutschland – as well as to my prodigal parents and to the President Emeritus of Colgate Rochester Divinity School, W. E. Saunders.

9th April 1966   J. A. P.

CHAPTER I

Biography

Dietrich Bonhoeffer's heritage embodied everything enlightened, temperate, humanitarian and responsible in nineteenth-century Germany.[1] On his mother's side he counted a grandfather who had served as chaplain to the emperor; his great-grandfather was the eminent church historian, Karl von Hase. Both men had known imperial disfavour and even imprisonment for their liberal views.

Dietrich and a twin sister were born in Breslau on 4th February 1906. The two were the sixth and seventh of a family of eight. Berlin tradition holds that the native Berliner must be born in Breslau, and in 1912 the Bonhoeffer family moved to Berlin, where Dietrich's father occupied the first chair of psychiatry at the university. We know from Dietrich himself that he was greatly influenced by his father. In one of his letters in 1944, he acknowledged: 'I don't believe I have ever changed very much, except at two periods in my life, the first under the first conscious impact of Papa's personality, and the second when I was abroad.'[2]

There is evidence that the uncompromising mien Dietrich was later to reveal was in keeping with his paternal heritage as well as the tradition of the aristocratic von Hases. One significant incident concerning Professor Bonhoeffer is recorded in Ernest Jones' life of Sigmund Freud. Two professors at the University of Berlin invited Freud to contribute articles to an encyclopaedia of medicine they planned to compile. Freud was delighted, for it would have meant support for his psycho-analytical theories and official recognition of psycho-analysis as a part of medicine. On discovering after some months that Professor Bonhoeffer's

assistant had been assigned to the same subject, Freud wrote
to the editors for an explanation, suspecting (correctly as events
proved) that after their initial invitation the editors had been
'influenced by Professor Bonhoeffer, who was antagonistic to
psycho-analysis.'[3] Years later, the elder Bonhoeffer was to serve
as the *ex-officio* psychiatric adviser at the trial of van der Lubbe,
the Dutchman executed for complicity in the burning of the
Reichstag in 1933.[4]

Dietrich's own mistrust of psycho-analysis may have had its
roots in Professor Bonhoeffer's rejection of Freud and his followers, and may underlie his later unreceptiveness towards
theologies which made use of existentialist philosophy. We
shall later see just how restrictive his view became, especially
during the church struggle and when his experience in prison
impressed him first-hand with what he termed 'the morbid
character of introspection and concern for self'.

The wooded Berlin suburb of Grunewald offered a cultural
and intellectual environment for Bonhoeffer's upbringing. Hans
Delbrück and Adolf von Harnack were neighbours, and Ernst
Troeltsch was a frequent visitor to the Bonhoeffer household.
There were many memorable evening discussions between
Ferdinand Tönnies, Max and Alfred Weber, and Dietrich's
elder brothers,[5] ranging from contemporary sociology and Dilthey, Simmel, Dostoevski, Soloviev and Berdyaev, the *avant
garde* heroes of philosophy and literature, to the *Jugendbewegung*
with its anti-rationalistic 'philosophy of life'. Eberhard Bethge,
later Bonhoeffer's close friend and the editor of his posthumous
works, reports that Dietrich 'read very carefully all of Nietzsche'
and was profoundly influenced by his *Lebensphilosophie* with its
love for the earth and its creatures.[6]

In spite of what Bethge calls 'the careful agnosticism of his father
and his brothers',[7] Dietrich decided at the age of sixteen that he
would enter into theological study. Following a year at Tübingen
he matriculated at the University of Berlin with its breathtaking
roll call of Liberal scholars: von Harnack and Karl Holl, Hans
Lietzmann, the church historian, Ernst Sellin in Old Testament
studies, Adolf Deissmann, and Reinhold Seeberg, with whom
Bonhoeffer completed his dissertation at the age of twenty-one.[8]

After two years as an assistant with the German-speaking congregation in Barcelona, and work on his inaugural dissertation,[9] Bonhoeffer spent a year's leave of absence at Union Theological Seminary in New York. Professors Scott, Ward, Bewer, and Moffatt were lecturing, John Baillie was visiting professor, Paul Lehmann was attending seminars, and Reinhold Niebuhr had just begun to establish himself as a teacher. Judging from letters and the report which he delivered to his church upon his return, Bonhoeffer was horrified by the sociable, non-academic atmosphere which prevailed at Union.[10] Much of what he learned from his trip was consequently the product of extra-curricular activity. His work with Negro churches, unemployment, and the social Gospel movement made unforgettable impressions upon him. After a second visit to Union in 1939 Bonhoeffer revised his judgement of theological and church life in America, coming to understand that much of it was simply inaccessible to someone with a European theological and cultural background.[11] He later counted his travel abroad as one of the two really formative influences upon his life and work, turning him 'away from the phraseological to the real'.[12]

Bonhoeffer returned in the summer of 1931 to take up his duties in Berlin as a lecturer in systematic theology. During the weeks before he began his work, however, two memorable events occurred. In June, he delivered an address on behalf of 'the youngest generation of theologians' at a memorial service for his beloved Adolf von Harnack, who had died shortly following his complete retirement from his teaching post at Berlin.[13] Bonhoeffer had always been very close to his teacher and his world, so much so that years later, deeply committed to the 'theology of revelation' against which Harnack had battled with all the strength of his last years, Bonhoeffer thought of himself as 'still a student of Harnack's'.[14]

In July Bonhoeffer spent two weeks at a seminar in Bonn, conducted by Karl Barth. The association was to last for the rest of his life. He wrote in letters to his Swiss friend Erwin Sutz of his fascination with Barth, confessing that he 'scarcely regretted an omission in his theological past more than not having come earlier'.[15] The theological movement of which Barth was the centre deeply affected Bonhoeffer's theology for the remainder of his life, and he became very personally dependent upon the older man.[16]

The great years of academic brilliance at the University of Berlin were behind when Bonhoeffer delivered his introductory lecture. He subsequently taught a variety of theological subjects and struggled with his additional duties as chaplain to the technical college, ecumenical youth secretary, and leader of a notoriously difficult confirmation class of young workers.[17] Of Bonhoeffer's pre-1933 work several sermons, articles, reviews, reports and lectures remain, including the study of Genesis 1–3 published as *Creation and Fall*, and a reconstruction of his lectures on Christology.[18]

With the collapse of the Weimar Republic and the rise of Adolf Hitler to power in 1933, there began the bitter struggle of the German Evangelical Church to preserve her identity. From the outset of the church struggle no one doubted on which side Bonhoeffer stood. Two days after Hitler had been installed as chancellor, Bonhoeffer's radio address attacking the Nazi leadership principle was interrupted by the authorities. He expanded it and delivered it a month later before a young audience at the *Deutsche Hochschule für Politik*.[19] In April of the same year the 'law for the restitution of the civil service', which dismissed Jews, including university professors, from government positions came into force.[20] Events moved swiftly in the church. In July, rigged elections returned an overwhelming percentage of 'German Christian' supporters of the régime into the governing bodies of the church, and the 'Brown Synod' in September prohibited anyone of Jewish blood or marriage from church office, including the pastorate.[21]

By November the Bethel Confession which Bonhoeffer had helped to draft had been published under the editorship of Martin Niemöller, expressing the belated but unequivocal opposition of the 'Pastors' Emergency League'.[22] But Bonhoeffer was no longer in Berlin. Sick at heart with the dismissal and persecution of Jewish-Christian pastors he had numbered among his friends, and disgusted with the vacillation of his university colleagues, he had accepted the leadership of two German congregations in London.[23] Here he renewed his interest in the ecumenical movement, now so important to the opposition in Germany, and attempted to interpret the true nature of the struggle within the German church to its leaders.[24] In 1934 the synods of Barmen and Dahlem,[25] under the aegis of Barth, declared the church government heretical and created the Confessing Church Brethren Councils which Bonhoeffer represented at numerous ecumenical functions. During the following year he was recalled to Germany.

At twenty-nine years of age Bonhoeffer directed an 'illegal' preachers' Confessing Church Seminary at Zingst and later at Finkenwalde, in Pomerania; and, in connection with it, founded an experimental community known as the *Bruderhaus*. Some of Bonhoeffer's most influential writings were produced during this period of communal life and work, notably *The Cost of Discipleship* in 1937 and *Life Together* in 1938. Both the Finkenwalde seminary and the *Bruderhaus* were dissolved by force in 1937 but the former maintained a clandestine, peripatetic existence until 1940. By this time, Bonhoeffer's own activities had been greatly restricted by the Gestapo.

An attempt by Reinhold Niebuhr's 'committee of two', the other member of which was Paul Lehmann, to get Bonhoeffer to safety in America, succeeded for a few months.[26] But when war became inevitable Bonhoeffer felt that he had to share in whatever the fate of his country might be, and he returned to Germany in the summer of 1939. John Baillie invited him to Edinburgh to deliver the Croall lectures for 1940 but travel soon became impossible.[27] Bonhoeffer continued work on the talks he was unable to deliver (even after he was forbidden to preach, write, or remain in Berlin and his later books had been banned), and the fragments of his work which were not destroyed and which were kept out of the hands of the authorities, were published posthumously in 1949 as *Ethics*.[28]

Before the war, Bonhoeffer had been strongly influenced by pacifism. During his time in London in 1934 and 1935, he had even made the preliminary arrangements for a discussion with Gandhi about the most effective methods of passive resistance.

17

But when war began, his brother-in-law, Hans von Dohnanyi, was committed to the resistance group which eventually sought Hitler's death, as an assistant to General Oster of the Intelligence Service. He urged Bonhoeffer to serve as a *V-Mann (Verwendungsmann)* or civilian agent with the *Abwehr* (the counter-espionage department), 'partly in order to save him from conscription, partly in order to use his knowledge for the resistance'.[29] This service (which, as is now well known, was deeply involved in underground activities) enjoyed unusual freedom from Gestapo interference, and Bonhoeffer was assigned to the Munich office as a courier.[30] The extent of his involvement in resistance affairs is not entirely clear, but it is known that he made two journeys on behalf of the resistance, and planned others. He lived for a time at the Benedictine monastery of Ettal in southern Germany and travelled in 1941 to Switzerland to deliver certain documents to W. A. Visser't Hooft.[31] With remarkable good fortune he was able to disclose the plans for the overthrow of the Nazi government at a meeting in neutral Stockholm in 1942 with George K. A. Bell, the late Anglican Bishop of Chichester.[32] But in April of 1943 Bonhoeffer's activities were suspected and he was arrested and imprisoned at Tegel, near Berlin. Most of the letters and papers which have since been published in Germany as *Widerstand und Ergebung*, in England as *Letters and Papers from Prison*, and in America as *Prisoner for God* were sent to his parents and his friend Eberhard Bethge during the days at Tegel.[33] After the failure of the spectacular bombing of Hitler's headquarters on the 20th July 1944, more stringent measures were enforced and he was placed in close confinement in the prison on Prinz Albrecht Strasse. The drama of his last days began the following February and he was removed to Buchenwald, Schönberg, and finally to the gallows at Flossenbürg, where he was hanged.[34] On Easter morning of 1952, the pastors of Bavaria dedicated a tablet in the village church at Flossenbürg, with a simple inscription which reads:

> *Dietrich Bonhoeffer, a witness of Jesus Christ among his Brethren. Born 4th February 1906 in Breslau. Died 9th April 1945 at Flossenbürg.*

CHAPTER 2

Bonhoeffer as a Theologian

Organizing Bonhoeffer's Theology

The publication of the fragmentary *Ethics* in 1949 and the appearance in 1951 of a collection of letters and papers from his wartime imprisonment signalled the beginning of post-war biographical and theological interest in Dietrich Bonhoeffer. Since that time, and due largely to the dedication of Eberhard Bethge, the whole of Bonhoeffer's pre-war theological work and the letters, essays, documents, lectures, and sermons of the five volume *Gesammelte Schriften* have been made available.[1] Two lengthy studies of Bonhoeffer have appeared: John Godsey's *The Theology of Dietrich Bonhoeffer* in 1960, and Hanfried Müller's *Von der Kirche zur Welt* in 1961. Bonhoeffer has been the subject of innumerable articles scattered throughout various theological journals, and the more important of these, together with the proceedings of a circle of theologians influenced by him, who have met four times during the years to discuss problems raised by his thought, have been preserved in four issues of a journal entitled *Die mündige Welt*.[2] An American symposium of critical essays appeared in 1962 which bears the title *The Place of Bonhoeffer*.

Although Bonhoeffer research is still handicapped by the lack of a detailed biography (now being prepared by Bethge), the collection and presentation of the source material is complete.

A quick look at the production of Bonhoeffer's eighteen years as a theologian reveals the unsystematic character of his thinking. The biographical aspects of his career often affected his theological work, and it is a basic assumption on the part of many of his interpreters that the history of the time through which and in which Bonhoeffer lived is an important factor to be considered in any assessment of his thought. Especially during the church struggle he wrote largely as occasion demanded, as professor, preacher, pastor, and protagonist of the Confessing Church. The surviving writings from the end of his life – the *Ethics* and the prison letters – appears on the surface to be retractions (or at least extensive revisions) of much that he had written before. One of the initial tasks of our present study must be to discover the essential homogeneity of his outlook and to try to see the reasons for the diversity, at times contradiction, in his expressions of that outlook.

It will be useful first to examine the methods which have been used by other interpreters. Characteristic has been a chronological organization which seeks to relate Bonhoeffer's life and theological output to the history of the times in which he lived. Thus, Godsey and Müller have sought to overcome the problem of consistency by drawing a very close connection between the events of Bonhoeffer's life, the historical events in Germany between 1918 and 1945, and the theology which he taught while he lived, and forecast just before his death.

Both John Godsey and Hanfried Müller recognize the difficulty of presenting a 'theology of Dietrich Bonhoeffer' which attempts to relate the later, fragmentary works to any of those written within the preceding ten years. The famous essay on 'cheap grace',[3] written in 1937, protested against grace without discipleship and faith without obedience in uncompromisingly biblical terms, drawing a visible boundary line between the world and the community of saints. Yet only seven years later, Bonhoeffer was meditating in his prison cell upon the theme of 'religionless Christianity', the dangers of 'positivism of revelation', and worldliness as the necessary and proper concern of the Christian. This abrupt shift of focus from elaboration of the basis, structure, and life of the church to concern for the problem of the revelation of God in Christ and the life of the Christian in a mature, 'godless' world presents to the interpreter a formidable problem which needs to be thoroughly examined.

Godsey attempts to build Bonhoeffer's thought into a coherent pattern by setting life, work, and world history together in chronological sequence. His study divides Bonhoeffer's life and work into three periods, corresponding historically to pre-Hitler Germany, the 1933–40 church struggle, and the wartime catastrophe ('theological foundation', 'theological application', and 'theological fragmentation'). He links these periods together theologically by seeing the whole of Bonhoeffer's concern as Christological and ecclesiological, a concern for what Bethge has called 'the concretion of the revelation' (a phrase which we will define shortly). Godsey's implicit assumption thus far is typical of Bonhoeffer's interpreters: recapitulation within a chronological scheme, allowing Bonhoeffer to speak for himself with a minimum of interpretation, will dissolve any problem of inconsistency.

But in Bonhoeffer study, organization itself cannot escape being interpretation. Presentations of Bonhoeffer's theology will differ (whether the difference is acknowledged or not) by the choice of 'phase' in his life and work through which the whole of his development is to be seen. Godsey seems to have chosen the second, the period of the church struggle and *The Cost of Discipleship*. If this is true, then we can better understand the unsupported conclusions which he reaches at the close of his book and discusses without the help of additional evidence or analysis. The most important of these is that 'the last development in Bonhoeffer's theology, while indeed unexpected, does in no sense represent a break with the theology of the former periods, but rather a bold consummation of the same!'[4] Godsey proceeds to question the value of certain important clues to the meaning of the prison letters (among them, the attack on Barth's theology and the characterization of Bultmann) in an attempt to bring them and the *Ethics* into agreement with the more tractable biblical and theological works which preceded them. He appears to be pointing to his own organization, especially the biographical material, as the basis for this judgement of the prison letters. He imagines, no doubt, that this will provide an objective view of Bonhoeffer's development, and demonstrate in a self-evident manner that this development is continuous and coherent.

But we need to know more; the problems are much deeper and must be squarely faced and discussed. Godsey leans heavily upon his chronological-biographical-bibliographical organization as the solution to these problems. It is certain, however, that although biographical and chronological organization can be a useful tool for organizing and interpreting Bonhoeffer's theology, it cannot relieve us of the task of a more critical investigation to determine the reasons for any shifts or breaks in his thought.

Hanfried Müller also makes it clear in his study that he has laid much emphasis on the fact that the periods of Bonhoeffer's theological development begin and end on dates highly significant for German political and cultural history. In 1933 Hitler assumed power, in 1939 the war began, in 1944 the end of Nazism was certain.[5] A convinced Marxist and an East German, Müller sees Bonhoeffer's theological output almost as a foil of German history: the break-up of the Weimar Republic (Bonhoeffer's search for community), the Nazi take-over (counter-offensive), and the break-up of fascism (shattering of the *bourgeois* society in which Bonhoeffer had participated, and his vision of a new world order). Müller counters anticipated criticism by stating at the outset that he is not interested in an objective presentation of Bonhoeffer's theology – in 'making a dead man speak', as he later put it. He wishes frankly to 'make use' of Bonhoeffer in order to develop his own position. But he *does* think, in spite of this, that he has done no violence to Bonhoeffer's thought. In so far as Müller indicates that he believes he understands Bonhoeffer, it is necessary to criticize him not only by asking whether his system does not itself fall victim to his own instinctive dislike of attempts to systematize Bonhoeffer, but also by pointing out certain difficulties with the historical dates upon which he has staked so much of his interpretation. The foundation for *The Cost of Discipleship*, for instance, was laid in 1932; Müller sees the work as 'the theoretical outcome of the practical experiences of the church struggle' which began the following year.[6] *Life Together* describes the *Bruderhaus* experiment which went hand in hand with the thought of *The Cost of Discipleship* and has some of its roots in

Bonhoeffer's 1927 dissertation; Müller conveniently characterizes this work (which does not fit into his system) as a 'detour'.[7]

But there is undoubtedly a measure of truth in the thesis Müller shares with so many of Bonhoeffer's interpreters: Bonhoeffer *was* deeply involved in the life and spirit and affairs of his country, and his thought could not have been unaffected. What one wishes to see, however, is sufficient regard for the 'arisotocratic' Bonhoeffer who, in Karl Barth's words, 'seemed to move on ahead in another dimension'.[8] Bonhoeffer's *freedom* from time and place and circumstance characterized him beyond all else and astonishes all who read the prison letters.[9] His theology can hardly be summed up as a theology of reaction. It was much more a theology of the *unexpected* – as his friends continually recognized both to their delight and their bewilderment. Involvement need not preclude detachment (or *hilaritas*, as Bonhoeffer was to call it);[10] true involvement may in fact demand such an objective and independent attitude. An interpretation of Bonhoeffer's theology ought therefore to strive to maintain Bonhoeffer's freedom from the events of his life and of the time in which he lived, if we are to understand him and make use of his contribution. Neither Müller nor Godsey have paid sufficient attention to what can be called the *sine qua non* of Bonhoeffer studies.

Ecclesiology as the Clue to Bonhoeffer's Theology

If an interpretation of Bonhoeffer's thought is to be theological and sufficiently organized that it will be coherent, the interpreter must decide upon a particular vantage point from which to view the whole. Godsey and Müller agree that Christology and ecclesiology, taken together as a single theme, are the clues whereby the unity of Bonhoeffer's far-reaching thoughts may be discerned.[11] The approaches of the two men are very different in manner and style – the importance of Bonhoeffer resides for Godsey in the message to the church to 'be what it is in Christ'; while for Müller (who places a greater valuation upon the *Ethics* and the prison letters), Bonhoeffer shatters the boundaries of a church whose structure has been determined by Western ideology, in order to understand the whole of society as redeemed and taken up in Christ. But both locate the key to Bonhoeffer's development in his concentration upon the problem of how Christology takes concrete form as ecclesiology.

Godsey is convinced that Bonhoeffer remains in the realm of Christology and a generally orthodox ecclesiology throughout the various turnings of his argument. The basic concern remains Christological, 'but because Christ is not without his body, Christology includes ecclesiology within itself. . . . Bonhoeffer passionately believed that revelation continues to take place only in a concrete form, namely, as Jesus Christ lives and takes form in a concrete community, in his church.'[12]

Does this statement remain true for the last period of Bonhoeffer's thought? Godsey has little difficulty demonstrating Bonhoeffer's virtual identification of Christology with ecclesiology during the first periods of his work, drawing heavily and rightly upon *Sanctorum Communio (The Communion of Saints)*, *Act and Being*, *The Cost of Discipleship*, and *Life Together*. Examining the *Ethics*, he points to Bonhoeffer's stress on the church as 'Christ taking form in the world', and (though less certainly, for this is in fact only a small part of the *Ethics*) his thesis can still be defended. It is with the prison letters that Godsey has the greatest difficulty. Eager to see that Bonhoeffer's sudden interest in 'worldliness' should not be misunderstood as a devaluation of the church, he writes:

. . . he does not mean that in becoming worldly, the church would cease to be the church, but that it can only *be* the church in the true sense when its own attitude towards the world parallels God's attitude, when its life in the world is patterned according to Christ's life, when it takes with utmost seriousness its role as vicarious representative and deputy for the world. That the notion of Christian worldliness does not dissolve the identity of the church nor exclude its essential functions is easily proved, because Bonhoeffer speaks of its ongoing task of proclaiming the word of God, its secret discipline, its cultus and its task of intellectual discussion with the world.[13]

Godsey is probably correct in saying that Bonhoeffer did not envisage a total disappearance of the church in favour of 'worldliness'. But he misses the significance of the fact that the letters discuss the implications of Bonhoeffer's discoveries for the church *only as a side issue* and in a very sketchy fashion. As in much of the *Ethics*, the church is set off to one side. The discoveries themselves are not ecclesiological. No reader of the prison letters can fail to miss the polemical nature of the thoughts on 'religionless Christianity' and the fact that this polemic is directed towards the church and her traditional apologetic. Up to the beginning of the *Ethics* in 1940 the church was the central theme in his thinking. But there follows an unmistakable break with this pattern. Bonhoeffer's correspondent, surprised at the direction of the former's thoughts in prison, wrote expressing his concern, and received the answer: 'You ask whether this leaves any room for the church, or has it gone for good? . . . I'm breaking off here, and will write more tomorrow.'[14] Tomorrow did not come, and Bonhoeffer's vision remains incomplete. Should we complete the picture by pointing towards Bonhoeffer's previous interest in a doctrine of the church? If not, does ecclesiology remain the best path into the *Ethics* and prison letters?

It is at least certain that Bonhoeffer has not swept the church aside with a stroke, but has set ecclesiology to one side in order to clear his mind of pressing preliminary questions. The conclusion of Müller's study is that Bonhoeffer has moved steadily from his ecclesiological concern of 1927, under pressure from historical events, to its consummation in 1945. But unlike Godsey, Müller sees a radical development in Bonhoeffer's ecclesiology, or at least in the function it performs, during these years. *Gemeinschaft* is replaced by *Gesellschaft*, the community of saints by the godless, secular society. Müller sees in the 'religionless Christianity' of the *Letters and Papers from Prison* the final vindication of man's freedom from the religious worldview of the Christian West, so that the Christian may take up a secular *Weltanschauung*, which requires neither a formal concept of God nor the institutional church for its completion. The 'coming of age of the world' (the phrase which occurs in Bonhoeffer's letters), by which he means the continuing historical movement of the world towards ultimate secularization, demands a theology based not upon Christ's redemption of an elect community, the church, but upon his suffering Lordship

over the whole of society. One is thereby enabled to live a life
of faith within a world which formally declares itself to be what
it has in fact become: a 'godless' world in which the 'comrade'
replaces the neighbour as the bearer of the Word, and community is manifested in the Communist society.

Müller's argument should be studied carefully by theologians
in the West for its own sake; it is vitally new in Christian
thought and we cannot afford to dismiss his work or the experience of the church in eastern Europe out of hand. He does not
claim to be drawing conclusions from Bonhoeffer's thought that
Bonhoeffer himself would have drawn. The question, as he puts
it, is not 'where would Bonhoeffer stand today?' – this is pointless
– but rather, 'who may rightly receive Bonhoeffer today?'[15] Bonhoeffer was of course thoroughly dedicated to his own *bourgeois*
life and culture, and it seems that he was never really conversant
with Marxist sociological analysis or political theory, despite
his keen interest in sociology. One feels obliged to allow Müller
to make use of Bonhoeffer in order to understand the difficult
position of the Christian in a Marxist land. But as a presentation of Bonhoeffer's theology itself this cannot be allowed to stand.

What Müller does not appreciate is that his argument has
taken Bonhoeffer's 'religionless Christianity' as a *last word*. Because there is no ecclesiology as such in the letters, this does not
mean that Bonhoeffer had done away with it, nor does it
justify the thesis that society may properly assume the role of
the institutional church. We have enough clues (though they
are no more than clues) in the prison letters to know that
Bonhoeffer wanted to discuss the role of the church in the area
of the 'secret discipline',[16] and that he regarded this as the
dialectical partner and corrective of 'religionlessness'. Müller's
theology of the cross, which he finds in Bonhoeffer, turns (in
Bethge's words) 'essentially into a negation of *any* ecclesiology.'[17]
Where he begins with a genuine dialectic between the secret
discipline and the liberated life of the world come of age, this
dialectic soon resolves itself in favour of the utter invisibility of
faith and the disappearance from the scene of the peculiar
content of Christian doctrine and any peculiar response of the
believer to a peculiar revelation.[18]

26

The central difficulty in Müller's and Godsey's interpretations seems to be their choice of ecclesiology as a vantage point. Godsey can hold Bonhoeffer's position together as a thoroughgoing ecclesiology only by dismissing the very important and significant final criticism of the church and of Barth, whom Bonhoeffer identified with its mistakes; directing us towards the latter's earlier and undoubtedly passionate interest in ecclesiology. Müller, on the other hand, points to the virtual identification of Christology with ecclesiology in *Sanctorum Communio*, and then to the meditation on 'religionless Christianity' in the letters (with their final, but surely temporary, silence on ecclesiology), in order to argue that Bonhoeffer was seeking a way to *replace* the body of Christ with the godless (Marxist) 'world come of age'. He finds it necessary in this to minimize or deny the significance of the products of the second phase of Bonhoeffer's work, *The Cost of Discipleship* and *Life Together*.

Whatever Bonhoeffer was concerned with in the *Ethics* and the prison letters, it was *not* primarily ecclesiology. To base an interpretation of his thought in its entirety on the ecclesiological concern of his earlier thought or to argue from the silence of the letters that he has thrown it over will make it almost certain that he will be misunderstood. There are so many problems bound up with any attempt to see Bonhoeffer's theological progression as a logical and inexorable movement from ecclesiological beginnings to mature ecclesiological (or anti-ecclesiological) conclusions that ecclesiology simply has no usefulness as a basic interpretative principle for understanding the *whole* of his theology.

The Christological Perspective

What seems more fruitful as a guide through Bonhoeffer's thought is a characteristic which undoubtedly did carry through all three phases of his thought, and which has been recognized by practically all of his interpreters (including Godsey and Müller).[19] Bonhoeffer's emphasis on Christology, particularly on a Christology which exhibited certain definite and constant tendencies, *is* a basic clue to his thinking. One cannot escape it in any assessment, and it has been adopted in this study as the light which can illuminate the dark places, narrow passes, and turnings of Bonhoeffer's path.

The danger of turning to Christology, as Ebeling notes, is that of retreating into a kind of Christomonism, reducing all problems to the dogmatic, Christological sphere. We have no wish to do this. The implications must constantly be explored, without obscuring issues by resorting to a traditional terminology in which we may feel more at home. It will therefore be our task to uncover the Christological motivation for the various shifts in Bonhoeffer's concern. Bethge has described this motivation as 'the quest for the concretion of the revelation,'[20] by which he means that Bonhoeffer struggled, throughout his life, to give adequate expression to his conviction that the revelation of God in Jesus Christ was visible, tangible, concrete, apprehensible by all men. Almost to the end of his life, he demonstrated this concretion by pointing to the church as the Body of Christ, where Christ was present. In his last years, he explored the possibility of pointing to this reality and 'participating' in it within secular, worldly life, without undue concern for the ecclesiological implications of his discoveries. Bonhoeffer's Christology *developed*; to say that it was a constant motif of his thought does not mean that it remained an *idée fixe* by which he measured the utterances of fifteen years. His theology issued from the tension, we shall argue, between unreconciled elements in its Christological centre. Thus, in 1940, he found that his ecclesiology could no longer serve as the conceptual partner of his Christology, and he set aside the former to concentrate on the development of the latter.

A liberated and many-sided but always *concrete* Christology therefore becomes our guide to the development of Bonhoeffer's theology.

The Usefulness of a Study of Bonhoeffer's Theology

A study of the development of Bonhoeffer's theology is of undoubted interest simply for its own sake. The man seemed to embody in what he called his 'bastardized theological heritage' many of the struggles of Protestant theology which have decided its present-day shape. His involvement in the battle of the church against Nazism opens out the whole history of the church struggle, from which theology and the ecumenical church still have so much to learn. As a human story, one can hardly match the dedication of this man to his church, country and heritage, his involvement in a conspiracy to eliminate a false leader, his courage in the face of betrayal, his theological insight from within his prison cell, the disappointment of all his hopes, and death at the hands of the hangman.

Certainly, a presentation of Bonhoeffer's theology is justified if it does nothing more than confront us with this 'open and rich and at the same time deep and unnerving man', who somehow 'shames us and comforts us', as Karl Barth was to describe him.[21] Bonhoeffer's theology, like the man himself, has this disturbing quality about it, and it is good for us to be disturbed in this way.

But it is not possible, especially after Müller's study has been written, to content ourselves simply with an objective presentation of Bonhoeffer's thought. It would be easy, and therefore cheap, to dismiss Müller's subjection of Bonhoeffer to his Marxist presuppositions as a bit of opportunism.[22] But this book, unlike the majority of Bonhoeffer studies, will not let one go. Müller has demonstrated with his militant, exciting, vital, disturbing book that Bonhoeffer's *spirit* can and should cast a long shadow over any words that are written about him. Bonhoeffer wished above all to be 'useful', and we would not escape bad consciences if we contented ourselves simply with a systematic recapitulation.

Finding a way out of Bonhoeffer's theology is therefore as important as finding a way in. If it is true that many of his battles are the battles that Protestant theology fought and continues to fight, may it not be that Bonhoeffer's discoveries can suggest ways out of the stagnation of our present-day theological situation and the deadlock to which our theological history has led us?

Theologians, students and laymen have returned again and again to the prison letters of Bonhoeffer because they are cheered, disturbed, and stimulated by what they find there: a demand that fresh ground be broken; a declaration that the old battles, however nobly fought, have been left behind by the course of world history, and that to remain waiting warily on these battlefields for the next enemy attack is to surrender the central, renewing hope of the Christian Gospel. In the final section of our study we will be examining the final and most productive period of Bonhoeffer's life and thought, not with the aim of setting in order and completing the fragmentary visions of the *Ethics* and the *Letters and Papers from Prison*, so that Dietrich Bonhoeffer may be assigned his place in the history of theology – rather, we must take the fragments seriously as fragments, clarifying and relating them only so that they might excite, anger, disturb and enlighten us the more. Only in this way can we fulfil Bonhoeffer's intention: opening out new and fresh possibilities for the future direction of theology.

The final judgement of our investigation must be, of course, whether or not Bonhoeffer has helped us to find that which he sought: a vision of Jesus Christ which will enable us to live and work and love as disciples who seem to have more than the customary measure of unbelief in our belief. At the least, Bonhoeffer can help us to clear away some of the nonsense (including that in his own works) which has obscured our theological task, so that we might take our bearings on the next several years and prepare for them. A theologian who can help us in even this little has helped us a great deal.

CHRIST AND THE CHURCH

Before the war we lived too far from God; we believed too much
in our own power, in our almightiness and righteousness. We
attempted to be a strong and good people, but we were too proud
of our endeavours, we felt too much satisfaction with our
scientific, economic, and social progress, and we identified this
progress with the coming of the kingdom of God. We felt too
happy and complacent in this world; our souls were too much at
home in this world. Then the great disillusionment came. We saw
the impotence and the weakness of humanity, we were suddenly
awakened from our dream, we recognized our guiltiness before
God and we humbled ourselves under the mighty hand of
God. . . . We had to recognize the limits of man and that means
we discovered anew God in his glory and almightiness, in his
wrath and his grace.

Lecture. Autumn 1930. GS I, *pp.69–70*

God is not free *of* man but *for* man. Christ is the Word of his
freedom. God *is there*, which is to say: not in eternal non-
objectivity but . . . 'haveable', graspable in his Word within the
church.

AB, *p.91*

CHAPTER 3

Discovering God Anew

The church must get out of her stagnation. We must once again get out into the open air of intellectual discussion with the world. We must also risk saying controversial things, if this is to be one way of raising the vitally important questions. As a 'modern' theologian who still bears within himself the heritage of Liberal theology, I feel myself obliged to open up these questions. There will not be many of the younger genera-tion who combine both trends in themselves. How much I could use your help!

3rd August 1944. Letters, p.128

A Crisis of Vocabulary

Protestant theology was in a state of upheaval when Bonhoeffer began his theological training at Tübingen. In that year, 1923, a prophetic exchange of letters took place between the two men who were to have the most profound influence upon his life: Adolf von Harnack, the great figure of the last years of nine-teenth-century evangelical theology, engaged Karl Barth and his 'theology of crisis' in the pages of the Liberal journal, *Die christliche Welt*.[1] If one were to judge by the strange new phrases which were suddenly appearing in this and similar debates – the 'Wholly Other' who breaks in 'perpendicularly from above', revelation 'thrown like a stone', the 'infinite qualitative distinc-tion' between God and man – one might have called the critical situation a 'crisis of vocabulary',[2] perhaps the first great turning-point of this kind since the time of Schleiermacher. Barth and congenial thinkers called for nothing less than a precipitous break with the theological development which had been successfully asserting itself for two or three centuries.

At the turn of the century Adolf von Harnack had said in his famous lectures, *The Essence of Christianity*, that 'those of us who possess more delicate and therefore more prophetic perception no longer regard the kingdom of love and peace as a mere Utopia'.[3] But confronting a world whose foundations had been shaken by the First World War and the resultant chaotic situation in Germany, young theological students began to look elsewhere for guidance. Bonhoeffer spoke of the recognition of the impotence and weakness of humanity, and the glory and almightiness, wrath and grace of God. God was real, perhaps more real than he had ever been – but his reality was his distance from man in his majesty. The revolution was given its classic text in Karl Barth's *Epistle to the Romans*:

The more profoundly we become aware of the limited character of the possibilities which are open to us here and now, the more clear it is that we are farther from God, that our desertion of him is more complete . . . and the consequences of that desertion more vast . . . than we had ever dreamed. Men are their own masters. Their union with God is shattered so completely that they cannot even conceive of its restoration. Their sin is their guilt; their death is their destiny; their world is formless and tumultuous chaos, a chaos of the forces of nature and of the human soul; their life is illusion. This is the situation in which we find ourselves.[4]

Barth was later to compare the beginning of his theological revolution to someone ascending a dark church tower who clutches, instead of the stair rail, the bell rope, accidently striking the great bell. But if this bell roused students at Berlin to shocked awareness of the theological situation, their teachers were at first startled, then puzzled, and finally angered. Influential schools of Liberal theology looked to Berlin for guidance and found little. Ernst Troeltsch died before Bonhoeffer arrived at the university; Karl Holl while he was still in attendance. In 1931 Harnack himself died at the age of eighty, leaving, of the four, only Seeberg, the 'learned but colourless'[5] historian of dogma and perhaps the most vulnerable to the criticisms of dialectical theology. But if the University of Berlin was in a state of decline when Bonhoeffer matriculated, it is also true that too much emphasis in the study of Bonhoeffer has been placed upon his reaction against his teachers and too little on the great influence they exerted upon him. It is well, therefore, that we begin by examining the central motifs in the theologies of his four teachers.

Harnack, Seeberg, Troeltsch and Holl had trained in the theology of Ritschl and Herrmann and represented various modifications of the thought their teachers had expressed. The first three shared a movement away from Ritschl's disinterest in culture and philosophy of religion and his isolation of theology from other intellectual disciplines.[6] From this point the three separated from each other in their ideas. Seeberg concentrated upon the church, developing both the theme of the redemptive community as the basic theme of dogmatics, and a synthesis with the Hegelian metaphysics Ritschl had mistrusted. He was thus enabled to place a conservative view of church history at the service of the Liberal spirit.[7] Harnack remained loyal to the wider interests of Herrmann, substituting for the centrality of ecclesiology in Ritschl's thought a broad sweep of cultural interests and an individual spirit which drew its strength from the heroic transcendence of history and nature.[8] But the most radical reaction against Ritschl, and against Herrmann and Harnack as well, came from the History of Religions school and the systematic theologian of that movement, Ernst Troeltsch.

Ernst Troeltsch

'Perhaps the greatest and most modern of the modernists,'[9] Troeltsch rejected the kernel-and-husk methodology by which Harnack, Holl and Seeberg sought an irreducible 'essence' or minimal 'absolute principles' of Christianity, and set out with tremendous self-confidence, a profound understanding of the secular world, and an instinctive mistrust of half-measures, to 'build' a modern Christianity.[10] He thought of himself as one whose task it was to complete Schleiermacher's revolution. Like Schleiermacher, he saw Christianity as a matter to be dealt with in the area of the philosophy of religions, the psychological analysis of religious consciousness and the religious idea as it manifested itself in history. History and religiousness were self-evident facts; the problem was how to relate them.

Troeltsch had been deeply affected by Hegel and Lessing. For the former, 'religious faith grows out of history' but 'in its inner truth and validity it is not dependent on history'. Troeltsch coupled this with Lessing's dictum: accidental truths of history cannot furnish the proof for the necessary truths of reason. Thus, what Troeltsch felt required of him was an absolutely fearless attitude towards historical relativism, and because the historical element in the incarnation is 'no more than the means of introducing the Christian idea into history' – an idea which can now maintain itself by means of its own intrinsic resources – the 'illustrative' historical facts may be given over to textual criticism.[11]

The result is that Christianity, as a religion, must recognize that it is limited and conditioned; a search for 'absolutes' or an 'essence' asks for what history cannot, by definition, provide. An impartial study of religions will, however, show Christianity to be the 'highest', the synthesis of the legalistic and redemptive religions of mankind, and the perfect expression in its central affirmations of the philosophical truth of the unity of God with man. Troeltsch's enemy was 'absolute authority', and he felt it his duty to guard a secular world from ecclesiastical encroachments. The course of history had freed the world from absolutes and laid bare its own underlying religiousness. In *Protestantism and Progress*, he wrote:

If the absolute authority has fallen which, in its absoluteness, made the antithesis of the divine and human equally absolute, if in man an autonomous principle is recognized as the source of truth and moral conduct, then all conceptions of the world which were specially designed to maintain that gulf between the human and divine, fall along with it. With it falls the doctrine of the absolute corruption of mankind through original sin, and the transference of the ends of life to the heavenly world in which there will be deliverance from this corruption. In consequence, all the factors of this present life acquire an enhanced value and a higher impressiveness, and the ends of life fall more and more within the realm of the present world with its ideal of transformation.[12]

'The conceptions of the world which were especially designed to maintain that gulf between the human and divine' seem to include, first, a certain picture of divinity itself. It was basic to Troeltsch's thought that the world is 'a product of the divine will into which divinity does not enter',[13] and those earthly-heavenly structures which imagined that they somehow embodied this divinity must be done away with. These are removed from this world, but they do not disappear altogether. In 'the life beyond the world', Troeltsch wrote in the enigmatic closing paragraph of his *Social Teachings*, divinity acts upon the world as 'the inspiration of the life that now is'.[14]

Secondly, 'absolute and immediate divine revelation embodied in the church is no longer tenable', and Christianity is left 'capable of freely combining with all of the interests and factors of life'.[15] Thirdly, dogmatics as 'firmly established, unchangeable truth' is replaced by a kind of dogmatics which is 'emerging from the great self-revealing movement of history, and is conscious of working in the direction of an absolute end'.[16] Fourthly, the Bible, which in Protestant scholasticism replaced the authority of the church with the authority of an infallible, divinely inspired Scripture – is to be made completely subject to the criticism of historical science.[17]

The departure of 'divinity' or 'absolute authority' embodied in the institutional church does not leave the secular world comfortless, however. In Troeltsch's thinking, the place of divinity is taken by an 'autonomous principle' in man, which is 'the source of truth and moral conduct'. Troeltsch's picture of 'the secular' permits – indeed, it embraces – an innate religious quality in the world which is embodied in 'the clear requirements of the moral consciousness'.[18] This religious quality is not the possession of a particular community, although the church could symbolize in its cultus and ethics its presence and its special characteristics. But if Troeltsch had no place in his thinking for a self-conscious, revelatory, redemptive community, one should also remember that he regarded radical individualism with equal mistrust and spoke of a movement of history, guided by the religion which it bears and which at the same time transcends it, towards 'a new civilization of restraint'. He thought it his duty to ask the church to be in some way the bearer of that message and, in its life, to prefigure that civilization.

A student who took part in Troeltsch's seminars could never

have included his teacher's name in any general characterization of 'Liberal theology' as unduly optimistic about the future course of world history. Troeltsch had no illusions concerning the outcome of the growth of what he called 'militaristic, nationalistic *bourgeois* states'. Still, the students of Bonhoeffer's generation might have remarked bitterly in 1933 about that prophecy, barely a decade before, that a 'new civilization' based upon 'restraint' and 'the autonomy of man' represented the future of Germany. Troeltsch had found the doctrine of original sin a relic of the past, outmoded along with the old conception of divinity, and colleagues who had been greatly influenced by him found themselves defenceless in the face of the tragedy which confronted them in Hitler.

In spite of the fact that Troeltsch died before Bonhoeffer could sit in on his lectures, the bold sociological approach to the doctrine of the church which he presented in his *Social Teachings* remained in the air at Berlin and determined the subject and approach of Bonhoeffer's student dissertation. Bonhoeffer chose for himself an exceedingly difficult task: to produce an understanding of the church which 'rejected the possibility of grasping her sociological facts from outside' – i.e. in terms of general religious principles – while setting forth her structure in terms of a sociological analysis carried into the service of dogmatics. Troeltsch had ruled out any understanding of the church on the basis of revelation, and his *Social Teachings* concentrated instead on its 'historico-sociological shapes and conditions – the non-theological factors'[19] or, in Troeltsch's own words, 'the intrinsic sociological idea of Christianity, and its structure and organization'.[20] Bonhoeffer now wished to reassert the *vertical* dimension of the church, to 'liberate a genuinely theological concept of the church . . . with every philosophical and sociological tool at his command'.[21] But this was not the whole of his concern. He wanted to insist, at the same time, that Troeltsch was correct in seeing the church as an empirical structure because 'revelation means nothing beyond, but an entity in this historically and sociologically shaped world'.[22]

But if Bonhoeffer had taken over Troeltsch's sociological

tools, he did not really confront the presuppositions which determined the way in which Troeltsch wielded them. It is too bold a claim for Bonhoeffer's champions to say that here, in his first writing, he had encountered Troeltsch directly. While his contemporaries engaged in discussion over the temporal problems of faith and history, Bonhoeffer turned to the spatial question of faith in the community – thereby anticipating, no doubt, concerns which the 'theology of revelation' still has not properly considered.[23] But by beginning where he did, he left begging as many questions as did Barth, who summarily pronounced Troeltsch's theology a cul-de-sac.

Not until the writing of the *Ethics* and the time of his imprisonment was Bonhoeffer to attempt to come to terms with the basic questions Troeltsch had raised, and we shall see how greatly these questions disturbed him. Emil Brunner once wrote of Troeltsch as the one 'to whom belongs the credit of having discerned and shown the irreconcilable contradiction which modern theology had so long attempted to hide . . . : the chasm which separates modern theology from the theology of the reformers and of the ancient church'.[24] And in a prison letter in which Bonhoeffer wrote that contemporary theology would have at last to face the questions raised by a liberalism which, if it lost the battle, at least had the courage to enter it, he added parenthetically the one name: Troeltsch.[25]

Karl Holl

Karl Holl published a collection of his monographs on Luther in 1923, as the first volume of his *Gesammelte Aufsätze zur Kirchengeschichte*. Hans Lietzmann described the publication as 'like a sudden and mighty revelation', while Harnack, his older colleague at the university, called him 'the renewer of Lutheranism'.[26] Troeltsch had dismissed Luther as a medieval man and placed the beginning of neo-Protestantism in the eighteenth century. But Holl was certain that Luther could speak in his own words to the twentieth century. He based his study upon exacting historical and philological examination of sources, relating Luther to the whole spiritual development of the West, including that of the modern world, and took Luther out of the hands of the subjectivists to present him as a genuinely theocentric theologian. Within the decade following publication Holl's work had been questioned from many quarters. It was said that his assertion of Luther's theocentricity against the Christocentric conception of Luther's doctrine (which originated with Ritschl and was accepted at the time) masked a Kantian prejudice, and that he had oversimplified Luther's teaching on justification, with the result that in his presentation, 'justification becomes merely the initial groundwork for God's continuing dealings with men'.[27] Like Seeberg, Holl seemed to Scandinavian scholars to overemphasize the new life of the Christian, and thus to suggest that sanctification was a 'growth into a real righteousness of one's own, given . . . by God', which becomes the 'real continuing ground of one's standing with God'.[28] Regin Prenter accused both men of setting Luther's doctrine into an idealist frame and thus piously identifying the 'new man' in Christ with the 'converted man'.[29]

But at the time of their writing, Holl's essays seemed to many of his contemporaries to constitute 'an important medium between Barthianism and Liberal theology'. Harnack had expressed surprise that, in his own study, he had seemed able to make so little sense out of Karl Barth's vocabulary, and Holl's work was expected to provide him with an 'aerial'. Instead, it brought forth only criticism both from Barth and from many Liberals, none of whom was willing to accept the Luther Holl had presented.[30]

The difficulty was that Holl had seen in Luther's theology a 'religion of conscience' to which he himself subscribed. The effect of this was most evident in his understanding of New Testament Christology, as he outlined it in his popular *Distinctive Elements in Christianity*. Jesus lived, he wrote, because 'an extraordinary individual was necessary – one who knew how to walk along the dizzy path where satanic and divine are divided from one another'.[31] The irrational element in Christianity 'made evident the actual truth, that what offended the common sense of mankind, commended itself to the thoughtful as the revelation of a deeper and supremely convincing truth concerning God and man – herein lay the conquering power of Christianity'.[32] Holl saw in this the clue to Pauline theology. 'Over and above what the ordinary man may achieve . . . Paul recognizes a still higher plane where, in virtue of a special endowment, freedom and certainty of action join forces in a distinctive way. . . .'[33] The 'higher plane' is the sphere of conscience, a place in man where God might encounter him and show him his possibilities, enabling him to reflect upon the divine answer to his human striving and to choose then for good or evil.

Bonhoeffer, along with the dialectical theologians who were his contemporaries, reacted strongly against the notion that any point of contact between God and man can be spoken of. Consequently, he seriously questioned Holl's presentation of Lutheran theology. His reaction played a major role in his rebellion against the theology of his teachers, as we shall see in coming pages. But it was in Holl's seminars, Bethge writes, that 'Bonhoeffer got a magnificent introduction and came to love Luther above anyone else. . . .'[34] Nor could Bonhoeffer rid himself of the problem of 'conscience'. This troubled him in both of his earlier books, in the 1932–3 lectures on Genesis, and twelve years later in the pages of his *Ethics*. From prison, Bonhoeffer was to write of 'the time of religion', which he thought had come to an end, as a time of 'inwardness and conscience'.[35]

Reinhold Seeberg

Bonhoeffer wrote his doctoral dissertation under the guidance of Reinhold Seeberg, the historian of dogma who completed his valuable *Textbook of the History of Doctrines* while Bonhoeffer was his student. We may thus expect to encounter a substantial amount of Seeberg's teaching and reaction against this teaching in the pages of *Sanctorum Communio*. Seeberg led the 'Modern Positivist' revolt against Ritschl's refusal to relate religion to metaphysics and the dismissal of dogmatics by the History of Religions school, and attempted 'at once to reaffirm the Apostles' witness to Jesus and to conserve to the full the unity of the divine life'.[36] The Modern Positivist school was '"positive" in that it sought to preserve the full unity of Christian faith in the final revelation of God in Jesus Christ; ... "modern" in that it attempted to express this faith not by a repristination of old dogmas, but in a form intelligible to modern man and in harmony with the best thought of today.'[37] The programme is not unlike certain present-day interests of contemporary apologetical discourse. In the preface to *The Fundamental Truths of the Christian Religion*, a series of open lectures delivered in Berlin in 1911, Seeberg wrote:

Everywhere in our day we are confronted by the great task of preserving Christianity for the modern mind. This can be accomplished only if the modern world can be brought to the consciousness that even at the present day the deepest wants, needs, and problems which move men find their answers in the Gospel, and that the Gospel need fear no progress of science and culture. But for this purpose no pains must be spared in translating the thoughts of the Christian religion into the speech and modes of our time. No element of real Christianity may thereby be surrendered, yet the particular way of stating the problems raised by the spirit and need of our time must receive minute attention. The old truth must be taught in new wise.[38]

Seeberg went about his task in a highly original way. The studies of Lutheran theology and church dogmas in which he engaged were undertaken with the assumption that dogma 'is only the form in which the Christian society expresses its knowledge of the saving truths of faith'. Thus, dogma can be 'separated from the historic forms in which (the saving truths of faith) found expression in the past'.[39] Dogma can and should be rewritten for a modern age, and the proper language for such a reformulation is that of contemporary metaphysics.

Bethge thus calls Seeberg the 'mediating spirit between idealism, orthodoxy, and modernism'.[40] The latter developed what Sidney Cave called a 'bold and simple' Christology expressed by means of a peculiar vocabulary which mediated between the traditional language of dogma and a universal religious metaphysic. The best example of this mediating spirit remains his conception of the 'religious *a priori*', a notion which Bonhoeffer strongly rejected as providing the point of contact between God and man, a common denominator for theology and philosophy and the ultimate surrender of the concept of revelation. 'God can only be conceived as a reality,' Seeberg wrote, 'if there is in man an organ for this purpose.'[41] This organ was the mind, the realm of the Spirit, personal will, voluntarism. It possessed an 'intrinsic capacity' for 'becoming aware of the being and activity of the supramundane God, and accordingly for receiving the content of His revelation, as divine, into the soul'.[42] God enters the mind as 'a supernatural, living energy which has unlimited power over everything worldly'.[43] The basis of theology is thus for Seeberg the immediate reality of the new life in Christ in the consciousness. From this basis, he unfolds his Christology and ecclesiology.

A Christo-ecclesiology was at the centre of Seeberg's system. He saw the church as the visible, tangible, incarnate Holy Spirit, and related the church to the Holy Spirit in the same way that the *logos* is related to Jesus.[44] He maintained a 'historical' understanding of the Trinity, whereby the church exists in the 'time of the Holy Spirit', *as* the Holy Spirit in the process of being realized. The relationship between Christ and God thus determined, at the same time, his understanding of the relationship between the Holy Spirit and the church, and between the individual consciousness and God.

We shall be treating Seeberg's ecclesiology in more detail in the following chapter of this study. Here it is useful to point to its Christological basis, and see how closely God and 'operative spiritual will-power' in the church and the individual were identified, as they manifested themselves in Jesus. 'Jesus' disposition and Jesus' will,' Seeberg writes, 'is holy, almighty love-energy.' 'Therewith is Christ's nature known. This is, at the same time, knowledge of God. The God who is revealed to us in Christ is holy, almighty love-will.'[45] This God-will created the man Jesus for its 'organ', and 'what he felt, willed, thought, said, and did was worked in Him by the personal God-will that dwelt in Him'.[46] Seeberg formulated this doctrine of the Trinity by substituting for the traditional persons three co-eternal and co-terminous volitional acts. The second person is Jesus, in whom the personal God-will worked in the form of an energy which was 'the divine person himself'.[47] The Holy Spirit is thus the God-will as it manifested itself in the church.

Seeberg attempted in this way to relate the significance of

the church to spiritual history in general, and thus to find a new basis and significance for dogma and church history. Bonhoeffer took this attempt seriously, and wrestled with Seeberg's doctrine of the church throughout the pages of his dissertation. He reworked much of his teacher's terminology and used it for his own purposes, attacking at the same time his metaphysical presuppositions. Not until he attacked Seeberg's religious *a priori* in *Act and Being* was Bonhoeffer entirely independent of the concerns of his teacher.[48] But it was Seeberg's work in the history of dogma that ironically enabled Bonhoeffer to ground himself in the Reformation theology which he was to use as the basis of his protest against the Liberal theology in which he had been trained.

There was little theological *rapport* between Bonhoeffer and his teacher once his dissertation was completed. One suspects that Seeberg never had the personal influence over Bonhoeffer that Harnack and Barth enjoyed. In a letter to a friend in 1930 Bonhoeffer wrote of one of Seeberg's sermons which he had recently heard as 'shameful . . . a religious chat'.[49] Both Seeberg and Bonhoeffer were teaching at the university for the next several years, but after 1931, Bonhoeffer never mentioned his teacher in his writings again.

Adolf von Harnack

Much of the blame for the creation of the false alliance between Protestantism and culture in Germany which collapsed in 1918 has been laid at the feet of the man who most influenced the Christian world in which he lived, Adolf von Harnack. His *Essence of Christianity*, which Barth has called a climax in the history of nineteenth-century evangelical theology, went into several printings – perhaps indicating that the society to which Harnack spoke understood these lectures as a powerful and optimistic expression not only of the Christian faith, but also of trust in the progress of the modern world. Yet Harnack's understanding of history was not a simple one. He insisted that 'all meaning resides exclusively in the supernatural world', and that religion must transcend history and nature as the realm of death. At the same time, history and nature are redeemed by religion through the elevation of the individual spirit 'above heaven and earth'.[50] In his own personality, Harnack embodied just such an individual spirit and became one of the truly impressive figures in modern Protestant church history.

Troeltsch thought of dogmatic theology as a possibility for neo-Protestantism, but only in a form which made no divine claims for itself. Seeberg wished to reclothe dogma in modern, metaphysical dress. But Harnack, in his masterwork, *The History of Dogma*, saw the Reformation as the culmination and conclusion of the development of dogmatic theology.[51] The history of dogma was the story of the obscuring of the Gospel through Hellenization. Luther discarded dogma and substituted for it an evangelical view. But, only half understanding what he had done, he left behind him the material for the reconstruction of dogma in Protestant scholasticism. What Luther discovered was that 'theology is not the analysis and description of God and of the divine acts from the standpoint of reason as occupying an independent position over against God, but it is the confession on the part of faith of its own experience, that is, of revelation'.[52] Not reconstruction of dogma, but completion of the destruction of dogma was the task of contemporary theology. And Harnack closed his great work with these words:

Therefore the goal of all Christian work, even of all theological work, can only be this – to discern ever more distinctly the simplicity and the seriousness of the Gospel, in order to become ever purer and stronger in *spirit*, and ever more loving and brotherly in *action*.[53]

The centre of Christianity was thus what it did to shape one's life. And no one ever lived his teaching more than Harnack. The breadth of his interests and the depth of his scholarly insight made him at home in almost any faculty of the university. During the summer following Harnack's death, Bonhoeffer delivered the address on behalf of the last generation of students to have sat at the feet of Harnack, and spoke of him as 'the old master, to whose opinions the entire cultural world listened attentively', the enemy of all false knowledge, narrow-mindedness, and prejudice, 'above all, a theologian'. He regretted that future generations of students could know nothing of 'the world which this personality embraced' and which he carried with him wherever he went, 'constraining honour for a life which was conducted in the spirit and battle for the truth'.[54]

Bonhoeffer never lost a profound respect for the world of Harnack, which he himself had known in his youth. In prison, he read one of von Harnack's histories and confessed that it drove him to melancholy with the feeling that this kind of life could never again be achieved.

... Our generation [he wrote to his parents] can no longer expect as yours could a life which finds full scope in professional and private activities, and thus achieves perfection and poise. And to make matters worse, we have the example of your life still before our eyes, which makes us painfully aware of the fragmentariness of our own.[55]

Bonhoeffer saw the task of his generation as that of 'saving ourselves out of the debris, as a brand plucked from the burning ... to keep our lives going rather than to shape them, to endure, rather than to forge ahead'.[56] He was in fact remarking on the vast gulf between his age and that of von Harnack, and perhaps on the gulf between the theology which he had come to accept and that of his teacher. For von Harnack had rejected the age of Luther, so similar to Bonhoeffer's own, and had constructed his theology for an age which had passed away:

In [Luther's] age, when life still continued every day to be threatened by a thousand forms of distress, when nature was a dread, mysterious power, when legal order meant unrighteous force, when terrible maladies of all kinds abounded, and in a certain sense no one was sure of his life – in such a time there was necessarily no rising beyond the thought that the most important earthly function of religion is to give comfort amidst the world's misery. Assuagement of the pain of sin, mitigation of the evil of the world – this Augustinian mood remained the prevalent one, and assuredly it is neither possible nor intended that this mood should ever disappear. But the task that is set to Christian faith today is no apocryphal one. ... It must be able to take a powerful part in the moulding of personality, in the productive development of the dominion over nature, in the interpenetrating of the spiritual life with the spirit, and to prove its indispensableness in these directions, otherwise ... the great course of our history will pass on its way.[57]

Bethge sums up the formative influences on Bonhoeffer from

his Berlin education as follows: 'Troeltsch's interest in the sociological realities of Christianity, Holl's reawakening of the genuine Luther, Harnack's intellectual incorruptibility, and Seeberg's philosophical openness.'[58] Most important, Bonhoeffer remained 'one of those who love and share the tradition of a great society, who regard its shame and glory as their own, and who die a little with it, when it falls to the revolution'.[59] No one has put better than Paul Tillich what it meant to have loved and shared this nineteenth-century tradition:

Belonging to the nineteenth century implies life in relatively peaceful circumstances and recalls the highest flourishing of *bourgeois* society in its productive grandeur . . . a consciousness of the Christian humanist values which underlie even the anti-religious forms of this society, and which made and make it possible to resist the inhuman systems of the twentieth century. I am one of those in my generation who, in spite of the radicalism with which they have criticized the nineteenth century, often feel a longing for its stability, its liberalism, its unbroken cultural traditions.[60]

Upon reading Harnack's history of the Prussian Academy in his prison cell, Bonhoeffer wrote to his parents:

There are so few nowadays who have any real interest or sympathy for the nineteenth century. . . . Hardly anyone has the slightest idea what was achieved during the last century by our grandfathers. How much of what they knew has already been forgotten! I believe people will one day be utterly amazed at the fertility of that age, now so much despised and so little known.[61]

CHAPTER 4

Christ Exists as the Church

Five years before Karl Barth rewrote and retitled his *Christliche Dogmatik* as *Kirchliche Dogmatik*, Dietrich Bonhoeffer had completed his *Sanctorum Communio*, with its argument that the 'inner logic' of dogmatics demands that theology begin at that point where it acknowledges the irreducible claim of the church to a reality based upon the revelation of God in Christ. The theme of Bonhoeffer's work, 'Christ exists as the church', was developed in view of both the 'religious community' of his Liberal teachers and the destructive individualism and radical views on transcendence of the dialectical critics of Liberalism.[1] He thus attempted to construct a Christo-ecclesiology which would 'understand . . . the reality of the church of Christ which is given in the revelation of Christ' at the same time that it unfolded this revelation 'from the standpoint of social philosophy and sociology'.[2] In Godsey's succinct formulation, *Sanctorum Communio* was to be 'an investigation of the social structure of the "fellowship of the saints" in which the insights of social philosophy, with its genetic interest in human sociality and sociology, with its systematic interest in the structure of empirical communities are made fruitful for Christian dogmatic thinking about the church'.[3]

Perhaps it was inevitable not only that such a task should suffer from methodological obscureness but also that Bonhoeffer should have found no one to take his work seriously.[4] Dialectical theology was not prepared for a sociological and philosophical approach, in spite of the fact that Bonhoeffer's thesis was wholly in keeping with the logic of the dialectical method. The care with which Bonhoeffer developed his 'Christian

48

sociology' obscured the tension which carried through the work and made it seem what he certainly did not intend: a compromise. The style was that of a doctoral dissertation, pedantic and technical. Bonhoeffer borrowed and adapted his terminology from his teachers (notably Seeberg), social science (Tönnies, Simmel and the 'formalistic' school), and personalist philosophy (the language of I and Thou). The manner in which he then adjusted this terminology to fit the dogmatic and biblical presuppositions of the latter half of his dissertation never, in spite of his efforts, became wholly clear.

In an excellent essay on *Sanctorum Communio*, Peter Berger argues convincingly that Bonhoeffer made a poor choice when he selected the sociological theory which served as one partner in his conversation, turning his back on Marx and Weber to stand within 'a long tradition of German conservative ideology'.[5] Bonhoeffer wished to display the church as, above all, an empirical reality – but he chose a social philosophy which was 'anxious to safeguard a very high and distinctive level of abstraction'.[6] The result was that empirical data never really became a factor in Bonhoeffer's argument. It is important, in view of a renewed interest at the present time in the sociology of the church (which looks to Bonhoeffer's work as a legitimatizing classic) to emphasize that he worked with a sociology few sociologists of today would accept.[7]

But, as Berger admits, Bonhoeffer's sociological presuppositions are 'foils for an essentially dogmatic argument'.[8] And despite the eccentricities of his methodology, Bonhoeffer's polemic against the Berlin systematizers does clearly and forcefully emerge: 'Not religion, but revelation, not religious community, but the church: that is what the reality of Jesus Christ means.'[9] The strategy was to take sociology out of the hands of those who had used it to describe the church, by means of an outside standard, as a 'religious community'. Arguing that the church cannot be understood from any viewpoint other than that of Christian revelation, Bonhoeffer then used sociological concepts for his purpose of describing the visible and unique form which the revelation assumes among the secular structures of society.

One of the peculiar and unfortunate aspects of *Sanctorum Communio* is its avoidance of any direct encounter with the greatest of the liberal socio-theological thinkers, Ernst Troeltsch.[10] There is an implicit conversation with Troeltsch throughout Bonhoeffer's dissertation – which was surely inevitable – but his thesis simply argued the contrary of Troeltsch's position without confronting his presuppositions. These were that a correct historical understanding makes impossible any 'spatial' definition of the church as a community embodying the revelation of Christ, 'resting in an immediate authority with a strictly defined sphere'.[11] An ecclesiological structure which explains itself in terms of a revealed 'Word' inaccessible to objective study was for Troeltsch an anachronism. There can be no 'revelation' of this kind where all truth is subject to the relative conditions of history. 'Revelation' must therefore be replaced by a religious view of mankind as a whole, embodied in the person of Christ and the worship of him as 'the necessary symbol of the cult'.[12] The old church with her divine authority, her scriptural or hierarchical ideal of unity, has been irrevocably shattered by the Reformation and the rise of historical science. Her religious power is now manifested in the life and social structures of the secular world.

Bonhoeffer, like Barth, seemed in 1927 to feel that the only way to move beyond Troeltsch's position was to disregard it. Turning his back on the historical analysis which was to affect him so profoundly in later years, Bonhoeffer took up the theme of the 'spatial' aspect of the church and defended sociologically what was essentially a traditional Lutheran conception. Here he found himself struggling with the ecclesiological thought of his doctoral adviser, Reinhold Seeberg.

Seeberg's understanding of church dogma and his insistence on the validity and relevance of metaphysics as the realm of contemporary dogmatics would allow him no dissolution of the church into an independent organization for the production of ethical ideals and human inspiration. 'The church stands in a fixed relation of infinite importance to the world,' and must 'hold itself inwardly free from the world' if it is to give its service to the world.[13] At that point where Troeltsch had ended

50

his discussion, Seeberg began describing how the church receives and participates in Christ. He did not, however, develop this participation in Troeltsch's social and ethical terms, but rather with his characteristic metaphysical-psychological terminology. The combination of traditional ecclesiology with Christology and metaphysics led him to centre his general religious view of mankind in the church, concentrated, formally defined, and structured. The church as it participates in Christ, not the absolute personality of Christ, is the source of energy and stimulation for mankind. Holiness in the world thus resides in the church.[14] The church is the coming kingdom of God, which 'is and will be', and 'in which the will of God determines the course of humanity'.[15] The church is 'social life in the deepest sense', where egoism is overcome in the fellowship of believers.[16] From his conservative Lutheran background (the effect of which will clearly be seen in his pupil) as well as his metaphysical presuppositions, Seeberg could speak of the church as the 'incarnation' of the third person of the Trinity.[17]

Bonhoeffer's relationship to his teacher's conception of the church is not easy to determine. His theme, 'Christ existing as the church', was certainly directed against any attempt to ignore the brute fact of revelation. Seeberg and Troeltsch alike had substituted for 'revelation' (a conception inaccessible to scientific inquiry) the notion of 'religion'. But Seeberg's line of attack, because of his metaphysical presuppositions, was more difficult to get clear. Bonhoeffer was certain that no outside measure, no general concept of religion, could be allowed to determine the nature of the church and describe her forms and her future. The church can be understood, he argued, only from within and in terms of her revelational foundation in Christ:

The concept of the church is possible only in the sphere of reality based on God; that is, it is not deducible. The reality of the church is a reality of revelation, part of whose nature is to be either believed or denied. So if we want to find an adequate criterion for justifying the church's claim that it is the church of God, this is possible only if we place ourselves within it, if we submit in faith to its claim.[18]

From this basis, Bonhoeffer *could* have developed a thesis which engaged Troeltsch in conversation, showing how and in what way a conception of revelation was tenable in view of the historical process. He chose instead to consider his statement axiomatic, thus dismissing Troeltsch with a stroke and directing himself to the second question: can a particular limited space which especially contains Christ (Seeberg's concept of the church) be said to contain him 'religiously' or as 'revelation'? Within the boundaries Seeberg defined, discussion with Troeltsch could only occur in secondary issues, such as the particular morphology of the visible church. Bonhoeffer made axiomatic the inadequacy of Troeltsch's definition of the church, because 'in the foreground stands an historically fortuitous social construction'.[19] Thus the question of the relationship between the revelation embodied in the church and the historical dissolution of 'the fixed and objective ideal of unity' of the church never arose.

In its argument with Seeberg, Bonhoeffer's thesis depended largely upon the successful adaptation of the socio-philosophical terms of his teacher to his own purposes. The degree to which this was achieved, and the general direction of Bonhoeffer's dissertation as a whole, is most clearly indicated in his development of a term taken from Seeberg's writings: the 'objective spirit'. Following Seeberg (and Hegel),[20] Bonhoeffer defines this objective spirit as 'the bond between the sense of history and the sense of community, between the intention of a community in time, and its intention in space. Objective spirit is the will effectively operating upon the members of a community.'[21] We thus have to do with that spirit which, filling a community and the sphere of her existence, determines her nature. In the church, in Seeberg's view, this spirit would be that which made her distinctly 'religious' as opposed to the objective spirits of other human communities.

Bonhoeffer's point of departure for his discussion of the problem of community is a presentation of man as essentially *homo socialis*. He quotes with approval from Seeberg's *Dogmatik*: 'The sociality of the human spirit is revealed as a primal force. . . . It is a tremendous reality, which first teaches us to understand the secret of humanity and its history, and to place hope in the future of mankind.'[22] He notes that Seeberg was 'the first since Schleiermacher' to present sociality as something belonging to human nature. It is not clear, however, whether Bonhoeffer would have wished to question the latitude Seeberg granted to this idea in his ecclesiological argument. In the *Fundamentals of the Christian Religion*, Seeberg founded the church on the *a priori* structure of the sociality of man: 'The will of Christ that his church exist needed human nature with its tendencies and inclinations as the means for raising the structure. Man lives not solitarily, but socially.'[23]

Objective spirit is therefore a conception pertaining to *all* human communities. Where Seeberg elaborated its meaning for the church, he often substituted the more dynamic term, 'operative spiritual will-power'. Given Seeberg's metaphysical understanding of the relationship between God and the world, one cannot avoid suspecting that Seeberg wished to identify this 'spiritual will-power' with the Holy Spirit itself. At one point, Seeberg wrote: 'We . . . experience the Spirit from above as operative spiritual will-power.'[24] The relationship between members of the community seems identical to that between man and God:

Where one wishes to make another subject to the sovereignty of God, he wills it from God, and his own word takes effect in so far as it is heard at all, and works psychologically as almighty divine will. We all . . . speak God's word in so far as we speak of God's sovereignty, for our speech is the vehicle of the power of God.[25]

The danger here is readily apparent: Seeberg virtually identifies the action of God with dynamic, interpersonal relationship and personal will. The church is *Christus prolongatus*, the Incarnation of the Holy Spirit.

In his development, Bonhoeffer distinguished between the 'possibility' and the 'necessity' of the church from the standpoint of human sociality, dismissing the second from any proper understanding of the church:

If it is nevertheless a fact that religion is for the most part social in character, this is primarily accounted for by various psychological factors of a more or less accidental nature (e.g. the need to communicate – Schleiermacher, the receptive-active nature of man – Seeberg). These factors indicate that religious community is possible, but not that it is necessary. This leads us back from the general idea of religion to its concrete form, which for us means the concept of the church.[26]

Here again, as with Troeltsch's view of history, Bonhoeffer simply sets his own view alongside the opposing one. For he is arguing that the basis of the church cannot be derived from any socio-religious characteristic of human nature. When he arrives at his presentation of the objective spirit of the church, he neatly reverses Seeberg's argument:

> The empirical church is not identical with a religious community. Rather, as a concrete historical community, in spite of the relativity of its forms, its imperfect and pretentious appearance, the empirical church is the Body of Christ, the presence of Christ on earth, for it has his Word. It is possible to understand the empirical church only by looking down from above, or by looking out from the inside, and not otherwise. Once this fact has been grasped it is of course in principle possible once more to define the church as a religious community, always bearing in mind that it is really based on God. Thus if we now apply to the church what we said about the objective spirit, we have the claim of the objective spirit of the church to be the bearer of the historical work of Jesus Christ and of the social action of the Holy Spirit.
>
> The historical church *claims* that it possesses the Holy Spirit and is the effective custodian of the Word of God and of the sacrament.[27]

Bonhoeffer is perfectly willing to grant his Liberal teachers their conception of the church as a 'religious community', provided they have first understood it as a community whose determination is solely from God. And one notices the dependence upon dialectical methodology: the church cannot simply be identified with the Holy Spirit. The church *claims* that the Holy Spirit has been *entrusted* to her. She is the community of revelation only *in faith*. And here Bonhoeffer recreates all of the tensions Seeberg had carefully resolved. The time and space correlates of the objective spirit check one another, and Seeberg's question of the relationship between objective spirit and Holy Spirit is undercut by a necessary theological distinction between realized and actualized church. Because of human sin and limitation, and because the church is an institution in history, an identification between the two can be made only eschatologically. Thus Bonhoeffer speaks of the 'sanctification' of the objective spirit by the Holy Spirit.[28]

But this rejection of Seeberg's identification of the spiritual content of the church with the action of God comes into conflict with Bonhoeffer's thesis – which is, after all, to demonstrate that the community of revelation is, at the same time, a wholly empiric community. He resolves this conflict by pointing to the visible, 'sociological' forms of the church – preaching and the sacraments – as vehicles through which the Holy Spirit operates. As Godsey summarizes Bonhoeffer's position:

Christ and the Holy Spirit *use* the historically given forms of the objective spiritual life in the upbuilding of the empirical church: the historical tendency of the Christ-Spirit works in the form of the objective spirit, and the Holy Spirit uses the objective spirit as the bearer of his social activity. But both confirm their presence to the church solely through the word, which means that the ever-changing, imperfect, sinful objective spirit of a human 'religious fellowship' must *believe* that it is the church, 'Christ existing as community,' *sanctorum communio!* The identity cannot be confirmed historically and will remain invisible until the *eschata*. Yet a beginning has already been made in that *the Holy Spirit uses the objective spirit as the bearer of certain visible forms that he himself guarantees to be efficacious.*[29]

One may question the wisdom of attacking a conception which guarantees the presence of God within a religious spirit by setting against it divinely instituted, virtually *ex opere operato* forms which then have simply to be 'believed'. But Bonhoeffer was not as concerned with protecting his theory against the charge that he pictured revelation as a heteronomous power which arbitrarily violated the structures of the world, as he was with attacking the conception of the church as an organism which lived as an exalted communal feeling of value or worth. Perhaps his sociology betrayed him and left dubious his claim that 'revelation means nothing beyond, but an entity in, this historically shaped world'.[30] But if his dissertation confused more than it illuminated, at least his intention was clear. He concludes his argument:

The church is not first made real by assuming empirical form, when the Holy Spirit does his work; but the reality of the church of the Holy Spirit is one which is founded on revelation, and it is a matter merely of believing in that revealed reality in its empirical form.[31]

Bonhoeffer does not see how the experience of revelation will be distinguished from 'religious exp rience' or 'spiritual exaltation', but he attempts, by means of an explication of what he called 'everydayness', to differentiate theologically between the two. The church is God's downward movement, not the upward movement of an association of human beings. In a fine passage, he wrote:

... It is precisely in the commonplace surroundings of every day that the church is believed and experienced, it is not in moments of spiritual exaltation, but in the monotony and severity of daily life, and in the regular worship of God that we come to understand the church's full significance. . . . Our age is not poor in experiences, but in *faith*. Only faith can create true experience of the church, so we think it more important for our age to be led into belief in the church of God, than to have experiences squeezed from it which as such are no help at all . . .[32]

The purpose of Bonhoeffer's thesis was thus to reverse the standpoint from which the question of the church is asked. The church is indeed a community and, in view of its activity, a 'religious' one. But the determination of the church is solely from God and his revelation. No value over and above the value of any other human community can be ascribed to the church, independent of the reality given by Christ.

Bonhoeffer intended to maintain his conversation with his Liberal teachers by insisting that his concept of revelation was empirical, but they remained unimpressed by this kind of mediation. In fact, *Sanctorum Communio* already bore the marks of Bonhoeffer's impatience with Liberal methodology and he soon surrendered all attempts to mediate between Liberal and dialectical theologies. But he never surrendered his insistence that revelation is 'an entity in this historically shaped world' and he retained, for the next several years, the assertion that the revelation in Christ is an *ecclesiological* reality as the basis of his own theology. His more decisive battle with his Liberal teachers followed the publication of his dissertation, and took place in the pages of *Act and Being*.

CHAPTER 5

Ecclesiology as
the Ground of Revelation

Logically considered, the sequence of Bonhoeffer's first two major works is reversed. While *Sanctorum Communio* developed the forms and structures of the community of revelation, *Act and Being* is concerned with the preliminary thesis: A Christian conception of revelation must, by definition, be an ecclesiological statement. Thus many of the tensions and concerns within and behind the argument of *Sanctorum Communio* (especially the Christological ones) first became clear in *Act and Being*.

Although he discarded the problematic sociological development of his earlier work, Bonhoeffer remained loyal to his basic thesis. *Act and Being* confronts various philosophical and theological solutions to the problem of revelation which were prevalent in 1930, and orders them into two categories: those based upon a transcendental thesis and those which emerge from an ontological foundation. Bonhoeffer then questions the validity of each group for a specifically Christian conception of revelation:

The problem is one of forming genuine theological concepts and of choosing whether one is to use ontological categories in explaining them or those of transcendental philosophy. It is a question of the 'objectivity' of the concept God, of an adequate concept of knowledge, of defining the relation between the being of God and the mental act which conceives it. In other words, there has to be a theological interpretation of what the 'being of God in revelation' means and how it is known, of what may be the interrelation of belief as act and revelation as being, and correspondingly of where man stands when seen from the standpoint of revelation.[1]

57

Arguing that neither act nor being alone is an adequate category within which Christian revelation may be discussed, Bonhoeffer presents his thesis that 'the idea of revelation must be re-envisaged within the concretion of the idea of the church, i.e. in a sociological category where both kinds of analysis encounter each other and are drawn together in one'.[2]

A decision must now be made as to the best procedure to adopt in tracing out and holding together the various threads of Bonhoeffer's developing ideas: his ecclesiological theme, his encounter with Liberal and dialectical theologians, the philosophical considerations which now appear, and the underlying problems of revelation and Christology. The large number of persons and ideas which pass through the pages of *Act and Being* makes it impossible to reproduce Bonhoeffer's argument, even in summary form. In addition, it is systematically necessary that we anticipate themes which will occur in Bonhoeffer's later work. We must choose from the conversations remaining within the earliest phase of Bonhoeffer's life and work those which are closest to the centre of his concern and which will, at the same time, relate most clearly to the chapters which are to follow.[3]

Among the questions raised in *Act and Being* is one concerning the religious *a priori*, a general form of religious awareness in man, as set forth by Bonhoeffer's teacher, Reinhold Seeberg.[4] Bonhoeffer's attack on this notion signalled the end of Seeberg's influence upon him. In early writings from New York and Berlin, Bonhoeffer also confronts the problem of conscience as it appeared in the work of another of his teachers, Karl Holl. Although neither of these discussions is crucial to the specific thesis Bonhoeffer is developing, both point directly to what lies beneath his concern. We shall therefore focus our attention on the relationship between Bonhoeffer and his teachers and continue our discussion of the problem of revelation *versus* religion.

The outcome of *Sanctorum Communio* was the rejection of 'religious community' as a definition of the essential nature of the church, in favour of 'Christ existing as the church'. Seeberg's religious *a priori* and Holl's conscience were for the Liberal doctrine of man what religious community was for the

Liberal concept of the church: 'spaces' within which man might directly encounter God as a religious reality. 'Religious community', 'conscience', and 'religious *a priori*' have to do with man's awareness of God within a sphere which mediates the divine and the human. We shall continue to develop Bonhoeffer's wrestling with the question of whether such a sphere existed, and how this question related to the problem of revelation.

Finally, Bonhoeffer's relationship to the figure who most influenced the direction and form of his attack on Liberal theology becomes clearly defined in his writings during the years from 1930 to 1932. Bonhoeffer discovered, beneath the religious conceptions of his teachers, the Idealist philosophy which Karl Barth had held responsible for the major errors of nineteenth-century theology. Both men rejected this philosophy and the theology which had accepted it and turned to the Reformation for guidance and support. But now, for the first time, it becomes clear that Bonhoeffer and Barth have turned to the Reformation in quite different ways. We shall have to develop this as well.

The Religious *a Priori*

The religious *a priori* was a development of nineteenth-century evangelical theology which, in its simplest form, described the *capacity* in man for apprehending and comprehending the divine. It had its basis in Schleiermacher, who spoke of man's innate and essential capacity to 'sense and taste the infinite', and it was later taken up and developed by Troeltsch. Reinhold Seeberg articulated this concept as a part of his *Christian Dogmatics*. This clear and systematic work attempted to affirm on the one hand the independent, transcendent *being* of revelation over against man, and on the other the reality of the revelatory event within the consciousness of man – 'the clearest juxtaposition.' Bonhoeffer wrote, 'of theology's two great concerns'.[5] In Seeberg's formulation, the act of awareness or encounter of God and man within man's consciousness takes place in such a way that 'man consciously and willingly himself performs, in consciousness of his freedom, the movement performed in him by the mind of God'.[6]

It will be recognized that Seeberg's style is consistent with that of his ecclesiology and Christology which we have previously outlined: God and man perform together a single, simultaneous action. Yet here we have the disarming insistence that God *transcends* consciousness as Lord and Creator: 'The unconditional requirement of Christian theology' which, Bonhoeffer remarks, is 'elaborated by Seeberg throughout his dogmatics'.[7] At the same time, however, Seeberg sees the supernatural as having 'no existence other than that it enjoys in the religious movements of the human will, the religious intuition of the human mind'.[8]

'God can only enter the consciousness as a reality,' Seeberg writes, 'if there is in man an organ for this purpose!'[9] Seeberg thus speaks of man as 'charged with the capacity' for 'becoming directly conscious of pure mind'. This capacity he calls the religious *a priori*.

As a formal mental disposition, the religious *a priori* has no content of its own. The positive content of faith is dictated by revelation; the *a priori* is simply the intrinsic capacity, within this context, for becoming aware of the being and activity of the supramundane God, and accordingly for the receiving of the content of his revelation, as divine, into the soul.[10]

It is the picture of what Bonhoeffer calls 'a mould in man wherein the divine revelation may pour' that Bonhoeffer finds intolerable and, significantly, attacks on the basis of the Reformer's *cor curvum in se* of the natural man:

If revelation is to come to man, he must be wholly transformed. Faith itself must be created in him. In this case there can be no ability to 'hear' before the 'hearing'. These are thoughts which Seeberg expresses, and refers to in Luther. But faith stands as the work of God in a sense inapplicable to natural religiosity, for which the religious *a priori* noted by Seeberg certainly holds good. According to Luther, revelation and faith are bound to the concrete message, and the Word is the mediator of the contact between God and man, admitting no other 'directness'. But then the idea of the *a priori* can only be understood to imply that certain mental forms are preposited for the formal understanding of the Word, in which case, it must be admitted, a specifically religious *a priori* loses meaning. All that pertains to personal appropriation of the fact of Christ is not *a prioristic*, but is owed to the contingent action of God on man.[11]

After five years of wrestling with Seeberg's difficult theology, Bonhoeffer has at last freed himself from the influence of his teacher. The implications of his rejection of the religious *a priori* reached far beyond the four pages his argument occupied in his dissertation. He broke off what were at the time fruitless attempts to converse with his teachers, and turned his attention towards determining his own place among his contemporaries in terms of the theology of revelation. Throughout essays and lectures written at the same time as *Act and Being*, one now watches Bonhoeffer return again and again to the *oppositional* character of revelation: God stands over and against all human structures, institutions, and attempts to contain him. At the same time as he made his final departure from Seeberg, Bonhoeffer produced an essay on 'The Religious Experience of Grace and the Ethical Life'. Here he distinguished between the objective-psychological understanding of grace as 'a superhuman power which is in essence dynamic and which, as far as it is experienced, enters the realm of human feeling, willing, and thinking, and so gives finiteness an eternal worth and character'; and a theological understanding of grace, 'directly opposed to every human being, to human experience of value and good'.[12] Bonhoeffer does not mention Seeberg, but his teacher could well have been the target of his criticism.

Bonhoeffer now reacts instinctively against any theological *a priori* which, dependent upon a divine-human continuum, circumvented the whole problem of revelation. He expressed his indebtedness to the criticism of the Liberals which Karl Barth had made at this point, and virtually identified himself with Barth's revolution:

Theological thinking is not constructed *a priori*, but *a posteriori* as Karl Barth has maintained. Therefore, it has to be conscious of its limitations. As thinking *per se*, it is not excepted from the pretensions and boundlessness of all thinking. But the property of theological thinking is that it knows its own insufficiency and its limitations. So it must be its highest concern to guard these limitations and to leave room for the reality of God, which can never be conceived by theological thinking. This means that there is not one theological sentence which can presume to speak truth unless it refers to the reality of God and the impossibility of embracing this reality in theological sentences.[13]

Seeberg carefully insisted that 'the religious *a priori* has no content of its own; the positive content of faith is dictated by revelation . . .' Formally, the religious *a priori* remained an *empty* space which did in fact 'leave room for the reality of God'. But viewing this formulation from the vantage point of Seeberg's metaphysical approach to the problem, taken as a whole, Bonhoeffer could only suspect that God filled this space as a religious extension of humanity, 'the religious movement of the mind'. 'God' thus becomes superfluous. The use of general *a priori* categories to define the action of God could only lead to the final elimination of the transcendence which Seeberg, as a sensitive and incisive theologian, knew he was obliged to protect.

Karl Holl and the Religion of Conscience

Bonhoeffer's criticism of Seeberg and Barth's influence upon the direction of the former's line of attack disclosed a variety of Liberal targets. Bonhoeffer soon confronted the 'religion of conscience' of the man who had introduced Luther to him, Karl Holl. The direct criticism of Holl occurs in *Die Frage nach dem Menschen*, Bonhoeffer's inaugural lecture at Berlin in 1930. Here he pictures Holl as 'an impressive representative of the overwhelming majority of contemporary theologians' who, imagining that he was thinking along genuinely Lutheran lines, saw revelation as 'man understanding himself through reflecting on his conscience, where God encounters him'.[14] As with Seeberg's religious *a priori*, revelation is said to be available to man within a prescribed space within him, into which God enters and within which he encounters him.

In his inaugural lecture, Bonhoeffer brought the critism of the dialectical theologians to bear against Holl's conception of conscience, which he described as man's becoming-aware of his own 'possibilities'. He wrote:

There is in man no point where God can win space in him; indeed, it belongs to his essence to be *incapax infiniti*. With his limited nature it is impossible for him to unite himself directly with the infinite. . . . His thought and his ethically responsible conscience, indeed, his religiousness, remain hopeless attempts to anchor the I in the absolute. They belong to the *phronema sarkos*, whereby man seizes the honour of God in order to escape insecurity, in securing at least his self-understanding. He explains himself for good, he explains himself for evil; both are the attempt, whether for good or for evil, to be secure – without recognizing his guilt before God in his good and evil, which rests precisely at that point where he attempts to secure himself.[15]

In *Sanctorum Communio*, Bonhoeffer had spoken of conscience as 'just as well the ultimate prop for self-justification as the point at which Christ strikes home at man through the Law'.[16] In *Act and Being*, Bonhoeffer quoted Luther to telling advantage against Holl, sharpening his attack on conscience as man's 'final grasp at himself':

The conscience and remorse of man in Adam are his final grasp at himself, the final confirmation and justification of his self-lordly, self-masterly attitude. Man makes himself the defendant and exhorts himself upward to his better self. But the cry of conscience serves only to dissemble the mute loneliness of his desolate isolation, it sounds without echo into the world that is governed and construed by the self. Man in Adam reaches the confines of his solitude but, misreading his situation, continues to 'seek himself in himself': he hopes by remorse still to preserve his sinful existence. . . . Therefore this conscience is of the devil, who leaves man to himself in untruth, so this conscience must be mortified when Christ comes to man.[17]

The relationship of conscience to revelation is thus that of Law to Gospel. Rather than a sphere reserved for the encounter of God with man, it is the place where man confronts only his prideful self. Holl used conscience as Seeberg used his religious *a priori*, and both were unconsciously attempting to circumvent the question of revelation *from outside*, apart from man's understanding of himself and his world. Bonhoeffer turned to Barth and the Reformation in order to overthrow these conceptions. But the background of this battle was for Bonhoeffer, as for Barth, the bankruptcy of the philosophy of Idealism.

The Attack on Idealism and the Influence of Barth

Holl's 'conscience' served as the point of departure for Bonhoeffer's rejection of the Idealist background of Liberal theology in general. Although Seeberg dissociated himself from the

Idealism Holl openly embraced and attributed to Luther, it was difficult for Bonhoeffer to see the theology of his teacher as differing to any great extent from the main outlines of 'the gospel of Mind'. Throughout Bonhoeffer's early writings there thus runs the characterization of Liberalism, in so far as it was based upon an Idealist philosophy, as 'limitless'. By this he meant that Idealism, in its presumption, seized transcendence and placed it under the control of the ego. Once a 'space' has been posited within man where both God and man may be encountered and understood, where religious values and possibilities may be grasped as indubitably divine, the all-embracing ego cannot but assert its limitlessness, boundlessness, and autonomy. This was the understanding with which Karl Barth had attacked Idealism as the inevitable falsification of philosophy and theology, and responsible for all of the major errors of Liberalism. Bonhoeffer, in a 1930 essay on 'The Theology of Crisis and its Attitude Toward Philosophy and Science', vigorously set forth Barth's position:

Here (in Idealism) the ego is found as not only a reflecting, but even a creating ego. It creates the world itself. The ego stands in the centre of the world, which is created, ruled, overpowered by the ego. The identification of the ego with the ground of everything which has been called God is inevitable. There are no limits for the ego, its power and its claim are boundless, it is its own standard. Here all transcendence is pulled into the circle of the creative ego. . . . Man knows himself immediately by the act of the coming of the ego to itself, and knows through himself essentially everything, even God. God is in man; God is man himself. Barth and his friends discovered in this philosophy the most radical, most honest, and most consistent expression of the philosophical enterprise as such.[18]

Thus Bonhoeffer summarizes Barth's position. But he began his own *Act and Being* with much the same valuation of post-Kantian Idealism:

The gospel of mind finding itself in God and God in itself was preached too seductively by Idealism for theology to resist its blandishments, and all too readily it reasoned thus: If being is essentially consciousness, God must 'be' in religious experiences, and the reborn I must find God in reflexion upon itself. Where else could God be found but in my consciousness? Even if I can never pass beyond it, it must be what constitutes being in general. God, then, is the God of my consciousness. He 'is' only in my religious consciousness.[19]

Bonhoeffer therefore dismisses absolutely any theological attempt to make direct use of Idealist epistemology, and there is the implication that his reasoning holds equally good for his rejection of conscience, religious *a prioris*, and the 'religious' understanding of the church. Karl Barth's attack on Idealism as 'the most dangerous grasping after God, in order to be like God, and thus to justify man by his own power'[20] is unquestionably behind Bonhoeffer's thinking. Again in *Act and Being*, Bonhoeffer states:

... In the whole of Idealism, the inmost identity of I and God, underlying everything, is simply an expression of the proposition: like is conceivable only by like. If God is to come to man, man must already be in essence divine. If theology is to grasp the relationship of God and man, it can only do so by postulating the profound likeness of one to the other and finding there, exactly, the unity of God and man. One is like the very God one conceives ...

Thus intensified, such propositions are exposed as theologically intolerable. It is not because man is by nature divine that God comes to him – on the contrary, he would not then need to come – but because he is utterly unlike God and never shapes his concept of God according to his own image.[21]

The centre of Barth's attack on Liberalism was the rejection of all form of religion and religious awareness which depended on natural theology; the breaking down of all theological, philosophical, cultural, and especially ecclesiological structures which owed their conception to the positing of a continuity between God and man. This has, indeed, remained the heart of Barth's theology. Followers of Barth's encounters with various opponents, since 1920, will recognize that Barth has battled most impressively when the basis of his view of revelation, the absolute qualitative distinction between God and man, has appeared to be threatened. But where does Bonhoeffer distinguish his own view from that of Barth?

Thus far, the vigour and clarity with which Bonhoeffer singles out the issues and champions Barth's position against his opponents makes it difficult to distinguish between his exposition of Barth and the development of his own position. Both men exposed what they saw to be the pretentiousness of Liberal theology with its religious structures, showing them to be but endless attempts to avoid the embarrassment of revelation, by circumventing it and rendering it superfluous. The conception of God as Wholly Other than man, God over and against man, ruled out from the beginning any philosophical approach to the problem of God. Bonhoeffer, in his essay on 'The Christian Idea of God', signalled the close of a phase in his theological development. He wrote:

No religion, no ethics, no metaphysical knowledge may serve man to approach God. These are all subject to the judgement of God, they are works of man. Only the acknowledgement that God's Word alone helps and that every other attempt is and remains sinful, only by this acknowledgement is God received. And this acknowledgement must be given by God, as the Holy Spirit, in faith. That is the foolishness of the revelation of God and its paradoxical character – that just there, where the power of man has lapsed entirely, where man knows his own weakness, sinfulness, and consequently the judgement of God upon him, that just there God is already working in grace, that just and exactly there and only there is forgiveness, justification, restoration. There, where man himself no longer sees, God sees, and God alone works, in judgement and in grace. There, at the very limits of man, stands God, and when man can do nothing more, then God does all.[22]

The 'Community of Revelation'

It is in the positive content of Bonhoeffer's position that his early divergence from what he considered certain unhealthy tendencies in dialectical theology becomes visible. His general acceptance of the basic outline of dialectical theology, the theology of revelation as set forth by Karl Barth, was strongly and clearly stated in various writings between 1930 and 1932. But Bonhoeffer also developed, in his earliest writings, what he imagined to be a corrective of dangerous shortcomings in the dialectical method. The corrective was the thesis which he expressed in *Sanctorum Communio* and carried into the pages of *Act and Being*: the church is the 'community of revelation', Christ exists as the church.

Sanctorum Communio begins any discussion of Christian revelation with a concept of the church:

If at the conclusion of a dogmatics the concept of the church is presented as a necessary consequence of evangelical faith, nothing else is meant than that the inner reality of the church is connected with the general reality

66

of revelation. Only if the concept of God is understood alone in connection with a concept of the church can the latter be deduced from the former on the basis of a technical presentation. It would be well if a dogmatics were to begin not with the doctrine of God, but with the doctrine of the church, in order to set a clear structure over the inner logic of dogmatics.[23]

Bonhoeffer was disturbed by the characterization of the church in Barth's *Epistle to the Romans*, the latter's only major work until 1927, as an institution in which 'human indifference, misunderstanding and opposition attain their most sublime and their most naïve form'.[24] Dialectical theology possessed strong individualistic tendencies, directing the man before God to his utter inability to save himself and to the saving grace of what seemed a formal and impersonal God. What was necessary, to Bonhoeffer's mind, was an unequivocal affirmation of *both* sides of the dialectic; directing the sinner towards a community which was, however sinful, the chosen instrument of God's redeeming grace. Therefore, 'revelation is an entity in this historically shaped world'. The reality of human indifference, misunderstanding, and opposition did not alter the fact that here, in this community, God was revealing himself in Christ:

[In the *communio sanctorum*] the old ontic relationships are not radically annulled, every empirical formulation will necessarily be subject to the ambiguity inherent in all human actions. . . . In this we can perceive a special will of God which it is not open to us to belie by condemning everything that has taken on a form as the handiwork of man.[25]

During the year in which Bonhoeffer's dissertation was completed, Barth published his *Die christliche Dogmatik*, strengthening Bonhoeffer's suspicion that the former lacked a clear and positive conception of the role of the church as the ground of revelation. Barth's picture of God's transcendence was, if anything, even more formal and impersonal, and Bonhoeffer detected a 'characteristic wavering between use and rejection of temporal definitions of the act of belief'.[26] Continuing his insistence on the freedom of God from all human control, Barth presented the church (in terms borrowed directly from the *Epistle to the Romans*) as a 'parable', an analogy which pointed to God's action but which in no way participated in it. This was the logical outcome of Barth's basic position: man's knowledge is non-knowledge. God remains always and eternally in the realm of free address, always and eternally subject. The empirical actions of man in 'belief', 'obedience', etc., can only witness to God's activity and do not in themselves involve the participation of God. God's freedom in revelation means that he is bound by nothing, is utterly free and unconditioned.

If Bonhoeffer had accepted Barth's protest, he did not accept this conclusion. God was personal, not a formal construction. God offered himself to men, he did not turn away from them. God was hidden, but he was apprehensible in his hiddenness. God did not exist for himself, but for his creation. Through faith, God revealed himself in Christ within a community of men:

The whole situation impels one to ask whether a formalistic understanding of God's freedom in contingent revelation, conceived wholly in terms of the act, is really the proper groundwork for theology. In revelation it is a question less of God's freedom on the far side of us, i.e. his eternal isolation and aseity, than of his forth-proceeding, his *given* Word, his bond in which he has bound himself, of his freedom as it is most strongly attested in his having freely bound himself to historical man, having placed himself at man's disposal. God is not free *of* man but *for* man. Christ is the Word of his freedom. God *is there*, which is to say: not in eternal non-objectivity but (looking ahead for the moment) 'haveable', graspable in his Word within the church.[27]

This understanding of the relationship between ecclesiology and revelation ran directly counter to Barth's insistence that revelation, once having occurred, is not thereby absorbed into or merged with finite processes. As Bonhoeffer summarizes Barth's position in the 1927 *Dogmatik*: 'God can give and withdraw himself absolutely according to his pleasure; in either action he remains free. He is never at man's discretion; it is his honour and glory to remain utterly free and unconditional in relation to everything free and conditional.'[28]

Bonhoeffer is less interested in the logic of Barth's argument than in defending the *concrete* nature of revelation. What is behind his argument? If we remember that the 'community of revelation' is at the same time '*Christ* existing as the church', it becomes clear that the basis of Bonhoeffer's position, and the ground of his disagreement with Barth, is Christological. Where Barth writes of God's honour and glory in remaining free and unconditional, Bonhoeffer quotes Luther's famous statement on the nature of the sacrament:

It is to the honour and glory of our God . . . however, that giving himself for our sake in deepest condescension, he passes into the flesh, the bread, our hearts, mouths, entrails, and suffers also for our sake that he be dishonourably . . . handled, on the altar as on the cross.[29]

Here is the Christ who exists solely 'for others', the suffering Christ who gives himself to the world, who will appear with such power in Bonhoeffer's last writings. Recognizing that Luther's view of the sacrament, his theology of the cross, and his conception of the church were of one piece (growing out of Luther's understanding of the Augustinian *corpus Christi mysticum*), Bonhoeffer elaborates a Lutheran doctrine of the church as a Christology of condescension. The various strands of his thought are brought together into a view of revelation as God's 'haveableness' in the church. While Barth turns to the Reformation and follows the Calvinist path back to the present, protecting God's freedom and transcendence, Bonhoeffer runs the risk of a Lutheran Christology, pointing to God's committed presence in Christ for his community.[30]

Summary and Prospectus

We have watched Bonhoeffer free himself from his fruitless conversations with his Liberal teachers and their various views of religion and religious awareness, in order to insist that revelation is an event which comes to man *from outside*. His essential agreement with the theology of revelation led him, at the same time, to insist that revelation is concrete and apprehensible in the community of revelation, the church. The dangers of his position are reasonably clear: His view of revelation *as* the church leaves open the question of the relationship of Christ and the church to the world *outside* of the church. We would like also to see a Christological expression of Christ 'outside' of the church, as her Redeemer and Judge and Perfector, perhaps in the form of a doctrine of Scripture – which might distinguish his position from the self-contained ecclesiology and revelation of Rome.

For a few years, Bonhoeffer attempted to work out the difficulties of his position and to broaden the basis of his theology in order to make it more flexible. But history intervened and turned these thoughts inward once more, into an even more radical and exclusive and forceful presentation of his Christo-ecclesiology. We shall see in the following section how this came about.

THE CONCRETION OF A
NEW CHRISTOLOGY

Following Christ . . . what that is is what I want to
know.   *Autumn 1934.* GS I, *p.41*

The restoration of the church will come from a new
kind of monasticism . . .

January 1935. GS III, *p.25*

CHAPTER 6

The New Christology

I remember a conversation I had with a young French pastor at A., thirteen years ago. We had put before us, quite simply, the question what we really wanted to do with our lives. He said he wanted to become a saint (and I think it possible he did become one). This impressed me very much at that time. Nevertheless, I argued with him and said something to the effect that I wished to learn to believe. For a long time I did not recognize how far we were apart. I thought I could learn to believe by trying to live a similarly holy life. At the end of this phase I wrote *The Cost of Discipleship*. Today I see clearly the dangers of this book – although, of course, I still stand by what I wrote as before.

21st July 1944. Letters, pp.124–5

Introduction

'The planned path of Bonhoeffer's life,' Bethge writes, 'seems to have been robbed of its own initiative by Nazi history. . . . There is no question but that there is a turn in Bonhoeffer's thought.'[1] It is possible to speak of *two* changes in Bonhoeffer's development between 1931 and 1939. The first of these moved him away from the restrictions of his ecclesiological theory in order to develop a variety of interests in ethics, the relationship between church and state, the person and work of Jesus, and an original and radical exegetical method. Bonhoeffer did not seem particularly concerned with the ambiguities and inconsistencies in his doctrine of the church which these new interests might have revealed. In any event he showed no interest in systematizing his thought. But if the basis of his thinking in his writings of 1932 and 1933 was not ecclesiological, it nevertheless remained purposefully Christocentric. The suggestion, then, is that the writings of 1932 and 1933 show Bonhoeffer to be searching for a means whereby the concreteness of 'the community of revelation' might be preserved, freed from the ecclesiological limitations of 'Christ existing as the church'.

The second major alteration of his thinking came in 1934 and 1935, when Bonhoeffer gave himself without reserve to the Confessing Church, created officially in 1934. Participation in the church opposition meant, for Bonhoeffer, the placing of the whole of his theology at the service of his church and the effort to define her peculiar status and mission. Whatever the achievement of this 'narrow pass' in Bonhoeffer's theological development – and it was considerable – the restrictions which were thus imposed proved disastrous for his future course. Not only the strength of Bonhoeffer's position during the church struggle but also the radical exclusiveness and 'other-worldliness' of this phase of his life and work resulted from the marriage of the 1927–31 ecclesiological theory to the practical questions of the church struggle. What is more important, this combination created the conditions against which Bonhoeffer was to react in 1939: a defensive concentration on the internal problems of the church.

What appears to have happened to Bonhoeffer's development is this: throughout his various theological concerns from 1931 to 1933 a common theme may be traced; an emerging Christology of the person and work of Christ, separate from and in some opposition to his 'Christ existing as the church'. The church struggle, however, forced him to subsume his interests, along with the new Christology he had developed and which underlay all these interests, under a strict ecclesiological scheme. The latter was the result of drawing his early doctrine of the church into service for the ecclesiastical battles which were fought with such vehemence from 1933 until 1939. As long as the issues of the church struggle remained clear, an uneasy balance between these two Christologies was possible. But in 1939, removed almost entirely from church life and work by government decree and surrounded by men of affairs of widely different creeds and political persuasions, all working for the future of Germany, Bonhoeffer once more broke free from his intractable ecclesiological theory. The *Ethics* represents his attempts to set these two Christologies together without the sectarian overtones of *The Cost of Discipleship* and *Life Together*. These experiments proved fruitful but not wholly successful and, in the prison letters, Bonhoeffer set his ecclesiology to one side altogether, in order to meditate on the problems he had been skirting, without regard for the consequences of these meditations. In a final, brief vision he eventually united his two Christologies.

The first part of this hypothesis will be developed in this section of the book. We have first to discuss the emergence of the second Christology and then to show how Bonhoeffer 'concretized' it by uniting it with his new concerns, scripture and discipleship. At the conclusion of this section we shall be able to see more clearly the 'dangers' of *The Cost of Discipleship* to which Bonhoeffer referred in his prison retrospection on this phase of his work, as well as the reasons why he would 'still stand by' what he wrote.

Christ and the Transcendent

In the summer of 1933, Bonhoeffer applied his energies to a task which proved to be his last major teaching assignment at the University of Berlin: the delivery of a series of lectures on Christology.[2] He later confessed them to be the most difficult he had ever had to prepare. In the course of these lectures, Bonhoeffer freed his Christology from the limitations of his ecclesiology and provided a basis for a conception of revelation quite different from that of his two early dissertations. The former theme, 'Christ existing as the church', the 'community of revelation', was made subservient to a concept of Christ as the 'transcendent person'.

The effect of Bonhoeffer's having asserted his Christology in this new manner was not immediately felt. The reason for this was that his new formulation lacked the concrete application of his earlier, ecclesiological theory. In these lectures, Bonhoeffer attempted in a similar fashion to 'ground' his Christology. The notion of 'Christ existing as the church' was joined by notions of the 'form' and 'place' of Christ as Word and Sacrament; the Mediator within the individual, human history, and the state. But the actual 'concretion' of this Christological theme of Christ as the transcendent person came in *The Cost of Discipleship* where Bonhoeffer combined his new Christology with the exegetical method he had developed, creating an original and exciting conception of discipleship. From that point on, the theme of discipleship could not be separated from the theme of revelation.

We shall investigate several aspects of the 1933 Christology lectures, focusing upon Bonhoeffer's doctrine of the person and mediatorial work of Christ and the initial formulation of his theology of the cross.

The Christian Concept of Person

The concept of person had occupied in *Sanctorum Communio* a position subordinate to the basic theme of 'Christ existing as the church'. Bonhoeffer introduced the former in the opening pages of his dissertation, preparatory to developing the theme that Christ is the 'corporate person' of the community.[3] This phrase provided Bonhoeffer with the tool with which to shape the central thesis, i.e. that it is the *person* of Christ which is present temporally and spatially in and as the community of revelation. In his *Act and Being*, Bonhoeffer appears to have lost interest in the phrase and to have recalled in its place the conceptions of 'person' and 'corporate person' from *Sanctorum Communio*.[4]

Bonhoeffer argued in his earliest dissertation that, as opposed to the Idealist picture of an apersonal Mind in which every man participates and to which he must surrender his individuality, the Christian concept of person posits the individual as an ultimate willed by God. The multiplicity of persons and the integrity of the individual remain *irreducible* – even within the community of revelation. Community is thus the area of encounter between individuals in which, in the moment of decision, 'the individual again and again becomes a person through the other'. In community, I encounter and am encountered by, create and am created by, unique, ultimate, inviolable persons who directly affect me at the same time that they remain free from my control.[5]

Act and Being reworks this idea in a more directly Christo-logical and ecclesiological context. 'The being of revelation,' Bonhoeffer wrote, '. . . is person – the revealed person of God and the personal community of which that person is the founda-tion.'[6] Christ is the corporate person of the community of persons. In revealing himself in the church as a person, 'Christ has come the very nearest to humanity, has given himself here to his new humanity, so that his person enfolds in itself all whom he has won, binding himself in duty to them, and them reciprocally in duty to him.'[7] Thus Bonhoeffer makes direct use of his conception of person for his theory of revelation. As a person, Christ is free to 'withold himself from a cognitive intention';[8] as in *Sanctorum Communio*, the person is free from the grasp of the one he encounters and creates.

Person and Transcendence

Closely related is a special notion of transcendence. This was introduced together with the concept of person in the opening pages of *Sanctorum Communio*. In that work, two arresting sen-tences occur which prefigure Bonhoeffer's later Christological usage of these terms. 'The other man,' Bonhoeffer wrote, 'presents us with the same problem of cognition as does God himself.' And again: 'In principle, the nature of the Christian concept of community can be reached as well from the concept of God as from the concept of the person.'[9] Notice the free movement between Bonhoeffer's idea of person in general and his conception of God. He brought together all three con-ceptions – person, transcendence, and God – in an essay in 1931:

The transcendence of God does not mean anything else than that God is personality, provided there is an adequate understanding of the concept of personality. . . . For Christian thought, personality is the last unit of thinking and the ultimate reality. Only personality can limit me, because the other personality has its own demands and claims, its own law and will,

77

which are different from mine and which I cannot overcome as such. Personality is free and does not enter the general laws of my thinking. God as the absolutely free personality is therefore absolutely transcendent. .... Where can I find his inaccessible reality which is so entirely hidden from my thinking? How do I know about his being the absolutely transcendent personality? The answer is given, and must be given by God himself, in his own word Jesus Christ, for no one can answer this question except God himself, in his self-revelation in history, since none can speak the truth except God.[10]

Bonhoeffer's view is that personality cannot be defined apart from the context of human community. Personality is created only in confrontation with others, which involves both 'being-for' and 'being-free-from' the other person. Transcendence would thus seem to signify that quality which a person possesses by virtue of the fact that he *is* person, of simultaneously being-for and being-free-from the other.

It is of considerable importance that Bonhoeffer, in his Christology lectures, framed his idea of the *logos* in just these terms of person and transcendence:

[The questioner] asks after the particular being of a strange being, after the boundary of his own existence. ... Transcendence puts his own being into question. With the answer that his *logos* has reached its boundary, he comes up against the boundary of his own existence. The problem of existence is the problem of transcendence. Theologically expressed: alone before God does a man know who he is.[11]

The development of this theme is highly interesting. Since Christ is person, and since transcendence is a personal quality, his otherness, impenetrability, and inaccessibility are all 'given', and may not come into question.[12] The initial problem of Bonhoeffer's lectures is the dismissal from Christology of all questions which fail to confront the *logos*, Christ, as irreducibly personal and transcendent. These questions he sums up as the one forbidden question. '*How* can you be the Christ?' This is 'the godless question', 'the question of the serpent', 'the question of immanence'. The only question appropriate for Christology is '*Who art Thou?*'; insisting upon the given integrity and inaccessibility, the *transcendent nature* of the person to whom it is directed:

If the counter-*logos* enters history not as an idea but as the Word made flesh, there is no possibility of taking it into one's own *logos*-order. Here there remains only the question Who art Thou? Speak thyself! The question Who art Thou? is the question of the dethroned, the unseated reason. But just so is it the believing question. Who art Thou? Art thou God himself? Christology has to do with this question. Christ is the counter-*logos*. Classification is no longer a possibility, because the being of this *logos* means the end of the human *logos*. Only the question Who art Thou? is the appropriate question.[13]

It must be kept in mind that thus far, Bonhoeffer has refused to define transcendence in terms other than those in which the personal quality of every human being can be defined:

The question Who art Thou? is present in daily life. . . . It is the question about other men and their claims, about other beings, about other authority. It is the question of the love of the neighbour. Transcendence and existence questions become the personal question. That means Man cannot answer this question himself. Existence cannot step out of itself; it remains occupied with itself and only mirrors itself in itself. Imprisoned in its own authority it asks still further after the How?[14]

The Inviolable Person of Christ

The transcendence of the person means that he is inaccessible and exists *extra me*. It means, above all, that the other person cannot be violated by my ego; his personal centre is not available to me. From this basic understanding of person Bonhoeffer moves subtly and probably too swiftly to a doctrine of the person of Christ. His argument runs as follows: If the structure of the other person is inviolable and out of my grasp, then it must follow that neither may the divinity of Christ be isolated from his humanity, nor his humanity from his divinity. This would destroy the unity of his personal structure, asking the forbidden question: *How* can you be the Christ? Christology can have nothing to do with this question, but must rather base itself upon 'the personal structure of being of the whole historical Jesus Christ'.[15] It may ask only one question: *Who* is this God-Man?

Who is contemporary, present, actual? Answer: the one person of the God-Man Jesus Christ. I do not know who the man Jesus Christ is if I do not at the same time say: Jesus Christ, *God*. And I do not know who

Jesus Christ, God is if I do not at the same time say: Jesus Christ, *Man*. Neither can be isolated, for they do not exist in isolation. God in his timeless eternity is not God; Jesus in his temporal limitation is not Jesus. Rather, in the man Jesus is God *God*. In this Jesus Christ, God is contemporaneous. The one God-Man is the entrance way into Christology.[16]

With this indivisible personal structure of the being of Jesus Christ established as his axiom, Bonhoeffer can run through the whole of historical Christology, dismissing all questions which cannot be reduced to the question *Who* this God-Man is. The problem of Christology, he repeats again and again, is not 'the relationship of an isolated God to an isolated man', but rather the relationship of the given God-Man to the world of the flesh.[17] Bonhoeffer would thus, in the last analysis, reject all questions which attempt to go behind the Chalcedonian formula. For Christological questions must be framed in such a way that they neither call the Godhood of Christ into question nor destroy his manhood. When they do, they fail to acknowledge Christ as person, and thus as personally transcendent; such views are not only wrong, but basically heretical.[18]

But it would seem that Bonhoeffer, in ruling out any question which is not finally rhetorical, has deprived Christology of any real purpose. With what questions is Christology concerned if the Incarnation itself is removed from discussion?

Christ pro me

The heart of Bonhoeffer's lectures is his argument that the total orientation of the personal structure of Christ is *pro me*: Christ's being-for-me is not some 'power' which he possesses but rather the definition of his being. His determination *pro me* is the centre of his personal structure. Two questions are thus proper to Christology: *In what form* is Christ present *pro me*, and *where* is Christ present *pro me*?

Christ as the absolutely transcendent person is absolutely out of my control. Absolute also is the claim which he makes upon me. His person is determined wholly by his being *pro me*. Christ does not exist in and of himself, but only in his existential bearing *pro me*. This is not an ontic nor historical power which he possesses; his person *is* this power. As *pro me* Christ is contemporaneous, not as an historically extended energy nor as a reconstructed 'inner life' but as the indivisible person of the God-Man.[19] Here again, Bonhoeffer's formulation enables him to by-pass 'illegitimate' questions:

The question *How* the man Jesus, bound to space and time, can be contemporary is impossible. There exists no such isolated Jesus. The other question, how God can be in time, is also impossible. There is no such isolated God. Only the question *Who* is contemporary, present, and actual is possible and meaningful. Answer: the one person of the God-Man Jesus Christ.[20]

The contemporaneity of Christ is *given*; it is the essence of his *pro me* structure which, in turn, is inextricable from his personal being. We may only ask after the *form* and *place* of his presence.[21]

Throughout his lectures, Bonhoeffer uses the sentence from Luther as his battle-cry: 'At this man thou shalt point and say that he is God!'[22] The problem of Christology is not the Incarnation but its *form*; that 'this man' exists in the scandalous form of the Humiliated. Encounter with Christ is encounter with the humiliated God-Man:

Wherein does the special manner of existence as the Humiliated express itself? In that Christ takes up the flesh of the sinner. The Humiliated is determined by the world beneath the curse. The Incarnation is based upon the first creation, the humiliation upon the fallen creation. In the humiliation Christ, of his own accord, enters the world of sin and death. He enters such that he is not known as the God-Man, but concealed in weakness. He does not enter as a *morphe theou* in the clothes of a king. The claim which he asserts as God-Man in this form cannot but excite rebellion and animosity. He goes incognito as a beggar among beggars, as a rejected man among rejected men, as a doubted among the doubters, as a dying man among dying men. . . . And here lies the central problem of Christology.[23]

This incognito is never broken through; Christ remains always in the form of humiliation and, in this form, is borne witness to as the Christ. 'The believer sees in him the signs of the divine act at the end of the world. He sees, bound to the incognito, something of the glory of God. "We saw his glory" (John 1.14). But the non-believer sees nothing.'[24]

Bonhoeffer's powerful and persistent theology of the cross

reminds us of the incognito, the humility of the empirical church in *Sanctorum Communio*.[25] The humiliated form of the God-Man, like the empirical church, remains when one turns to speak of the contemporaneity of Christ; indeed, it is central to the latter:

Jesus the man is believed as God. And indeed as man and not in spite of his manhood or apart from it. As man Jesus kindles faith in the Word. Jesus Christ is not God in a godly nature, *ousia*, essence; thus not in a discoverable and describable manner, but in faith. If Jesus Christ is to be described as God, this godly essence, omnipotence, and omniscience may not be spoken of but rather the weak man among sinners, the crib and the cross. When we deal with the divinity of Jesus we must speak only of his weakness. One looks in Christology upon the whole historical man Jesus, and says of him: This is God.[26]

The discussion of the contemporary, humiliated form of Christ as Word, Sacrament, and Community need not concern us here.[27] More important is Bonhoeffer's consolidation of earlier thinking in his notion of the 'place' of Christ.[28] Here he turns to an original treatment of Christ as Mediator within man, history, and nature. 'The essence of the person of Christ,' he writes, 'is to be temporally and spatially in the centre. He who is contemporary in Word, Sacrament, and Community is in the centre of human existence, history, and nature. Being-in-the-centre belongs to the structure of his person. . . . That is his essence and the manner of his existence.' The mediation of Christ in being-for man is expressed in an important but somewhat cryptic paragraph:

Where does he stand? He stands *pro me*. He stands there at my place where I should and cannot stand. He stands on the boundaries of my existence, on the other side, yet for me. . . . The boundary lies between me and myself, between the old and the new I. In the encounter with this boundary, I am judged. At this place I cannot stand alone. At this place stands Christ, in the centre between me and myself, the old and the new existence. Thus Christ is at the same time my own boundary and my newly-found centre, the centre between I and I and I and God. . . . In Christ man recognizes (his boundary) and thus, at the same time, finds his new centre again.[29]

The Lutheran *Kondeszens*-Christology to which Bonhoeffer directed us in *Sanctorum Communio* and *Act and Being* is clearly indicated: Christ is the humiliated one, Christ empties himself, Christ is *pro me*. But now Bonhoeffer has moved beyond the limitations of 'Christ existing as the church' to a conception of the person of Christ as both the centre and boundary of the individual believer. He has located the central Christological problem not in the relationship of God to Jesus nor of Jesus to the church, but in the manner in which Jesus is in the world, for others. Revelation becomes the act in which Christ, who comes to me in Word, Sacrament, and Community, the humiliated God-Man whose total existence is for me, is confessed as God. As the absolutely transcendent, he stands free from me on the boundary and at the centre of my existence; in his transcendence, I find my centre and my boundary.

We are ready to move on to the combination of Bonhoeffer's Christology with ideas concerning exegesis and obedience which arose at the time of these Christology lectures. These three – Christology, scripture, and obedience – were woven together into the powerful conception of discipleship which found expression in the pages of *The Cost of Discipleship*. The Christ of the 1933 lectures acts through the believer; the believer takes the form of Christ upon himself in meditation upon and obedience to the Word of scripture.

CHAPTER 7

Concrete Exegesis

A few years ago, when Bonhoeffer's early writings were again made available, readers of the *Ethics* and the *Letters and Papers from Prison* searched eagerly among the numerous biblical studies which he had produced through the years, hoping to find there some practical illustrations of 'the non-religious interpretation of biblical concepts', or clues to his understanding of the hermeneutical problem. They searched to no avail. The hermeneutical problem simply did not exist for Bonhoeffer prior to his imprisonment, and in his biblical studies, even those produced during his imprisonment, he regarded it with a great amount of hostility. *Creation and Fall* (1932–3), his early study of Genesis 1–3, demonstrates a complete disinterest in literary and historical questions in favour of an interpretation of the given text through the eyes of the theology of revelation and a cryptic, peculiar, and very personal existentialist philosophy.[1] The 'homilies' of *The Cost of Discipleship* pass quickly over the difficulties involved in determining the accuracy and origin of the text in order to stress, as they do so effectively, the unconditional demands and absolute commitment of discipleship. The heavy-handed Christologizing and typological investigation which occurs in many of Bonhoeffer's writings on biblical passages becomes especially tedious in his *König David* and his work on the Psalms. And in the collection of sermons and short studies in *Gesammelte Schriften* IV, whatever their other merits might be, there is hardly the critical awareness one would expect to find in a student of Deissmann, Sellin, Lietzmann and Harnack – much less the radical 'non-religious interpretation' of the prison letters.[2]

84

But although it is probable that contemporary exegetical method and biblical study will learn little from an investigation of Bonhoeffer's methods of scriptural interpretation, it is certain that his understanding and use of the Bible is a vital key to his own development. Scientific exegesis with the aim of disclosing the original form of a text or uncovering the historical setting of a particular passage was just not Bonhoeffer's concern. His question, by-passing textual criticism (and leaving for us the problem of the relationship between this and what he wished to do), was how to hear and obey the Word of God. He feared losing sight of this problem in textual and critical theorizing, and becoming interested in abstract literary concerns. Exegesis and ethics were not to be separated. His meditation upon and obedience to the Word of scripture was, therefore, not a side issue in Bonhoeffer's theology, but close to its centre. Recognizing exegesis as well as ethics to be a *Christological* problem, Bonhoeffer used his doctrine of scripture as the means whereby his new Christology might be 'concretized'. This was a process which Bonhoeffer called the 'concretion of the proclamation'.

This development, and the relationship between this movement in Bonhoeffer's theology and his involvement in the church struggle, emerges out of the biblical studies which he wrote, and some extremely self-conscious letters which attempted to explain his attitude. It was this movement in Bonhoeffer's thought that culminated in the writing of *The Cost of Discipleship*.

'Theological Interpretation': Creation and Fall

The origins of Bonhoeffer's scriptural approach are obscure.[3] In Berlin, he sat under some of the most brilliant exponents of the historical-critical approach, yet he praised only the biblicist Adolf Schlatter, whom he had come to know during his year at Tübingen, to his Finkenwalde students.[4] His first interests were in any case systematic theology, philosophy, and sociology. Neither *Sanctorum Communio* nor *Act and Being* is a 'biblical' study. But in 1932–3, Bonhoeffer lectured in Berlin on the first three chapters of Genesis, producing what he called a 'theological interpretation'.

The method of *Creation and Fall* (the title under which the lectures were later published) was to accept the Genesis material from beginning to end as a theological unity, divide the text thematically, and unfold the various themes as part of the single, declaratory message. Although he did not write a lengthy introductory apologetic for his methodology, the phrase 'theological interpretation' provides the clue to what Bonhoeffer imagined himself to be doing. As opposed to a history-of-religions approach which would seek out the sources of the material and engage in comparative study to determine its meaning, or a psychology-of-religions approach which would demonstrate the validity of the material in terms of outside, *a priori* psychological truths, Bonhoeffer proposed to interpret the texts 'from the church's point of view'. 'Theological interpretation,' he wrote, 'accepts the Bible as the book of the church and interprets it as such.' This involved the *a priori* assumption that Genesis speaks of one God and one God speaks through the Genesis texts. 'God is the one God in the whole of Holy Scripture,' Bonhoeffer wrote. 'The church and theological study stand and fall with this faith.'[5]

The first question we should wish to raise is the relationship between this 'theological interpretation' and the historical-critical methodology of Bonhoeffer's teachers. Writing of Bonhoeffer's method, Richard Grunow sees in *Creation and Fall* a 'disregard of all historical and literary questions raised by the text'.[6] It is indeed certain that if Bonhoeffer made use of historical-critical and literary research, he did so apart from and even in spite of his interpretation.

But it would not be fair to say that Bonhoeffer altogether denied the necessity and value of such questions as are raised by the critical approach. That he was aware of such difficulties is clear from his comments in his lectures on Christology, delivered during the following semester:

But is not every door and gate to enthusiasm thus opened? This is not the case, because the self-authentication of Jesus is none other than that which is finally delivered to us by scripture, and comes to us in no other way than through the word of scripture. *We have finally to do with a book with which we find ourselves in the sphere of the profane. It must be read and interpreted. It is to be read with all of the help of historical and philological criticism.* The believer, too, has to do this insistently and impartially. At every turn we must face the problem of having to preach on a word of Jesus which one knows, from historical-philological study, was never spoken thus by Jesus. In the interpretation of scripture, one finds oneself on strangely broken ground.

And even more emphatically:

. . . The Bible remains a book among books. One must be ready to allow the disguise of history and thus the way of historical criticism. But throughout the broken Bible the Resurrected encounters us. *We must involve ourselves in the difficulties uncovered by historical criticism.* Its importance is not absolute, but at the same time it is not inconsequential. Indeed, it is not the weakness but the strength of faith that the disguise of historicity belongs to the humiliation of Christ.[7]

How does the 'theological interpretation' of *Creation and Fall* reflect this understanding? Here we must distinguish between two questions. It is inappropriate to demand that Bonhoeffer, having announced a different approach to the scriptures, should concern himself at every point in the text with a preliminary resolution of all etymological, form-critical, and religio-historical considerations. Still, it is fair to ask that he come to terms generally with historical-critical methodology. Bonhoeffer does in fact claim that he has given the central question of historical-critical methodology its due, and he sees no dispute between this approach and his own:

'A myth, a childlike, fantastic picture of the grey, hidden times of old': thus speaks the world. 'God's Word, even in the beginning of our history, before history, beyond history, yet in history; *we ourselves* are confronted, intended, addressed, accused, sentenced, expelled. *God himself* is the one who blesses and curses. It is *our* pre-history, truly our own. It is the beginning, destiny, guilt, and end of every one of us': thus speaks the church of Christ.

Why dispute the one at the expense of the other? Why can we not understand that all our speaking about God, about our beginning and end, about our guilt *never* mentions these things themselves but always speaks only in pictures? Why can we not understand that God must reach out towards us with these ancient, magical pictures as well as with our technical, conceptual pictures, that he must teach us if we are to become

87

wise? . . . We must always assume that in either case it is we who are aimed at and we must readily and openly allow what was said in that age about the man of the magical world-picture to apply to us.[8]

'God encounters us' and 'is alone to be found' in this human document which, as such, is subject to the criticism to which any human discipline is subject. It is proper, however, that we ask whether the 'brokenness' of the Bible resulting from historical criticism has been reflected in Bonhoeffer's 'theological interpretation'.

Has Bonhoeffer not, after all, set his own methodology *against* that of historical criticism and 'disputed the one at the expense of the other'? In his Christology lectures he acknowledges the problem of the disunity of biblical texts. As the means of dealing with this 'brokenness' theologically, he turns to the words of Thurneysen: 'One may never halt at some particular place; one must move on through the whole of the Bible, from one place to another, just as one crosses a river filled with ice floes and does not remain standing on one, but jumps from one to the other.'[9]

This should mean that the brokenness of scripture remains for, and is indeed reflected by, any 'theological interpretation'. Yet the image of jumping between ice floes is not the picture one finally receives from *Creation and Fall*. Bonhoeffer gives each verse equal 'revelatory' weight and value within its immediate context. The text is treated as a single unit – a single story of God's dealing with man and man's relationship to him. Bonhoeffer accomplishes this unification by means of a highly original and systematic method of reflection, which combines an existential hermeneutic, psychology, and his own revelational theory. Nevertheless, his method would never be acceptable to anyone who takes the critical approach seriously.

What is not clear to us is how Bonhoeffer has moved from the assumption that 'God is the one God in the whole of Holy Scripture' to the indivisible theological unity of the text, nor is it clear why such a unity is necessary.[10] The brokenness of scripture which one discloses on the historical-critical level is not finally reflected in Bonhoeffer's 'theological interpretation'.

The 'Concretion of the Proclamation' and 'The Sacrament of the Ethical'

Bonhoeffer did not regard the relationship of historical criticism to theological interpretation as the most pressing of the problems concerning the approach to the scriptures. It is at least certain that his own development was not determined by this question. From the very beginning of his interest in the problem of scriptural interpretation, he was intensely involved with the question of *how one related oneself to scripture; how scripture became actual and concrete in life*. 'Scientific' exegetical thinking should grow from this basis, not vice versa. His thoughts on scripture were thus taken up along with his mediations on questions concerning Christian ethics and proclamation.

Following a visit to Karl Barth's seminar in Bonn in the summer of 1931, Bonhoeffer was persuaded that the greatest unsolved problems for the theology of revelation lay in the field of ethics.[11] He was perplexed by Barth's understanding of ethics, and Emil Brunner's *Das Gebot und die Ordnungen*, which appeared in 1932, did not raise the question with which he was most concerned, namely: 'the question of the possibility of proclaiming a concrete commandment through the church'.[12] By this Bonhoeffer meant the ability and duty of the church to proclaim the *commandment* of God in the same way that it proclaimed the *gospel*, and to have this ethical proclamation assume positive, concrete form. To a friend he wrote:

It is the problem of the concretion of the proclamation which moves me at present. It is simply not enough, and therefore false, to say that the principle of concretion can only be the Holy Ghost itself....The concretion of the proclamation of grace is of course the sacrament. But what is the sacrament of the ethical, the commandment?[13]

Various papers which he delivered at ecumenical meetings revolved around this theme, as we shall see in the chapter following. But it was the Sermon on the Mount which brought this difficulty home to Bonhoeffer, and led him to relate his concern for the concretion of the proclamation directly to the problem of how to read the Bible. In April 1934, Bonhoeffer wrote again to his friend Sutz of his fresh encounter with Matthew 5–7:

Do write to me sometime just how you preach on the Sermon on the Mount. I am just now attempting it – in an infinitely plain and homely manner, but always about *the keeping of the commandments without evading them*. Following Christ – what that is, is what I want to know. It is not exhausted in our concept of faith. I am sitting at a work which I might call *exercitien* as a preliminary step.[14]

Bonhoeffer's 'spiritual exercises' proved to be the initial experiments with the theme which later formed the central chapters of his *Cost of Discipleship*. The question of the concretion of the proclamation had led him back to the scriptures themselves, 'keeping the commandments without evading them'.

We must begin keeping dates before our eyes: the letter from which the last quotation was taken was written at the conclusion of Bonhoeffer's first half-year in London; the Barmen declaration, creating the Confessing Church, was issued only one month later. By January of 1935, Bonhoeffer had finally and self-consciously resolved the question of ethics and the concretion of the proclamation in 'simple obedience' to the Sermon on the Mount. He described his decision in a letter to his brother, Karl Friedrich:

It may be that in many ways I will seem to you somewhat crazy and fanatical. I am myself anxious about it. But I know that if I were to be 'reasonable' I would honestly, in the next few days, have to put the whole of my theology on a shelf. When I began with theology I thought of it differently – perhaps a more academic pursuit. Now it is something else entirely. But I believe that I am at least on the right track for the first time in my life. And that in itself is a pleasant thought. I am only afraid that in worrying about the opinions of others, I won't go any further, but remain stuck. *I believe that I first become really clear when I begin by taking the Sermon on the Mount seriously.*
. . . The restoration of the church will come from a new kind of monasticism, which has in common with the old only *an uncompromising life based on the Sermon on the Mount in the following of Christ.* I believe that it is time to assemble men for this task.[15]

Bonhoeffer took over his duties as leader of the preachers' seminary in Pomerania during the following April.

One might describe this outcome as a self-conscious turn towards legalism in Bonhoeffer, if by *legalism* we mean an understanding of the scriptures as direct, clear, and wholly relevant commands; and by *self-conscious* we mean that Bonhoeffer was fully aware of the dangers involved in the decision he had made. This overriding concern for obedience to the biblical Word had much in common with the approach of *Creation and Fall*, although in the final analysis, the former is far more radical. The ultimate suspension of all critical questions proved both more fruitful and more dangerous than anything Bonhoeffer had hitherto attempted, as we shall see by examining the effect of this action on Bonhoeffer's own life and work.

'The Last Authorities'

The most penetrating and revealing letter we have from Bonhoeffer's hand was written in April of 1936 to his brother-in-law, Rüdiger Schleicher. In it Bonhoeffer deals directly with his own approach to the scriptures, showing how the question of how one reads and responds to the Bible had touched the very centre of his existence. He wrote in response to a certain bewilderment, perhaps disappointment, which Schleicher had expressed over the direction Bonhoeffer's life and thought seemed to be taking. Bonhoeffer summarized the question he felt was at stake: 'How do I live a Christian life in the world of reality, and where are the last authorities for such a life, which alone make it worthwhile?' His letter continued:

I want finally to confess quite simply: I believe that the Bible alone is the answer to all our questions, and that we need humbly and persistently to ask in order to receive an answer. One cannot read the Bible simply as one reads other books. One must be ready really to ask. Only thus is it un-locked. Only when we least expect the answer is it given to us. And that is because in the Bible, God speaks to us. One cannot simply think God out of oneself, but one must ask after him. Only when we seek him does he answer. Of course one can read the Bible like other books; from the stand-point of the textual critic, etc. One may say nothing against that. Only that this usage merely skims the surface of the Bible, and does not unlock its essence.[16]

We noticed previously in Bonhoeffer a tendency to set historical-critical questions to one side. Textual criticism was simply an improper standpoint from which to approach the scriptures; a discipline necessitated by intellectual honesty but one whose questions were finally irrelevant to the hearing and understanding of the Word of God. While this outlook was previously directed towards the theological questions of exegesis, Bonhoeffer now speaks of the Bible as, in the first place, the *devotional* centre of the Christian life of faith. At the same time, he clearly recognizes that *two* approaches to the scriptures, a 'devotional' and a 'theological' approach, cannot finally be allowed.[17] Critical work had become meaningless for his devotional life – 'breaking the ground' of the Bible was now utterly beside the point. He therefore found it necessary to admit his willingness to suspend certain critical reservations in order to confront a Bible whose every part is theologically trustworthy and whose integrity and unity is unquestioned:

For all of this, is it now somehow understandable to you that I don't want to surrender the Bible as this strange Word at any point; that I want rather to ask with all that is in my power what God wants here to say to us? Every other place outside of the Bible has become uncertain to me. I fear only that I will come up against a 'divine double' *(göttlichen Doppelgänger)* of myself. Is it then somehow conceivable to you that I would rather be ready for a *sacrificium intellectus* just and only in this matter (and who doesn't at some place need his *sacrificium intellectus?)* – that is, the admission that one does not yet understand this or that place in the scripture, in the certainty that this also will some day be revealed as God's Word. That I would rather do that than to judge for myself: this is divine, this is human?[18]

One cannot help being deeply moved by the power and simplicity, the fascinating impossibility of this answer to the question how, in 1936, one 'lives a Christian life in the world of reality'. One opens the Bible; one questions God directly. If the text does not provide a simple and direct answer, demanding absolute obedience, one asks again and again until the answer comes. No dialectical escape, no evasion, no relativizing of the Word of God is permitted:

I will tell you personally: since I learned to read the Bible – and that is still not so long ago – it becomes each day more wonderful for me. I read mornings and evenings, often even throughout the day; and each day I take a text, which I have with me for a whole week, and try completely to immerse myself in it, in order really to hear. I know that without it I could not live rightly anymore. And also not believe . . .

It may be that this is a very primitive matter. But you don't know how happy one is to have found one's way back to this primitiveness after so many theological side-tracks. And I think that in matters of belief, we are really just primitive all the time.[19]

Bonhoeffer's thinking on the scripture was consummated in 1936 as disciplined involvement with the scriptural text by means of meditation and unquestioned obedience. It is inconceivable that this devotional application should not have affected Bonhoeffer's work and thought at every level. Fortunately, we have preserved for us a large fragment of a lecture which Bonhoeffer delivered in the autumn of 1935, on the subject of how the New Testament and the present-day Christian become contemporaries. Here Bonhoeffer's whole attitude towards the question itself cannot be understood apart from the undercurrent of his devotional life. He could see no motive behind the demand that the scriptures be made 'understandable' to modern man other than that of wishing to avoid direct obedience, of wishing to be both autonomous and Christian at the same time and, therefore, of asking that the biblical texts 'prove themselves before the forum of modernity'. His opposition was unequivocal:

It is the same approach [i.e., no matter whether such a demand be made in the eighteenth, nineteenth, or twentieth centuries]; namely, that the archimedian point, the immovable, outside question has already been found (be it reason, culture, or *Volkstum*) and the movable, *questionable*, uncertain element is the biblical message. And it is precisely the same method: namely, to take actualization [*Vergegenwärtigung*, 'making present'] to mean that one allows the biblical message to sift through the sieve of one's own experience, despising and shaking out what will not pass through; and one prunes and clips the biblical message until it will fit into a given space, until the eagle can no longer fly in his true element but with clipped wings is exhibited as a special showpiece among the usual domesticated animals . . .[20]

Even asking the question, as though the present day were the judge and jury at a trial of the New Testament, has no place in Christian thought in Bonhoeffer's view. Rather, the present is to be judged by the New Testament. 'No special act of actualization [*Vergegenwärtigung*] may be allowed apart from the content itself. . . . Where Christ and his Word are allowed to speak: *there* is actualization.' And again: 'God alone says what his Word is and that means God alone makes his Word contemporary; the Holy Spirit is the principle of actualization.'[21]

This unquestioning devotional-theological attitude towards exegetical questions had the effect of cutting off all conversation between Bonhoeffer and the critical approach to the scriptures. It is well to remind ourselves that April 1936 (the date of the letter to Schleicher) was the month and year of Bonhoeffer's well-known essay on church community which included the sentence which caused so much embarrassment and disagreement even in his own Confessing Church circles: 'He who knowingly separates himself from the Confessing Church in Germany separates himself from salvation.'[22] Here again, no escapes from concrete allegiance are allowed. At this time, Bonhoeffer was well under way with his experimental project, the *Bruderhaus* – a *vita communis* of recent seminary graduates which informally restored some of the traditional monastic vows and established a daily order of prayer, confession, and communal life among its members.[23] *The Cost of Discipleship* was published in 1937, after Bonhoeffer had lived for several years with its ideas. *Life Together*, the book which grew out of the experience of the *Bruderhaus*, appeared in 1939. During these years, biblical meditations and outlines followed in a continuous stream; including *König David* (1935), *Temptation* (1937) and, inevitably, a study of the Psalms (1940).[24]

The church struggle barred several legitimate directions from Bonhoeffer's theological consideration. But the element in his thought which provided the impetus for his decisions and determined his course of action was not simply the practical question raised by the church struggle. This 'concretion of the proclamation' had a Christological centre, and it was the marriage of his Christological thought to his strict doctrine of scripture which gave *The Cost of Discipleship* its remarkable freedom and excitement, and kept the work from a primitive, fanatic biblicism. The following chapter takes up the theme of the Christological-ethical interpretation of scripture as it finally appeared in *The Cost of Discipleship*.

CHAPTER 8

Christology and Discipleship

Bonhoeffer could never be satisfied for long with thinking in the abstract. Nor could he sustain an interest in the purely academic problems of scriptural exegesis. One nagging theological problem kept emerging whenever he set to work in his new field: how could the Christ revealed in the scriptures be shown to be truly present, actual, and apprehensible in the life of the world? In 1927 Bonhoeffer had sought the answer to this question by showing Christology to be concrete in ecclesiology: Christ exists in and for the world as the *church*. In 1936, Bonhoeffer attempted to wed his new understanding of the person and work of Christ to *an exegetical method*, as the solution to the problem of 'concrete' proclamation and 'concrete' obedience. The disciple encounters Christ in the scriptures and follows him by participating in the 'being for the world' which is thus revealed to him. But he cannot do this unless he enters into the work and life of the church. In Christ, in the church, confronted with the unequivocal call to obedience, the believer is freed from the world to be truly for the world. Such was the programme Bonhoeffer set forth in the pages of *The Cost of Discipleship*.

The Cost of Discipleship is a deceptively simple book. Within its pages, Bonhoeffer attempts to weave together the new Christology, the revised ecclesiology from his earlier works, and the themes of concrete proclamation and concrete obedience which emerged from his scriptural studies. Perhaps Bonhoeffer himself sensed his inability finally to shape these varied notions into a single theme: the first chapters of his book focus on the Christological implications of discipleship and scripture and he includes a special section (Part Four) which attempts to integrate the earlier chapters with the life of the church. The result, despite Bonhoeffer's missionary zeal, is not entirely convincing. His lack of success seems to have led him in his final chapter to attempt to break fresh ground in setting forth a protestant *imitatio Christi* – a bold and revealing venture whose possibilities attracted Bonhoeffer for the remainder of his life and work.

The present chapter of this study will show how Bonhoeffer connected his thoughts on scripture and Christology to those of discipleship and the problem of concrete obedience, beginning and concluding with a glance at the first version of the *imitatio Christi* which was to become so characteristic of Bonhoeffer's later thought. Chapters 9 and 10 will investigate the fate of 'Christ existing as the church' as this notion was pressed into service for the church struggle, showing what consequences followed for Bonhoeffer's further theological development.

Discipleship and the Imitation of Christ

Throughout the history of theology, doctrines of sanctification and the Christian life have been set forth frequently in the form of the *imitation of Christ*. This formula has been justified scripturally by pointing to the profound and puzzling phrases which abound in the writings of St. Paul: 'in Christ', 'through Christ', 'of Christ', 'you are Christ's', 'to live is Christ', and, most important, 'be imitators of Christ'. The most famous development of this method whereby the disciple, by emulating the life and work of Christ, comes to participate in his being, came, no doubt, from medieval monasticism. Protestant theology has traditionally been uneasy with formulations of this kind, but developments of the theme have emerged on occasion out of protestant soil. The German pietist movement can be described as an attempt to imitate Christ, to let Christ live within one's own life, and to be (as Luther himself had directed) 'Christs to one another'. The writings and hymns of those who led the Evangelical movement in eighteenth-century Britain reveal an undoubted interest in blurring the distinctions between the life of Jesus and one's own. And if the Liberal quest of the historical Jesus is being re-examined and re-evaluated in the present day, we should not neglect to examine the motivation which led to such a search and thus guided the very different paths of theologians such as Albert Schweitzer, Adolf von Harnack, and Walter Rauschenbusch: finding Christ in order to follow him through a kind of participation in his being.

Bonhoeffer's *Cost of Discipleship* was not, therefore, breaking entirely new ground in setting forth a kind of imitation of Christ in 'the keeping of the commandments'. But he remains the only theologian closely identified with the revolt against Liberal theology to have attempted to reopen this possibility. For his cue, he turned not to Liberal theology but to the Reformation itself, where one cannot but notice the remarkable similarity between Bonhoeffer's notion and certain aspects of Luther's doctrine of scripture. It is not really possible to isolate an exegetical method in the works of either man: discipleship is inextricably related to doctrines of Christ and sanctification and the reading and hearing of the scriptural Word. In Luther studies, the exegetical aspect of this combination has been called the 'tropological interpretation' of scripture.

Tropological Interpretation in Luther and Bonhoeffer

The Christological interpretation of scripture is one of the more familiar features of Luther's theology. One meets with this characteristic method of exegesis at every turn in his works: 'In all scripture, there is nothing else than Christ, either in plain or involved words.' 'The whole scripture is about Christ alone everywhere, if we look to its inner meaning, though superficially it may sound different.' 'The entire Old Testament refers to Christ and agrees with him.' 'If I know what I believe, then I know what stands in scripture, for scripture has nothing more than Christ and Christian faith in it.'[1]

Luther used the traditional (medieval) four-fold method of scripture interpretation: historical, allegorical, tropological, and anagogical. But he tended in time to concentrate upon the third part of this scheme, which stressed the bearing of scripture upon the individual Christian through the action of Christ *(de quolibet spirituali et interiori homine)*.[2] J. K. S. Reid, in his *The Authority of Scripture*, says the following concerning the importance of this conception for Luther:

[For Luther] the authority which scripture possesses is objectively grounded in a book which speaks of Jesus Christ. This authority, however, is established in the heart into which Christ enters, or (which is much the same thing) upon which the Holy Spirit works, to create the faith in which it is both recognized and obeyed.[3]

Tropology, then, is an exegetical-devotional process whereby subject and object are overcome through the action of Christ in confrontation with the scriptural Word. Christ's mediatory work grants to the believer the power both to comprehend and to obey. Through the scriptures, Christ comes to dwell in the individual by faith *(in ipsa fide Christus adest)*,[4] so that the individual shares in his victories and is united with him 'even more closely than the husband is coupled with his wife'.[5] 'If scripture contains Christ,' Reid remarks, 'it has something quite specific and objective to offer, but what it offers is something that takes up its residence within the subject, who then by faith acclaims its authority and yields to it.'[6]

Luther made extensive use of this method, especially in his writings on the Psalms,[7] and it is more than coincidence that Bonhoeffer, who turned so often to Luther in order to clarify his own thinking, found in the Psalms his greatest joy and comfort. In the introduction to his *Gebetbuch der Bibel: eine Einführung in die Psalmen* (1940), Bonhoeffer provided an example of this 'devotional-existential' method of exegesis which could have served as Luther's own:

In the Psalms it is the incarnate Son of God who lives with us men, praying to God the Father, who lives in eternity. In the mouth of Jesus Christ the word of man becomes the Word of God, and when we pray his prayer with him, the Word of God becomes the word of man! . . . Christ stands in our place and prays for us. . . . It really is our prayer, but because he knows us better than we know ourselves, because he was a truer man than we, it is also really his prayer and can only become our prayer because it was his.[8]

The question 'How do I lead a Christian life in the world of reality?' thus receives its answer in the 'new kind of monasticism' Bonhoeffer envisaged in 1935 as the end of his quest for 'the sacrament of the ethical'. One follows Christ by entering into a devotional circle wherein one confronts the scriptures, directly encounters Christ there, and receives at the same time the power to fulfil what he commands. Like Luther, Bonhoeffer saw exegesis as a problem of *discipleship* and proceeded to formulate his own 'tropological' interpretation.

Tropological Interpretation in 'The Cost of Discipleship'

Tropology, we have said, is the process of relating scripture and the Christian life to one another through their common orientation towards Christ. In *The Cost of Discipleship*, the individual confronts Christ's Word in the scriptures and, at the same moment and through the action of Christ, is apprehended by that Word and receives the power to obey whatever it commands. This 'infusion', as it were, of Christology with doctrines of scripture and the Christian life had startling consequences for the whole of Bonhoeffer's theology.

First, Bonhoeffer's Christology provided his 'unscientific' exegetical method with its justification. His notion of the absolute integrity of the Christ person, indivisibly God-Man and contemporary in his *pro me* structure, became in *The Cost of Discipleship* an exegetical concept. One simply approaches the scriptures as one approaches Christ himself. Historical criticism does not enter into Bonhoeffer's methodology because he equates it with the forbidden question 'How'?[9] This approach can only serve to provide the Christian with an escape from the clear call to obedience. The Bible is 'the strange Word of God' which is at the same time 'the sole answer to all our questions' – as is the person of Christ in Bonhoeffer's Christology, the Bible is itself *pro me, extra me*. It operates in the same inviolable sphere of the *transcendent*. Bonhoeffer can therefore speak of discipleship as 'a problem of exegesis':

By eliminating simple obedience on principle, we drift into an unevangelical interpretation of the Bible. We take it for granted as we open the Bible that we have a key to its interpretation. But then the key we use would not be the living Christ, who is both judge and saviour, and our use of this key no longer depends on the will of the living Holy Spirit alone. The key we use is a general doctrine of grace which we can apply as we will. The problem of discipleship then becomes a problem of exegesis as well.[10]

Secondly, one notices the persistent theme in *The Cost of Discipleship* of the 'adherence' of the disciple to Christ. Notice in the following passage the close proximity between discipleship and Christology:

Discipleship means adherence to Christ and, because Christ is the object of that adherence, it must take the form of discipleship. An abstract Christology, a doctrinal system, a general religious knowledge of the subject of grace or the forgiveness of sins, render discipleship superfluous, and in fact they positively exclude any idea of discipleship whatsoever, and are essentially inimical to the whole conception of following Christ. . . . Christianity without the living Christ is inevitably Christianity without discipleship, and Christianity without discipleship is always Christianity without Christ.[11]

Bonhoeffer defines this relationship to Christ primarily as a sharing in Christ's suffering and humiliation. 'Just as Christ is only Christ in virtue of his suffering and rejection, so the disciple is a disciple only in so far as he shares his Lord's suffering and rejection and crucifixion. Discipleship means adherence to the person of Jesus, and therefore submission to the law of Christ which is the law of the cross.'[12] An echo of Bonhoeffer's treatment of Christ's humiliation in his 1933 lectures rings throughout these pages. It was in this context that Bonhoeffer wrote his famous sentence, which has since become identified with his martyrdom: 'When Christ calls a man, he bids him come and die.'

. . . It is the same death every time – death in Jesus Christ, the death of the old man at his call. . . . The call of Christ, his baptism, sets the Christian in the middle of the daily arena against sin and the devil. Every day he encounters new temptations, and every day he must suffer anew for Jesus Christ's sake. The wounds and scars he receives in the fray are living tokens of this participation in the cross of his Lord.[13]

Thirdly, although *The Cost of Discipleship* nowhere specifically develops transcendence as a theme, it is never far away from Bonhoeffer's thinking throughout his book. We have seen this described in his early writings as 'the last limit of thinking', 'the ultimate reality', 'the demand and claim which I cannot overcome'.[14] Transcendence designates that quality belonging to personal being which enables one to be at the same time wholly for others and free from their control. Bonhoeffer thus spoke of transcendence as the very centre of Christ's being. As the absolute personality, Christ is absolutely transcendent. This is the understanding which Bonhoeffer carries into the work we are presently considering.

In confrontation with the scriptures, then, a devotional 'circle' comes into operation: from Christ, to the scriptures; from thence to the believer through the mediatory action of Christ; finally leading to the realization of Christ's being in concrete obedience to his Word. Through the participation of the believer in Christ and Christ in him, Christ 'continues to live in the lives of his followers'; he 'has entered my life and taken charge.'[15] In effect, one could describe this 'devotional circle' as a 'circle of transcendence', for Christ's impartation of himself to the believer through the scriptures enables the latter to share in his transcendent power. And what does 'share in his transcendent power' mean? It means that the disciple *participates* in *Christ's freedom from and determination towards the world*.

Finally: 'About this matter of the participation in the suffering of God,' Karl Barth wrote of the prison letters, 'it seems clear to me that this is a variation of the *imitatio* concept which he always and so rightly stressed. . . . Was Bonhoeffer of the opinion that the whole of theology is to be put on this particular basis?'[16] Almost alone among the many who have commented upon Bonhoeffer's prison meditations and their relationship to earlier phases of his theology, Karl Barth recognizes the connection between 'sharing in the sufferings of God' and 'religionless Christianity' and the doctrine of discipleship Bonhoeffer formulated during the church struggle. It is not simply coincidental that *The Cost of Discipleship* ends with a stirring call to the disciple to be 'like' Christ. Bonhoeffer clearly intended this to be the consummation of his meditations.

While conscious of the need for the proper checks and balances, Bonhoeffer nevertheless turned fearlessly to this theme in the concluding chapter of his work.[17] 'Those who follow Christ are destined to bear his image,' he wrote. 'The image of Jesus Christ impresses itself on the image of the disciple. . . . We cannot help bearing his image ourselves' (p. 269). No doubt 'we cannot transform ourselves into his image; it is rather the form of Christ which seeks to be formed in us. . . . We must be assimilated to the form of Christ in its entirety . . .' (p. 272). But there can be for Bonhoeffer no escape from the language of participation, assimilation, imitation. 'In the body of Christ we are become "like Christ".' Self-consciously and courageously Bonhoeffer concluded his work:

Now we can understand why the New Testament always speaks of our becoming 'like Christ' (*kathos Christos*). We have been transformed into the image of Christ, and are therefore destined to be like him. He is the only 'pattern' we must follow. And because he really lives his life in us, we too can 'walk even as he walked' (1 John 2. 6), and 'do as he has done' (John 13. 15), 'love as he has loved' (Eph. 5. 2; John 13. 34; 15. 12), 'forgive as he forgave' (Col. 3. 13), 'have this mind, which was also in Christ Jesus' (Phil. 2. 5), and therefore we are able to follow the example he has left us (1 Peter 2. 21), lay down our lives for the brethren as he did (1 John 3. 16). It is only because he became like us that we can become like him. It is only because we are identified with him that we can become like him. By being transformed into his image, we are enabled to model our lives on his. Now at last deeds are performed and life is lived in single minded discipleship to the image of Christ and his words find unquestioning obedience. (p. 274).

Tropology in 'The Cost of Discipleship' and the Prison Letters

It will be apparent to readers of the *Letters and Papers from Prison* that we have here, in this tropological formula, this imitation of Christ, a scheme into which the theological ideas of Bonhoeffer's last years might be set. Despite the vast differences in style and direction between these two works, the same problems are revolving in Bonhoeffer's mind: Christology, discipleship, and the interpretation of scripture cannot be separated. One cannot take up one element without taking up the other two at the same time. The impetus for both works is christological – *The Cost of Discipleship* is described at the outset as 'a . . . quest for him who is the sole object of it all, for Jesus Christ himself' (p. 29); the prison letters begin their theological meditation on 'religionless' Christianity by asking 'Who *is* Christ for us today?'[18] Christ is, for both works, the sole principle of exegesis and the basis for the action of the Christian. The centre of this Christology, in both works, is the transcendence of the person of Christ which is shared by the believer, leading the Christian to strike a certain attitude towards the world. What, then, is the difference in this 'attitude', the difference in the meaning of transcendence for *The Cost of Discipleship* and the prison letters?

Bonhoeffer was aware throughout *The Cost of Discipleship* of a 'boundary' between Christ and the world, a barrier set not by Christ but by the world which rejects him.[19] In a chapter entitled 'Discipleship and the Individual', Bonhoeffer wrote:

By virtue of his incarnation (Christ) has come between man and his natural life. . . . By calling us he does cut us off from all immediacy with the things of this world. He wants to be the centre, through him alone shall all things come to pass. . . . Since his coming, man has no immediate relationships of his own any more to anything, neither to God nor to the world. . . . This breach with the immediacies of the world is identical with Christ the Son of God the Mediator. . . . The call of Jesus teaches us that our relation to the world has been built on an illusion. All the time we thought we had enjoyed a direct relation with men and things. . . . We cannot establish direct contact outside ourselves except through him. . . . He stands in the centre between my neighbour and myself. He divides, but he also unites. Thus, although the direct way to our neighbour is barred, we now find the new and only real way to him – the way which passes through the Mediator.[20]

The resemblance between this statement and the definition of Christ as Mediator in the 1933 Christology lectures is striking,[21] but Bonhoeffer has now given one element of 'transcendence' a special emphasis. In Christ and by virtue of his call, the 'breach with the world' is revealed. In directing my gaze towards Christ, I see the rejected, crucified, humiliated Son of God. It is the world which has rejected, humiliated, and crucified him. In seeing and in following Christ, I am separated from everything outside of his Being. The cornerstone of *The Cost of Discipleship* thus remains Bonhoeffer's famous opening essay on 'costly grace', which utterly rejects the idea that Christianity and a worldly life are compatible:

The world has been made 'Christian', but at the cost of secularizing the Christian religion as never before. The antithesis between the Christian life and the life of *bourgeois* respectability is at an end. The Christian life comes to mean nothing more than living in the world and as the world, in being no different from the world, in fact, in being prohibited from being different from the world for the sake of grace. . . . I need no longer try to follow Christ, for cheap grace, the bitterest foe of discipleship, which true discipleship must loathe and detest, has freed me from that.[22]

For *The Cost of Discipleship*, transcendence means primarily freedom from the world (although, as we shall see in the chapters which immediately follow, Bonhoeffer saw this separation to be the only way in which the Christian could be *for* the world). This 'breach with the world,' made relevant and concrete in the issues of the church struggle, characterized this phase of Bonhoeffer's life and thought. His Christology became concrete in his radical doctrine of discipleship, and when he came later to question his attitude during this phase, he referred to it as a time when he thought he 'could learn to believe by trying to lead a . . . holy life'. Christology was given concrete form in discipleship, and discipleship meant nothing less than a 'breach with the things of this world'.

But in the prison letters, the 'boundaries' which delineated this breach with the world have disappeared. It is not merely coincidental that Bonhoeffer's interest in ecclesiology disappeared at the same time. What *remains* is the interest in the participation of the disciple in the transcendent being of Christ. There is, of course, a major alteration: in *The Cost of Discipleship*, being *for* the world in Christ could only mean separation *from* the world. The prison letters neatly reverse this, following the meditation on the 'worldliness' of Christ which begins in the *Ethics*: freedom from the world can only be spoken of as the participation in Christ's *being-for-others*.

The basic difference between the prison letters and *The Cost of Discipleship* is the *sphere* of Bonhoeffer's concern, the presence or absence of the 'boundaries' which he described in 1937. And this leads us to an examination of the joining together of Bonhoeffer's early ecclesiological-revelational theory to the Confessing Church and the practical necessities of the church struggle. This forced marriage was, we shall see, an unhappy one.

THE BOUNDARIES OF REVELATION

Extra ecclesiam nulla salus: outside of the Confessing Church there is no salvation.

Zur Frage nach der Kirchengemeinschaft 1936. GS II, *p.242*

The more exclusively we acknowledge and confess Christ as our Lord, the more fully the wide range of his dominion will be disclosed to us.

Ethics, p.180

CHAPTER 9

Revelation and the Confessing Church

All concrete questions are for us so difficult to answer, because we have not yet formulated clearly the pevious question: What space the church must claim for the power of the Word of God itself. Is the space only the mathematical point of the Word of God, which darts in here and there? The mathematical point of justification? Is it the case that as long as the church is allowed this space, everything is in order? The experiences of the last years have taught us that the church reacts more sensitively, above and beyond our theological knowledge, to certain boundaries of her body of which she was not previously aware. She discovers boundary situations where, dogmatically, she had thought to find no boundaries. . . . Theology and the question of the church develop out of the empirical experiences of the church in her conflicts. Blows befall her, and she recognizes: the body of the church goes this way or that. Question: How, then, is the recognized space of the church to be distinguished from other spaces round about her?. . .

'Sichtbare Kirche im neuen Testament'. 1935–6. GS III, *pp.325–6*

The formula 'Christ exists as the church' was a weapon with which Bonhoeffer seemed able to fight but one battle at a time. He had never intended that an ecclesiology wedded to the theology of revelation should disregard the formidable problem of the relationship between revelation – the church – and 'other spaces' of the world; rather, his dissertation and *Habilitationsschrift* found it necessary to circumvent these questions in order to fight on another front. As a result, Bonhoeffer's insistence that the church was a human sphere, subject to the same sociological laws as other human spheres, was frequently obscured by his emphasis that the sphere of the church comprised the revelation of God, subject to no human laws.

When he began his work at the University of Berlin in 1931, Bonhoeffer's interests were naturally broadened by the practical demands of his position. Lecture and seminar preparation led him to problems of ethics and exegesis, and he developed and deepened a Christology independent of the limited Christo-ecclesiology of his earlier works. At the same time, stimulated by his work with the infant ecumenical movement and as the leader of a communicants' class of young workers, Bonhoeffer began to raise the question he had circumvented in his early work: If the church, the 'community of revelation', is Christ, how does that which exists outside of the boundaries of this community apprehend and reveal Christ and serve him as Lord?

Bonhoeffer first set out this question, in 1932, in its traditional Lutheran form as the problem of the relationship between the two kingdoms, church and state. He described the state as a divine ordinance in which the created structure of the world is affirmed and preserved. But this interest was set aside and eventually discarded when Hitler came to power in Germany. Bonhoeffer found in his formulation no weapon with which to combat the Nazi-supporting German Christian Movement which had spread through the established church and, unlike many of his colleagues, he refused even a *careful* theological development of the relationship between church and state. Any discussion, he felt, might offer some comfort to the German Christians. He therefore ended conversation altogether and took up, once again, his original Christo-ecclesiology, infusing it with a confessional orthodox terminology and proclaiming it with prophetic vigour.

The church struggle and the birth of the Confessing Church at Barmen in 1934 reopened with special urgency the problem of the nature of the church. Not only so; it also forced the opposition to look upon those who remained associated with the *Reichskirche* – the established church – in a wholly new way. Attention was now directed towards the practical issues of membership, pastoral support, representation at ecumenical gatherings – in short, towards the constituency and boundaries of a church which claimed to be the one true church of Jesus Christ in Germany and which denied that coexistence with the *Reich* Church was a possibility.

We have seen that Bonhoeffer's ecclesiology was not (as was Barth's) based upon the analogous relationship of the church to the revelation of God; but rather upon the identification of the two. The church *is* Christ, the revelation. When this theory met with the practical issues of the church struggle, Bonhoeffer was left with the formula: *the Confessing Church is the revelation.* The boundaries of the church which the theoretical *Sanctorum Communio* never drew had now to be described boldly and concretely. Bonhoeffer accepted the situation and vigorously pressed his ecclesiology into service, drawing within its framework his new interests – Christology, ethics, and exegesis.

This action produced a steadfast champion of the Confessing Church and the book *The Cost of Discipleship*. Even in that remarkable work, however, it is apparent that the marriage of the two Christologies was not wholly successful. It was inevitable that when the time presented itself, the boundaries would be broken through as a result of the tension generated by juxtaposing two Christologies so different in conception and spirit. And when his association with the Hitler resistance and the enforced isolation from the church on the eve of the war reawakened interest in the themes which the church struggle had caused to be set aside, Bonhoeffer attempted to rework his theory in a way that might escape the restrictiveness of his ecclesiology. He remained certain that revelation must be stated concretely and therefore in a spatial manner, but he now attempted to make the spatial language more flexible, to release it from the Christo-ecclesiology of his earlier thought and therefore from the strict boundaries of the church struggle, and to formulate it in terms of his second, more dynamic Christology. These various experiments were collected as the *Ethics*. Finally, in the prison letters, Bonhoeffer's new understanding of the meaning of history caused him to turn away altogether from the attempt to locate in the world an empiric-revelational 'space' for Christ.

The church struggle thus set the stage for the inner conflict in Bonhoeffer's theological development without which, there would not have been the creative explosions of the *Ethics* and prison letters. This section will investigate this conflict and the situation within which it developed in *The Cost of Discipleship* and *Life Together*, and examine the attempt at reformulation in the *Ethics*.

Christ and the World, Church and State: 1927–33

If any remarkable, characteristic and instinctive impulse in Bonhoeffer's theological development can be discerned, it would be his determination never to lose sight of his own innate humanitarian concern. Worldly life and the life of the church were, at the outset of Bonhoeffer's theological career, contrapuntal themes. Because theological and church-political strategy made it necessary that the latter theme receive a special emphasis in 1927 and from 1934 to 1940, it is easy, in looking back over Bonhoeffer's early work, to lose sight of this worldly interest – and thus to understand the *Ethics* and the prison letters as radical departures from Bonhoeffer's basic theological convictions. We have thus to trace the theme of the worldly in Bonhoeffer's early thinking and, in greater detail, to examine the forms in which it emerged in his writings from 1931 to 1933.

Traces of the theme of worldliness appear in the very earliest products of Bonhoeffer's pen. In an unpublished diary from his period as a vicar in Barcelona (1928), Bonhoeffer humorously described a dilemma his theology was facing: 'I think I am becoming a humanist. Was Barth ever away from home?'[1] There were several factors which stood in the background of this outburst: Bonhoeffer's cultural and *bourgeois* heritage, the social-political situation in Germany, Spain, and America prior to 1933, his confrontation with the social gospel and his communicants' class, his absorption of the humanist spirit of Nietzsche, and the broadening effect of his travel and work with the ecumenical movement.[2] His humanitarian interest in 'the world and its creatures' was unquenchable. It was in Barcelona that Bonhoeffer lectured for the first time on 'the basic questions of Christian ethics', illustrating his thesis that ethics is a matter of history, 'a child of the earth', with the legend of Antäus, the giant whose strength could be overcome only when his feet were lifted from the earth.[3]

We have seen that *Sanctorum Communio*, in attempting to establish an ecclesiological basis for a theology of revelation 'from above downwards', wrestled primarily with Bonhoeffer's liberal teachers and humanistic, 'religious' social philosophers. The reader is apt to pay less attention to the infrequent but often passionate outbursts which stress that the church is a completely human structure, affected by human history and vitally concerned with the humanity about her.[4] Bonhoeffer qualified what he saw as an unduly negative view of the church, expressed by Karl Barth in the *Epistle to the Romans*. The fact that everything which the church says and does in the world is *human*, Bonhoeffer argued, does not affect the fact that in her, God reveals himself. The revelation assumes its empirical form in space and time as a *human* community, the church.

In 1932, Bonhoeffer developed this side of his thesis further in the form of an essay on the relationship between the church as revelation and the world of which it is a part. Interest in the worldly nature of the church is not a secondary matter. Rather, Bonhoeffer insists, the church cannot be understood apart from the assertion that she is of the world. 'We can only talk about what the church is when we ask at the same time what it is in relation to men and in relation to God.' Church and world are conceptions which must always occur together, since they exist solely for each other:

The church is a piece of the world; forsaken, godless, beneath the curse: vain, evil world – and that to the highest degree because she misuses the name of God, because in her God is made into a plaything, an idol. Indeed, she is an eternally forsaken and anti-Christian piece of the world in that she proudly removes herself from her solidarity with the evil world and lauds her own self. And yet: the church is a piece of qualified world, qualified through God's revealing, gracious Word, which she is obliged to deliver to the world which God has occupied and which he will never more set free. The church is the presence of God in the world. Really in the world, really the presence of God.[5]

Here is a concise presentation of Bonhoeffer's ecclesiological thesis for which one searches in vain in the pages of *Sanctorum Communio*. The influence of Barth's *Epistle to the Romans* is clear, but also Bonhoeffer's own characteristic 'and yet . . .' There are also clearly audible echoes from Bonhoeffer's past writings. 'Only he . . . who loves the earth and God in one,' Bonhoeffer writes, 'can believe in the kingdom of God.' There can be no flight from the world in the name of God, nor can there be any place in an understanding of the kingdom of God for 'Christian secularism' which views the church as an organ for religious and moral uplift:

He who evades the world cannot find God, but only his own, better, lovelier, more peaceful world, an 'other' world, but never God's world which breaks within this world. He who evades the world in order to find God finds only himself. He who evades God to find the earth does not find God's world, but only a stage for the conflict between the good and evil, the pious and the blasphemous. He who edifies himself finds himself. Whoever loves God loves him as Lord of the earth, just as it is. He who loves the earth loves it completely as *God's* kingdom on earth, but at the same time as God's kingdom *on earth*. This is because the King of the kingdom is the Creator and Preserver of the earth, because he has blessed the earth and has taken us out of the earth.[6]

Here is the 'affirmation of the earth, an entrance into its orders, its communities, its history'[7] which was later to form the theme of the *Ethics*. But Bonhoeffer's concern at this time is to define further the revelation in Christ by means of a positive theory of church and state. He does this by introducing the idea that 'miracle' and 'order' *(Ordnung)* are the 'two forms in which God's kingdom appears on earth; enters into it'.[8] The miracle is the Resurrection which breaks through the cursed world (which Bonhoeffer described in his *Creation and Fall*).[9] The church bears witness to this miracle of God's new creation which shatters all of man's earthly orders, establishes the new community, and overcomes man's egocentricity, sin, and death. But the state is positively related to the miracle as the kingdom of order, by which the world, with its laws and history and communities, is affirmed and preserved. Church and state must exist side by side, divided but mutually limiting one another, as long as the earth remains. Thus: the miracle breaks through and the order retains.

The direction in which Bonhoeffer's thoughts are moving suggests that he wished to unfold his theme as a notion of revelation in which the whole of humanity could be taken up, on the basis of a conception of God as Lord of the earth. But just at this stage in his development, Bonhoeffer found himself confronted with a political and ecclesiastical struggle in Germany which induced him to halt any meditation upon the nature of the state which suggested that it could serve positively as an instrument of God's will. John Godsey's summaries of Bonhoeffer's numerous essays concerning the nature of the response which the church should make to the church-political questions of 1933,[10] arranged as they are in chronological order, show clearly that the latter's thinking was deeply affected by a confrontation with these concrete, inescapable realities.

In his two essays (1932–3), 'What is the Church?' and 'The Church Confronting the Jewish Question',[11] Bonhoeffer still appears essentially conservative: The church does not engage directly in political action, as long as the state acts justly for the maintenance of order. Regarding the dismissal of Jewish-Christian pastors from their churches, Bonhoeffer saw the role of the church as one of criticism of the government and aid for the victims.[12] But he sensed early in the struggle that discussion of the relationship between the church and the state would require an approach very different from the traditional 'limitation of responsibilities' within a concept of the kingdom of God.[13] The problem was that he could provide no theological answer to these complicated questions which was not an evasion. (And no doubt, this confusion was a factor in his decision to go into the pastorate in the autumn of 1933.) 'Until now,' Godsey writes, 'the boundary between church and state seemed clearly defined, and one had only to guard the boundary and explain the duties of each in respect to the other. But all at once the situation changed, and the church found its clear view *vis-à-vis* the state clouded by treason within its own borders! The German-Christians, who professed to be the church . . . were able to confuse the issues to such an extent that the church struggle appeared to be an inner-church instead of a church-state affair.'[14]

The effect upon Bonhoeffer was so great that he immediately broke off theological conversation on the theme of church and state; in Bethge's words, he 'dropped the further development of his doctrine of Christ's Lordship over the world just as he had launched it'. Bethge continues:

Positive statements about the state ... disappear. The clever notion of the *Erhaltungsordnungen* (orders of preservation) he never mentions again. He drops it at the same moment when some prominent Lutherans (Künneth) take it up to develop their own concept of the two realms on this basis. He lost in 1933 any interest in discussing with Gogarten, Brunner, and their friends the doctrine of *Schöpfungsordnungen* (orders of creation) which gave a good scheme for providing a place in the Christian catechism for a tamed version of the German *Frühlingdoctrine* of a pure race (*Blut und Boden*, national 'blood and soil'). . . . Walking the easy way in picking out Luther's statements about world, state, and creation seemed now to Bonhoeffer the opposite of clinging to the concreteness of the message.[15]

In fact, one could say that Bonhoeffer broke off *theological* conversation altogether. What Bethge writes of the effect of the church struggle upon Bonhoeffer's life seemed equally true of his theological path: it was 'robbed of its initiative by Nazi history'.[16] When Bonhoeffer returns to the problem of ecclesiology, in 1935–6, it is clear that he has used a strict form of his original thesis to solve the church-political problem and that he has foreclosed any discussion on the theme of church and state: revelation and the Confessing Church can be equated. His interest now becomes the articulation of the revelation of Christ within the church and only within the church; his insistence upon the exclusiveness of the Body of Christ is determined by the practical demands of the Confessing Church and its struggle for existence in Germany. Virtually all of his theological thinking was drawn back into the sphere of ecclesiology, just as the whole of his life was placed at the service of the Confessing Church.

We already have had occasion to speak of the unfortunate result of this limitation to Bonhoeffer's thinking in his treatment of the hermeneutical question. The positive outcome of this concentration, however, ought not to be overlooked. Setting aside any dialectical escapes from the identification of the

Confessing Church with revelation itself made it possible for Bonhoeffer to proclaim his message with clarity, creativity, and vigour – and the result was *The Cost of Discipleship*. But the outcome which Bonhoeffer accepted as the only one for his theology heightened the tension between a restrictive ecclesiology and a dynamic new Christology until it reached the breaking point. The *Ethics* and eventually the prison letters were born of the battle between the two Christologies which Bonhoeffer had attempted to resolve in the pages of *The Cost of Discipleship*. We shall return to this shortly. At this point in his development, the central theological problem for Bonhoeffer has become the conquest of a living space for his confessing Church and the articulation, within its strict boundaries, of his thinking on Christology and discipleship.

The Articulation of the Body of Christ

The most obvious difference between the dissertation which Bonhoeffer produced in 1927 and his later writings on ecclesiology is the alteration in terminology. After 1933 we find no attempt to make theological use of secular language, either sociological or philosophical, to describe the form assumed by Christ in the community. Instead, the Christology which Bonhoeffer had made the centre of his theory becomes more explicit, and the language which he uses to develop his doctrine of the Body of Christ becomes more traditional. Not surprisingly, he first turns his attention to the most visible of the activities of of the church – preaching and the sacraments – and gives them both a Christological interpretation.

The *communio sanctorum*, Bonhoeffer wrote in his earliest book, takes the form of Christ. He then spoke of an 'objective spirit' which extended itself spatially and historically in the life of the community, bearing certain forms which Christ 'guarantees to be efficacious' and through which the Holy Spirit operates. Christ existing as the church means that Christ is present and the Spirit is at work in the church when the Word, in sacrament and preaching, is proclaimed. The centre of Bonhoeffer's ecclesiology thus became an original and dynamic theological-sociological exposition of these traditional marks of the church of the Reformers and the Lutheran confessions.

In the terminology of the 1933 Christology lectures, the explication of Word and Sacrament took the following form: 'The one and complete person of the God-Man Jesus Christ is present in the church in his *pro-me* structure as Word, Sacrament, and community.'[17] Bonhoeffer's characteristic Lutheran 'is' was at the centre of his discussion: Christ is present not only *in* the Word of the church but also *as* the Word of the church. This means that Christ *is* the spoken Word of the sermon and the acted and proclaimed Word of the sacrament. 'They do not signify something,' he insists, 'they *are* something.'[18] Word and Sacrament are the vehicles for Christ's manifestation of himself in and as his community. But Christ also reveals *himself* in Word and Sacrament, in his humiliated and *pro-me* form. Here Bonhoeffer's *theologia crucis* comes into play: the church, through Word, sacrament, and community, participates in this humiliation and takes it upon itself. Thus, preaching is described as 'Christ himself striding through the community as the Word', 'Christ bearing human nature', the *sacramentum verbi* which 'takes us up and bears us,' upon which 'all anxiety, sin, and death of the community may fall'.[19] Again, 'preaching is not the only means whereby Christ takes visible form. That is also done by the sacraments of baptism and the Lord's Supper, both of which flow from the true humanity of our Lord Jesus Christ.'[20] The concrete, personal, dynamic Christology of 1933 has here been drawn into the service of ecclesiology.

Bonhoeffer's spatial language, which had all but disappeared in the Christology lectures, reappeared in the latter chapters of *The Cost of Discipleship* in an even more dynamic form. He speaks of a 'space of proclamation'; that is, of the visible Body of the exalted Lord manifested in the preaching of the Word. 'The church of Jesus Christ claims space in the world for its proclamation. The Body of Christ becomes visible to the world in the congregation gathered round the Word and Sacrament.'[21] An essay written in 1936[22] on the subject of the visible church speaks of 'the space of proclamation and confession', and in

The Cost of Discipleship, Bonhoeffer writes of this same space as one which the church claims as 'an ordinance of divine appointment'.[23] There are other spaces to which the church lays claim: spaces for 'the office, offices and gifts'[24] and for 'the articulation and order' of the community.[25] But Bonhoeffer began to concentrate upon what he called the 'living-space' of the church: 'The church needs space not only for her liturgy and order, but also for the daily life of her members in the world. That is why we must now speak of the living space *(Lebensraum)* of the visible church.'[26]

The Living-space of the Church

'Bonhoeffer,' Bethge tells us, 'always added to the two classical notions of the church in the Lutheran confessions – Word and Sacrament – a third, the fellowship of men.'[27] This conception took a number of forms and served a variety of purposes during the course of Bonhoeffer's theological development. In *Act and Being*, the Word in Sacrament and preaching could not be considered apart from the fellowship, and all three terms merged in his organic conception of the church as the revelation:

In *reality* I hear another man declare the Gospel to me, see him offer me the sacrament: 'Thou art forgiven', see and hear him and the congregation praying for me; at the same time *I* hear the Gospel, I join in the prayer and know myself joined into the Word, sacrament, and prayer of the communion of Christ, the new humanity now as then, here as elsewhere; I bear it upon me and am borne of it. Here I, the historically whole man, individual and humanity together, am encountered, affected. I believe; that is, I know myself borne: I am borne *(pati)*, therefore I am *(esse)*, therefore I believe *(agere)*.[28]

The church is not an empty space; the dynamic movement of the community in its cultic activity, to which the presence of the Holy Spirit has been promised, constitutes the act-being unity of revelation.

The 1933 Christology lectures carry this notion further, and separate, for the purposes of definition, Christ as sacrament and preaching and Christ as the community of fellowship. 'The community is not only the receiver of the Word of revelation,' Bonhoeffer writes, 'but is herself the revelation and the Word of God. The Word is itself community, in so far as the community is revelation and the Word has the form of a created Body.'[29] Later, when Bonhoeffer attempted to relate his thinking on 'the concretion of the commandment' to 'Christ existing as a church', he wrote of a 'space of the Christian commandment (new life, discipleship)'.[30] Still later, the 'space of discipleship' becomes the 'living-space of the church'. This idea represents Bonhoeffer's attempt to give life to what could have become a static, institutionalized ecclesiology, to thrust the inner-directed and defensive Confessing Church, with her visible boundaries between herself and the world, out into the world. Into this living-space Bonhoeffer carried his tropological interpretation of scripture, with its interdependent Christology, devotional application to scripture, and concrete obedience.

The final chapters of *The Cost of Discipleship* and virtually the whole of *Life Together* may thus be described as Bonhoeffer's attempt to forge a weapon for the church struggle by uniting the early chapters of the former book (where Christology, scripture, and discipleship were combined with such a telling effect) with the Christo-ecclesiology (with its language of 'space') adapted from his earliest work. In this endeavour, the notion of the living-space of the church served as a catalyst. It is this uneasy alliance of two Christologies which makes the final chapters of *The Cost of Discipleship* and *Life Together* (as well as the *Bruderhaus* experiment) far more than the turn to piety and other-worldliness Bonhoeffer's interpreters have often found in them.[31] Even Bonhoeffer's examination of community life in *Life Together* constantly forces the Christian outward towards and into the active life of the world. The church's place is in the midst of the world, 'the Body of Christ has penetrated into the heart of the world in the form of the church.' 'To stay in the world with God,' Bonhoeffer reminds us, 'means simply to live in the rough and tumble of the world and at the same time remain in the Body of Christ, the visible church, to take part in its worship and to live the life of discipleship.'[32] Nor is the communal life of scriptural meditation and worship, confession and intercessory prayer described in *Life*

Together to be understood except as something taking place within this living-space which is thrust into the world. It is a *living*-space because it sends the Christian into the world to minister (as Bonhoeffer wrote in *Life Together*) through an 'attitude' of service, meekness, listening, helpfulness, bearing, and proclaiming.[33] This is thus a *worldly* space, but also a space of the church because, Bonhoeffer insists, even in isolation the Christian bears the community along with him in his confrontation of the Word, meditation, obedience, and action. For this reason, one cannot simply set the 'worldliness' of the *Ethics* and prison letters over against the supposed 'other-worldliness' of *The Cost of Discipleship* and *Life Together*. The disciple and his church move about in the world. What restricts Bonhoeffer's theology at this point is the boundary between the church and the world with which Bonhoeffer had to concern himself – a boundary, because of the peculiar relationship between revelation and the church in his theology, *between revelation and the world*. The church not only had to occupy a particular space, she had also to fight against the world to win and hold that space. The limits to worldliness in his theology were thereby fixed: worldliness *only within the bounds of the Confessing Church*. 'The limits and claims of the secular calling,' Bonhoeffer wrote, 'are fixed by our membership of the visible church of Christ, and these limits are reached when the space which the Body of Christ claims and occupies in the world for its worship, its offices, and the civic life of its members clashes with the world's claim for space for its own activities.'[34]

Extra Ecclesiam Nulla Salus

Thus far, we have seen Bonhoeffer's view of the church as it developed during the church struggle as essentially a purified and vigorous form of his 1927–30 'Christ existing as the church'. The church is visible, and she occupies space in the world as the revelation, the Body of Christ. But during the church struggle, the occupation of a bounded space by the Confessing Church involved her in a *claim* to space, to legitimacy. 'The Body of Christ takes up space on earth. . . . The Incarnation does involve a claim to a space of its own on earth. . . . A truth, a doctrine, or a religion need no space for themselves. They are disembodied entities.' But 'the *ecclesia Christi*, the disciple community . . . is made into one body, with its own sphere of sovereignty and its claim to living-space'.[35] This concern with the church's 'claim to space', the question of the boundaries of the Confessing Church and its right to point exclusively to itself as the Body of Christ, distinguishes this period of Bonhoeffer's theology and sets *The Cost of Discipleship* and *Life Together* apart from his other works.

Bonhoeffer was hardly a moderate in the struggle between the Confessing Church and the *Reich* Church. The Barmen Synod of 1934, strongly influenced by Karl Barth's theology and personality, established the Confessing Church with the charge that the *Reich* Church, controlled by supporters of the Nazi government and members of the German Christian movement, could no longer be called a church of Christ. Bonhoeffer's adherence to this declaration never wavered throughout the church struggle; he remained, if anything, more extreme in his support than the majority of his fellow churchmen. He made clear his position in a letter to the general secretary of the Faith and Order Conference concerning the problem of church representation at ecumenical conferences:

. . I must state that with regard to the German *Reich* Church, the position of my church is fundamentally different from its attitude towards all other churches of the world, as the Confessional Evangelical Church in Germany disclaims and wholly contradicts the *Reich* Church to accept [*sic*] our Lord Jesus Christ as God and Saviour. . . . The teaching as well as the action of the responsible leaders of the *Reich* Church have clearly proved that this church does no longer serve Christ but that it serves the Antichrist. . . . The Confessing Church has therefore (at the Dahlem Synod, last autumn) declared that the *Reich* Church government has dissociated itself from the Church of Christ. This solemn declaration has been given in full power and obedience to the Word of Jesus Christ; it states clearly that the *Reich* Church government can no longer claim to compose the Church of Christ in Germany nor any part of it.[36]

The tenacity with which Bonhoeffer held to this position soon proved to be an embarrassment to many members of his church, and the *Bruderhaus* experiment which he began in 1935 seemed to confirm the suspicions of many that he was moving blindly in a legalistic path towards a complete withdrawal from the world of reality. 1936 saw the publication of his highly controversial essay, 'Concerning the Question of Church Communion'.[37] This statement of Bonhoeffer's position regarding the constituency and boundaries of the Confessing Church came as the climax of this phase in his development, and is of considerable importance to our discussion. At no other place is the problem of 'the claim to space' so clearly put, and the answer so forcefully stated. And nowhere else is the dilemma which the church struggle forced on Bonhoeffer's theology more apparent.

From the summary which Godsey has provided,[38] we shall briefly examine Bonhoeffer's argument. Bonhoeffer begins by asserting that the 'true church can never wish to draw its own boundary, for God alone knows the real members of the church'. A church of the Reformation can never describe its own limits; when it declares itself to be the true church, the *world* fixes its boundary by refusing to answer the call of a confessional community. 'The limit of the church,' he writes, 'is fixed from without.' The question of communion with 'another church' (in this case, the neutrals of the *Reich* Church' must depend upon whether or not the church in question is 'bent on destruction'. Any decision based upon the limits which the world has set must remain an *opus alienum*, taken in order that the church may better perform her proper task of making distinctly the call of salvation. The synods of Barmen and Dahlem asserted that the *Reich* Church had excluded itself from the true church; this assertion must be taken with complete seriousness. No fellowship with the *Reich* Church is possible. It is true that the church may not speculate concerning the content of the church or the number and identity of those saved and damned. This is left to God. But she may and must declare, as a concrete act of obedience to the proclamation of the Gospel: 'Here is the true church!' Therefore, confessing her faith in the midst of her existential situation, the Confessing Church can only say, with Tertullian: '*Extra ecclesiam nulla salus*; outside of the (Confessing) Church there is no salvation.'

Bonhoeffer's statement aroused quick disagreement. An answer followed, written by Helmut Gollwitzer, protesting that the confession of the church can only *witness* to God's Word and can never be identical with it; that the Confessing Church is not in its 'visible, empirical circle of persons' but only *in hope* the true church of Jesus Christ in Germany.[39] In her relationship to the *Reich* Church, the Confessing Church represents 'the confessing remnant of the German Evangelical Church (the former united church)'. With this formula, Gollwitzer attempted to build a bridge between the neutrals – those who remained within the *Reich* Church but did not support the policies of the German Christians – and the Confessing Church.

For a 'wise tactician'[40] such as Gollwitzer, the legalistic views of Bonhoeffer – closing the door firmly upon a promising attempt to heal the breach between the neutrals and Confessing Church members and bring pressure to bear upon the heretical wing of the *Reich* Church must indeed have seemed unfortunate. What must be noticed, however, is that Bonhoeffer's position was the inevitable result of his ecclesiological theory. Having identified the church with the revelation, he was bound to accept the boundaries around his church as the concrete boundaries of the revelation in Christ. Gollwitzer expounded what was – and is – Barth's view of the church, maintaining the dialectical relationship between the church and the Word of God which Bonhoeffer had rejected as 'ambiguous' in *Act and Being*.[41] The Barth-Gollwitzer position left one the freedom to make decisions based on one's assessment of the situation and the various possibilities presented to one for altering that situation. But for Bonhoeffer there was no alternative, no room to manœuvre once he had cast his lot with the Confessing Church. Its boundary was the boundary of the revelation.

We saw at the beginning of this chapter that 'just on the eve of the church struggle, Bonhoeffer wished to speak with the greatest vehemence of the *openness* of the church'.[42] His essay defending the exclusiveness of the Confessing Church, however, moves in a direction opposite from his early interest. Yet even here, at his most exclusive and 'other-worldly', Bonhoeffer searched for breathing space for the basic movement of his theology out into the world. One of the means by which he thought to accomplish this was undoubtedly his notion of 'living-space'; the invasion of the world by the community of faith. Another was his insistence that it was the world, not the church, which set the boundaries. The Christology lectures of 1933 spoke of Christ's mediation between the disciple and the world, in which the disciple looks steadfastly and exclusively towards Christ and leaves it to the world to set its own limitations.[43] Bonhoeffer's argument concerning the position of the Confessing Church in relation to the world and other churches is based upon the same thinking; the church has no interest in her boundaries, but only in her confession of Christ. In looking upon Christ, she finds her boundaries described for her by a world which rejects her message, and thereby cuts itself off from salvation. Indeed, it is this breach with the world which demonstrates the being of Christ *for* the world.[44] Anything less can only mean a relapse into the 'cheap grace' which produced the German Christian movement.

But in spite of the safeguards Bonhoeffer provided in order to maintain his own freedom of movement, it can hardly be questioned that the period of the church struggle was a narrowly restrictive one for his own theological development. His position, and what he felt were the demands of a sound strategy in the church struggle, made impossible for him any interest in theological directions which seemed to provide an opening for compromise. Church and state conversations could not be enjoined nor, as we saw in the preceding chapter, could there be any discussion of 'hermeneutical' problems: The question of whether texts ought not to be 'interpreted' in accordance with modern forms of thinking only masked the desire to strip away the scandal from the Gospel, hence to destroy the Gospel itself.

More important was the fate of Bonhoeffer's own theological vision. His theology was no longer open, but besieged by the world. The boundary of the community of revelation became a battle line, to be defended at all costs. The world became the enemy of the church and the enemy of Christ. The effect of this on Bonhoeffer's development may best be judged by glancing, in passing, at the striking military images which first make their appearance in the final chapters of *The Cost of Disciple-ship*: 'The *ecclesia Christi*, the disciple community, has been torn from the clutches of the world.' 'The sanctification of the church is really a defensive war, for the place which has been given to the Body of Christ on earth.' 'The community of the saints is barred off from the rest of the world by an unbreakable seal, awaiting its ultimate deliverance. Like a sealed train travelling through foreign territory, the church goes its way in the world.' The church 'invades the world and conquers territory for Christ', 'invades the world and robs it of its children'. The church is 'always in the battlefield, waging a war to prevent the breaking of the seal. . . . The separation of the church and the world from one another is the crusade which the church fights for the sanctuary of God on earth.' Finally, we have the perfect statement of the apocalyptic vision which underlay Bonhoeffer's position concerning the church's 'claim to space' during the church struggle, which reads in startling contrast to so much of the prison letters: 'When the Christian community has been deprived of its last inch of space on the earth, the end will be near.'[45]

The restrictive boundaries of the church struggle dominated Bonhoeffer's thinking until the beginning of the war. We cannot be certain (although we shall try, in the next chapter, to suggest a number of possibilities) what factor or combination of factors were responsible for the disappearance of those boundaries. We shall probably never know whether the radical call to obedience of *The Cost of Discipleship* or the worldliness of the *Ethics* and letters from prison was behind his departure from a convinced pacifist position in order to begin active participation in the plot to kill Hitler. That question would surely have puzzled Bonhoeffer himself; whatever inconsistencies we may have noticed in his thinking, he did not seem to notice them or to be troubled by them. But it is true that the beginning of the war found Bonhoeffer deeply committed to 'activities in the secular sphere'.[46]

The opportunity presented itself almost by accident. The problem was how Bonhoeffer could be saved from conscription. A brother-in-law, active in the Intelligence Service and the resistance movement, offered Bonhoeffer employment which would allow him to meet and work with those working to overthrow Hitler – men with worldly interests, all too few of them orthodox Christians and churchmen. No more fittingly symbolic occupation could have been found: the dedicated Confessing Church leader, fresh from an experiment with monasticism, became a plain-clothes agent. At the same time, he engaged himself with a conspiracy which aimed to make good the debts of a social class and the crimes of a nation – most of it humanistic in outlook, part of it socialist and even atheist. Bonhoeffer, far removed from his church work, looked outward once more, beyond any boundaries, towards the duties and problems, successes and failures, experiences and helplessness which humanity bears in common.

When Bonhoeffer no longer found meaning and purpose to the question of boundaries and the claim to space, he dismantled his theory of revelation and attempted to combine the individual parts in different ways, such that the whole of worldly life could be subject to Christ, to the revelation. These experiments have come down to us in the posthumous collection, the *Ethics*.

CHAPTER 10

The Disappearance of the
Boundaries

Bonhoeffer's Progress to the 'Ethics' and the 'Letters and Papers from Prison

Returning from Stockholm in June of 1942, having delivered the plans for the overthrow of Hitler to the Bishop of Chichester, Bonhoeffer wrote to Bethge from his compartment on the Munich train:

Again and again I ponder my activities, which are still so strongly concerned with the worldly sector. I am surprised that I can and do live without the Bible for days – if I forced myself, it would be auto-suggestion rather than obedience. I know that such auto-suggestion could be and is a great help; it's just that I am afraid of falsifying a genuine experience and of receiving, in the last resort, no genuine help. Then, when I open the Bible once again, it is new and rewarding as never before, and I want eagerly to preach again. I know that I have only to open my own books to hear what should be said against all of this. I don't want to justify myself; rather, I know that I have been through periods which were much richer 'spiritually'. But I can feel in myself the resistance growing against everything 'religious'. Often to the point of an instinctive horror – and that surely isn't a good thing either. I am not naturally religious. But I do return again and again in my thoughts to God and Christ; the genuine things, life, freedom and mercy mean a great deal to me. It's just that the religious clothing is so uncomfortable. Do you understand? All these are not new thoughts or views, but because I think that something new is about to burst in upon me, I am letting things run their course without resisting. This is how I understand my present activity in the worldly sector. Please forgive these confessions, the long train ride is at fault . . .[1]

1937 saw the premature end of the *Bruderhaus* experiment following a Gestapo ban; 1942 found Bonhoeffer in the midst

of the 'worldly sector'. During the intervening years, his theological outlook appears to have done a complete about-face.
This movement is perceptible in his writings and can be
followed in the pages of the *Ethics*, the writing of which began
in 1940 and continued until after Bonhoeffer's arrest in 1943.
Here one finds at least four approaches to the problem of
Christian ethics, each moving farther away from the exclusiveness which characterized Bonhoeffer's church struggle theology
and further in the direction of the open worldliness of the prison
letters. But if this shift is discernible, the reasons for it are not
at all clear. It is well, then, that we pause for a moment in our
development in order to examine possible influences upon
Bonhoeffer's theological development between his return from
his trip to America and his imprisonment.

1. Bonhoeffer and the Confessing Church: 1937–41. By 1940 the Confessing Church's voice, to use Bethge's metaphor, had become
hoarse. Bonhoeffer had done more than his share in making
the call of the church loud and clear and ultimately, one must
confess, in making the voice hoarse. His activities did not go
unnoticed by the government. Step by step, Bonhoeffer was
forbidden the exercise of his customary church duties until, by
the summer of 1940, he was so hemmed in by government
restrictions that he could no longer count his church activities
as his primary occupation. His authority to teach in Berlin as
a *Privatdozent* was finally withdrawn in August 1936. In October
1937 the *Bruderhaus* and the Finkenwalde seminary were dis-
banded by the Gestapo. The latter divided into sections which
continued to meet secretly but this work was finally dissolved
altogether in 1940. In 1938, Bonhoeffer was forbidden participation in church activities in Berlin. During the summer of 1940,
he was ordered by the authorities to cease preaching altogether,
and to report at regular intervals to the police. Finally, in the
spring of the following year, Bonhoeffer's books were proscribed and he was not allowed to write or publish any further
work. He no longer had any official capacity in his church and
was forced to separate his activities from those of his fellow
Confessing Churchmen. Bonhoeffer's anguish over the fate of

his church brought him home from America after only a few months. But as Bethge writes, 'one of the things he did not realize then was how far he would drop out of the immediate church work and how painfully he would have to separate his doings from the church.'[2] This distance from the Confessing Church, imposed from without, provided Bonhoeffer with the opportunity to take a different perspective on theology and the task of the theologian than that of the Confessing Church apologist. In his search for a meaning for his work, he was thrown back upon himself and a new circle of associates.

2. *The Hitler Resistance Movement.* Hans von Dohnanyi first became involved with the men who were to be the principal figures in the resistance movement against Hitler early in 1938.[3] Upon Bonhoeffer's return from his second trip to America, his brother-in-law was appointed special adviser to General Oster, Admiral Canaris's staff officer in the Secret Service. Bonhoeffer had always been close to von Dohnanyi, and was easily persuaded that with his ecumenical contacts he could be of service to the resistance and that employment within the secret service organization was an excellent way of avoiding conscription. Moreover, the Gestapo allowed the secret service an incredible amount of freedom of movement of the kind Bonhoeffer needed. He therefore accepted employment as a civilian agent and took up residence in Munich, from where he would make several trips as a courier for the resistance, under the guise of his official position. Most of the restrictions on his movements were immediately lifted.

Working for the resistance movement could not but mean for Bonhoeffer a return to much of his liberal, humanitarian, middle-class past. He found himself surrounded by old and new acquaintances who professed a variety of religious, political, and personal beliefs and opinions; most were involved in secular professions and all were deeply committed to the cause of the resistance. There were Klaus, his brother, a legal adviser to Lufthansa; von Dohnanyi and Rüdiger Schleicher, his brothers-in-law, both eminent jurists; Ernst von Harnack, politician and son of Dietrich's teacher; Justus Delbrück, industrialist and son of the great historian. Friedrich Justus Perels, the lawyer and stalwart Confessing Churchman, was well known to the Bonhoeffer brothers. Through Klaus, Dietrich came to know Joseph Wirmer, the Catholic jurist, and Julius Leber, the socialist. Dohnanyi was close to the generals Beck and Oster as well as to Goerdeler, the Christian Humanist who once had been the mayor of Leipzig. The humanitarian and patriotic enterprise to which Bonhoeffer now dedicated himself played a decisive role in breaking down the last of the barriers to his freedom of thought and action which had been erected during the years preceding the war. He could now exercise what had always been a part of him: 'the freedom to encounter men of every background, rank, and conviction . . . cheerfully, imaginatively, and without doctrinaire exclusiveness.'[4]

3. Theological Influences. Bonhoeffer's report to his church concerning his trip to America took the form of an essay which he entitled *Protestantism Without Reformation.* Here, in a spirit very different from that which he had displayed in 1930, he asked his own church not to disregard American theology and church life after a surface appraisal, but rather to take seriously the historical, social, and political background of the American church; to ask 'what God is doing in and with his church in America, what he is doing for us through her, and for her through us'.[5] This was a prelude to the kind of openness he was to display in his *Ethics,* the writing of which was begun upon his return. Bonhoeffer always learned much from travelling abroad, and we may count the American adventure, however brief it may have been, as one of the experiences which broke down his resistance to the theme of worldly Christianity.

Of more direct literary-theological influences upon Bonhoeffer's development sufficiently strong to turn him from his Confessing Church exclusiveness to the theme of the *Ethics* and the prison letters, it is difficult to speak. Certainly his new preoccupation with the problems of post-war society required more of him than a retreat to dogma, and the reality and importance of questions of this kind must be kept in mind when one attempts to understand the *Ethics*. Bonhoeffer read and responded to William Paton's *The Church and the New Order*, published in 1941, on behalf of the Confessing Church and the resistance movement[6]. This task involved him directly in the problems of the new society of post-war Europe and the role of the church in determining the shape and purpose of that society. Other books absorbed Bonhoeffer's interest during the war years. This was the time, Bethge reports, 'in which Bonhoeffer read with new fascination *Don Quixote*, the honourable knight who became isolated from reality fighting for a principle'.[7] There were also the books which occupied Bonhoeffer's mind while he was in prison – though one cannot find more than a general thematic relationship between their subject matter and Bonhoeffer's new interest. These were minor classics of poetry and prose from the German romantic period, nineteenth-century histories (including works by Delbrück and Harnack), biographies, and introductions to the principles of natural and physical science.[8] Of theology, in the traditional academic sense of the word, Bonhoeffer read little. But he continued with his customary biblical exegesis and devotional reading, and remained profoundly moved and comforted by hymns and the daily *Losungen* (readings from a popular German devotional series). Taken on the whole, Bonhoeffer's reading without doubt readied his mind for the extension of his theology into the 'worldly sector'.

An important theological influence, perhaps the clearest of all, must be acknowledged. In the midst of the Confessing Church herself and while Bonhoeffer was still at work on the *Ethics*, there appeared, in 1941, Bultmann's famous essay on mythology and the New Testament. Bonhoeffer had hitherto contented himself with denying the right of the church even to raise the question of whether or not the Bible is intelligible to modern man. But Bultmann's essay finally impressed him with the seriousness of the hermeneutical problem. Bultmann had, he confessed, 'done intellectual integrity a service'; he had 'dared to ask what many repress in themselves, without overcoming it', and Bonhoeffer left no doubt that he included himself in the latter category.[9] On the other hand, he was shocked and deeply disappointed with the rigid refusal to listen to Bultmann on the part of the Confessing Church. The dangers of exclusivism and, by association, his own position were brought home to him. Bonhoeffer did not agree with Bultmann, but his rebellion freed Bonhoeffer of any misguided loyalty to a rigidly orthodox line of thinking. There is no doubt that he was inspired by this work to move on fearlessly in his own direction.

These, then, are at least some of the pieces of the puzzle of Bonhoeffer's change of direction between 1939 and 1944. More we do not know. Suffice it to say that the boundaries and restrictions were broken down, and Bonhoeffer's theological vision was directed outward, towards the world.

'Formation' and 'Conformation'

Bonhoeffer looked upon his *Ethics* as his first real theological contribution and hoped for nothing else in life than to be given the opportunity to complete his work.[10] Unfortunately, this was not to be: we have been left with a collection of scattered essays, some of them unfinished, for which no organization can be wholly satisfactory. But it is clear that these essays comprise a series of attacks upon a single question, a *prolegomenon* to the problem of the relationship between the Christian revelation and the life of the world. Once again, Bonhoeffer saw no way of confronting the question other than Christologically; once more, he turned to his notion of concretion for a point of departure.

Eberhard Bethge has recently suggested a method of re-ordering the essays of the *Ethics* so that they follow one another chronologically.[11] The result is most revealing. One notices, first, that Bonhoeffer's initial approach to the problem speaks the language of *The Cost of Discipleship* while stressing the one-ness of the world and God in the Incarnation. In the present *Ethics*, this comprises the fourth chapter and has been given the title, 'The Love of God and the Decay of the World'.[12] Bonhoeffer moves from the basis of his earlier thinking, prior to the church struggle, concerning the problems of man's knowledge of good and evil. There is a clear relationship between this section of the *Ethics* and portions of *Sanctorum Communio, Act and Being,* and the study of Genesis 1–3. Bonhoeffer's theme reflects both his loyalty to *The Cost of Discipleship* and his desire to move beyond the confines of that book; the exclusiveness of Christ is conjoined with the inclusiveness of his Lordship over the whole of the world: 'The more exclusively we acknowledge and confess Christ as our Lord, the more fully the wide range of his dominion will be disclosed to us.'[13] Once again, one sees how closely Bonhoeffer has bound together Christology and discipleship. Christ is the unifying factor for the Christian in the world. Because of the inclusiveness of Christ's being, the Christian can live 'in reconciliation and unity with God and with men', which means 'living the life of Jesus Christ'.[14] Here is an initial clue to the direction in which Bonhoeffer's thoughts will once more turn: towards an *imitatio Christi* as the proper form of the Christian life.

This chapter remained unfinished. Bonhoeffer had, however, become concerned with a theme which was to occupy his thoughts for the remaining years of his life. The *oneness* of Christ and the world must be illuminated because the Incarnation leaves one no other choice. But how is one to accomplish this without falling into 'cheap grace' on the one hand or a legalistic concern for 'boundaries' for discipleship and the church on the other?

Bonhoeffer's second approach to the problem finds him deeply involved with questions he had left unanswered in 1933: the impossibility of division in the world for one who sets his eyes on Christ; the inconceivability of a choice between Christ and the earth:

No man can look with undivided vision at God and the world of reality so long as God and the world are torn asunder. Try as he may, he can only let his eyes wander distractedly from one to the other. But there is a place at which God and the cosmic reality are reconciled, a place at which God and man have become one. That and that alone is what enables man to set his eyes upon God and upon the world at the same time. This place does not lie somewhere out beyond reality in the realm of ideas. It lies in

Jesus Christ, the Reconciler of the World. . . . Whoever sees Jesus Christ does indeed see God and the world in one. He can henceforward no longer see God without the world or the world without God.[15]

Here is a Christological restatement of Bonhoeffer's comment in his 1932 lecture on the relationship between church and state.[16] God and the world cannot be considered apart from one another. Here, however, he insists on the Christological basis of any such proposition. It is Christ, the worldly man who makes possible the unity of God and the world. One remembers that it was in 1932 that Karl Barth's influence over Bonhoeffer was growing very rapidly. It is striking how closely this portion of the *Ethics* (Chapter 1) resembles Barth's position since the latter's well-known 'change of direction' – which resulted in the fourth volume of the *Church Dogmatics* and which was expounded so self-consciously in the essay, *The Humanity of God*. For example, Barth writes in the latter work:

In Jesus Christ there is no isolation of man from God or of God from man. Rather, in him we encounter the history, the dialogue, in which God and man meet together and are together, the reality of the covenant *mutually* contracted, preserved, and fulfilled by them. . . . Thus in this oneness Jesus Christ is the Mediator, the Reconciler, between God and man.[17]

Bonhoeffer's form of this argument appears at several points throughout the *Ethics*, even in sections which are known to have been written as late as 1943. In one passage – interesting when compared with a criticism of Barth which comprised a footnote to *Sanctorum Communio* – Bonhoeffer wrote:

But Jesus Christ is man and God in one. In him there takes place the original and essential encounter with man and with God. Henceforward . . God cannot be conceived and known otherwise than in the human form of Jesus Christ. In him we see humanity as that which God has accepted, borne, and loved, and as that which is reconciled with God.[18]

But Bonhoeffer moved determinedly ahead with his theme of 'concretion', and he produced results of which Barth could not approve. Bonhoeffer was purposely (and characteristically) careless in not drawing sharp distinctions between Christology, revelation, and the Christian life. All, he argues, were part of the same problem: Christ's relationship to worldly life. He was searching once more for a visible, concrete, tangible way of expressing the relationship between the world and the revelation in Christ, the worldly man; taking seriously the world's structures, history, and dynamic. His first task, therefore, was an analysis of the historical situation of the western world. Up until the essay entitled 'Inheritance and Decay' we had no indication in Bonhoeffer's writings that he attached any theological importance to the dynamic movement of world history. But here we are given a foretaste of the thinking which we will encounter in the prison letters:

What has been utterly forgotten here is the original message of the Reformation that there is no holiness of man either in the profane or the sacred as such, but only that which comes through the merciful and sin-forgiving Word of God. The Reformation is celebrated as the emancipation of man in his conscience, his reason and his culture and the justification of the secular as such. The Reformers' biblical faith in God had radically removed God from the world. . . . While the natural scientists of the seventeenth and eighteenth centuries were still believing Christians, when faith in God was lost all that remained was a rationalized and mechanized world.[19]

Bonhoeffer describes, in a lengthy passage, the movement of the world away from God-consciousness and the counter-struggles of the church in its attempts to call the world back to God. Both, he argues, are based upon a misunderstanding of the Reformation. Within a few years he will see the matter differently, but at this point the secularization of the world is condemned rather than embraced. In the next section of this study, we shall examine the differences between 'worldliness' in the *Ethics* and 'worldliness' in the prison letters. Here our interest is in the effect upon Bonhoeffer's theme of his old concerns: 'the concretion of revelation is the space of the church'; 'the concretion of Christology is Christ existing as the church'.

This section of the *Ethics* represents Bonhoeffer's second approach to the problem, and it shows him to be troubled by the terminology he has brought with him from his own past. Can there be an unrestricted movement of his thinking into worldliness if he retains his spatial language? Christ had been bound to a particular 'space', the church, which stands over against the world. And clearly, Bonhoeffer wishes to avoid the division of the world into two 'spheres', 'the one divine, holy, supernatural and Christian and the other worldly, profane, natural and un-Christian'.[20] He attacks this view in a short but very important essay entitled 'Thinking in Terms of Two Spheres'. This kind of thinking, he charges, assumes that there are 'realities which lie outside of the reality of Christ', and supports the erroneous conclusion that one may live in the one sphere and have nothing to do with the other. But this, Bonhoeffer declares, is contrary to the thought of the Bible and the Reformation:

Ethical thinking in terms of spheres . . . is invalidated by faith in the revelation of the ultimate reality in Jesus Christ, and this means that there is no real possibility of being a Christian outside the reality of the world and that there is no real worldly existence outside the reality of Jesus Christ. There is no place to which the Christian can withdraw from the world, whether it be outwardly or in the sphere of the inner life. . . . Whoever professes to believe in the reality of Jesus Christ, as the revelation of God, must in the same breath profess his faith in both the reality of God and the reality of the world; for in Christ he finds God and the world reconciled. . . . His worldliness does not divide him from Christ, and his Christianity does not divide him from the world. Belonging wholly to Christ, he stands at the same time wholly in the world.[21]

Certainly Bonhoeffer has found the language of his own doctrines of the church and revelation unserviceable, and even embarrassing for his new interest. But he has not given up his determination that Christology be concretely expressed. He therefore introduces those two elusive formulations so characteristic of this second approach to *Ethics*: 'formation' and 'conformation'; 'Christ taking form' in the world and 'conformation with the Incarnate'.[22] In this manner, he seeks to free his Christology from his ecclesiology in order to describe a Christ moving about freely in the world; no longer a Christ identified with a church fighting against the world for her existence.

At the same time, Bonhoeffer is eager to show that he has not repudiated the church itself. He is still anxious that the church occupy a central place in his thinking. He therefore describes the church as 'nothing but a section of humanity in which Christ has really taken form', having to do with 'the whole man in the world with all its implications'.[23] And if he has found his 'spatial' terminology embarrassing, he has not thereby repudiated the serious questions he sought to answer with his older ecclesiological theory. 'Are there,' he asks, 'really no ultimate static contraries, no spaces which are separated from one another once and for all? Is not the church of Jesus Christ such a space, a space which is cut off from the world?'[24] His answer both defends the visible, spatial nature of the church and attacks the militant 'claim to space' of the last chapters of *The Cost of Discipleship*:

The church does indeed occupy a definite space in the world, a space which is delimited by her public worship, her organization, and her parish life, and it is this fact that has given rise to the whole of the thinking in terms of spheres. It would be very dangerous to overlook this, to deny the visible nature of the church, and to reduce her to the status of a purely spiritual force. . . . It is essential to the revelation of God in Jesus Christ that it occupies space in the world. . . . The church of Jesus Christ is the place, in other words, the space in the world, at which the reign of Jesus Christ over the whole world is evidenced and proclaimed. . . . It is the place where testimony is given to the foundation of all reality in Jesus Christ. . . . *The space of the church is not there in order to deprive the world of a piece of its territory*, but precisely to prove to the world that it is still the world, the world which is loved by God and reconciled with him. The church has neither the wish nor the obligation to extend her space to cover the space of the world. She asks for no more space than she needs for the purpose of serving the world by bearing witness to Jesus Christ and to the reconciliation of the world with God through him. *The only way in which the church can defend her own territory is by fighting not for it but for the salvation of the world.* Otherwise the church becomes a 'religious society' which fights in its own interest and thereby ceases at once to be the church of God and of the world.[25]

The Church occupies space in the world, but the nature of that space and the justification for its occupation need thoroughly to be rethought. This space of the church still is related to revelation in a special way, but it is no longer the only area within which the concept of revelation may be discussed. There is an important truth behind 'thinking in terms of two spheres', but its dangers (and, by implication, the dangers of Bonhoeffer's ecclesiology) lead one to search for 'another picture which is equally simple and obvious', which will 'conceive this distinction between church and world without reslaping into these spatial terms'.[26]

Thus, Bonhoeffer's Christology is liberated from his ecclesiology, and his search for 'another picture' leads him to develop a variety of new and exciting ideas. He writes, as we have seen, of Christ taking form and of man's conformation with Christ. His third approach (Chapter 3) introduces some truly fruitful products of his new thinking, freed entirely from his ecclesiological restrictions and defending his movement beyond them. Here, Bonhoeffer distinguished between the 'ultimate' and 'penultimate', introducing his concept of the 'natural'. The penultimate is validated Christologically as 'the encounter of Christ with the world'.[27] A correction of the traditional understanding of Luther's distinction between Law and Gospel is clearly intended, and his attack upon Barth's understanding of the relation of theology to worldly forms begins to take shape with the description and rejection of the 'ultimate' as the one and only interest of theology:

The radical solution sees only the ultimate, and in it only the complete breaking off of the penultimate. Ultimate and penultimate are here mutually exclusive contraries. Christ is the destroyer and enemy of everything penultimate, and everything penultimate is enmity towards Christ. Christ is the sign that the world is ripe for burning. There are no distinctions. Everything must go to the judgement. There are only two categories: for Christ, and against him. . . . What becomes of the world through this is no longer of any consequence. The Christian bears no responsibility for it, and the world must in any case perish. No matter if the whole order of the world breaks down under the impact of the word of Christ, there must be no holding back.[28]

But this solution, he argues, sets God the Judge and Redeemer against God the Creator and Preserver. Christology points the way to another solution. 'Jesus Christ the man – this means that God enters into created reality. It means that we have the right and the obligation to be men before God.'[29] The penultimate comes into its own as that which exists for the sake of the ultimate, but which really does exist and must be preserved. Manhood, humanity and goodness – the natural – can and must be claimed for Christ.

This chapter was set aside unfinished when Bonhoeffer

departed for his first trip to Switzerland in 1941, for the meeting with Visser't Hooft. When he took up his discussion once more, it was at another point. The fourth skirmish with the problem of ethics produced, among other things, the concept of the *Mandates*. This notion provides us with the clearest example of Bonhoeffer's struggle with the problem of how to embrace the whole of the world with the revelation of God in Christ without surrendering the concreteness and simplicity of his spatial terminology. The solution here is to speak of four 'earthly agents' – labour, marriage, government, and the church – in which Christ 'assumes concrete form in the world'.[30] A 'mandate' is defined as 'the claiming, the seizure, and the formation of a definite earthly domain by the divine commandment'. These divinely-authorized spheres in which revelation occurs are 'conjoined'; that is, they mutually limit and mutually support and are directed towards one another.[31]

Possibly by the time of his arrest, Bonhoeffer himself sensed the theological shortcomings of his theme. Barth spoke later of the 'north German patriarchalism' behind the idea of the mandates, and disliked the restrictions which they placed upon God's freedom of movement.[32] In the light of his own past restrictions, however, Bonhoeffer's notion is very clearly intended to free 'God' from 'the church' and to claim for him other worldly 'domains'. It is interesting to set Barth's criticism of the mandates alongside Bonhoeffer's own questioning of the extent to which he was restricted by his *bourgeois* past soon after the work on the *Ethics* was set aside for the last time.

The final approach to the problem of ethics had affirmed worldly order, responsibility, and 'the objective subordination of the lower to the higher'.[33] During the early days of his imprisonment at Tegel, Bonhoeffer attempted to write a play in which he put the argument for a reconstruction of *bourgeois* and aristocratic values into the mouth of a medical student named Christoph. The antagonist is Heinrich, a young worker who confronts Christoph with a quite different world. 'You have a foundation,' he tells Christoph. 'You have ground beneath your feet, you have a place in the world, for you some things are self-evident . . . because you know that your roots lie so deep that they will sprout once more. For you only one thing matters: to keep your feet on the ground. . . . Upon the ground beneath your feet depends the question of whether one will live – and this is the ground which we do not have. . . . Give me ground beneath my feet; give me the archimedian point upon which I can stand – and everything would be otherwise.'[34] The play ends with Christoph deep in meditation upon Heinrich's passionate plea for a place to stand which does not simply direct him towards a *bourgeois* tradition which he does not and cannot share. May we say that at this point, Bonhoeffer is at last ready for the fresh approach and truly radical breakthrough of his letters from prison?

The Archimedian Point

'Who is Christ for us today?' is the question with which Bonhoeffer opens his letter from prison on 30th April 1944. No sooner has he asked this question and advanced his belief that 'Christ must become the Lord of those with no religion', than he acknowledges: 'The questions needing answers would surely be: what is the significance of a church (church, parish, preaching, Christian life) in a religionless world? . . . Does the secret discipline or, as the case may be, the distinction (which you have met with me before) between ultimate and penultimate acquire fresh importance?'[35]

Bonhoeffer's failure, during the remainder of the prison letters, to turn his attention towards *these* questions has confused or saddened some of his interpreters and delighted others.[36] However that may be, Bonhoeffer chooses to explore the possibilities for 'non-religious Christianity' without being too concerned about the implications of his thoughts for a doctrine of the church. A 'non-religious Christianity' seems necessarily bound to a decisive and final rejection of 'spatial' descriptions of Christ as the church or any other limited spaces. 'You ask whether this leaves any 'space' for the church, or has it gone for good?' Bonhoeffer wrote to Bethge after describing the situation.[37] But the question simply remained unanswered. In their present form, the prison letters reflect the final separation of

Bonhoeffer's Christology and his conception of revelation from ecclesiology and the search for a *spatial* 'concretion'. Here is no 'community of revelation' or 'Christ existing as the church', no 'Mandates'. Here we do not even find 'conformation' or 'Christ taking form'. Bonhoeffer's interest is focused almost wholly upon the 'penultimate' half of his formula. Finding 'Christ for us today' must mean that one sets aside the careful drawing of connections between Christology and the concept of God and Christology and ecclesiology; and seeks instead to find the revelation, Christ, in the forms of worldly life. Christianity must speak of 'personal faith' in Jesus Christ and discipleship.

So Bonhoeffer sets out to reconstruct and reinterpret the combination of Christology, scripture, and ethics which he set forth at the beginning of *The Cost of Discipleship*. Once again, revelation must be described as an *imitatio Christi*, the living of the life of Christ in the world; the life 'for others' and for the world. But in a 'world come of age' this formula must be revised, especially as regards the relationship of scripture to the other two elements. Bonhoeffer seems at last to have decided for a non-spatial concretion of the revelation and especially to have refused to continue the development of his past efforts to ground revelation in the visible church.

The background of this revolution in Bonhoeffer's thinking was a new understanding of the historical situation of the western world. His positive acceptance of his own analysis of a world which has 'come of age' is the decisively new element which broke down the last of his reservations and opened up the flood-gates through which the exhilarating ideas of the prison letters flowed. We therefore move directly into our next section and the discussion of the historical problem which Bonhoeffer finally came to acknowledge as a vital one for theology.

THE WORLD COME OF AGE

The question is: Christ and the world come of age.
8th June 1944. Letters, p.108

CHAPTER II

The Theme of the Secular

The three phrases which have become most closely identified with Bonhoeffer's name – 'the world come of age', 'religionless Christianity' and 'sharing in the sufferings of God' – emerge out of a conception of human history and an assessment of its importance for the proper understanding of Christian faith and theology. This much is certain from any preview of the prison letters. There, Bonheoffer tells us that the world has 'come of age' – this means that it stands at the end of a historical process through which it has achieved a maturity and independence from ecclesiastical and religious guardianship. Christian faith and Christian theology which truly respond to the revelation of God in Christ must be expressed in ways which recognize and serve this maturity. Given the fact that the world is essentially historical, a description of the activity of God and man in the world must affirm this historical self-understanding. It was in searching for such a statement of Christian faith, that Bonhoeffer envisaged a 'non-religious' Christianity. Later, in an important modification and correction of his theory which pointed more certainly to the Christological nature of his quest, Bonhoeffer spoke of 'sharing in the sufferings of God at the hands of a godless world.'

We stated in Chapter 9 that Bonhoeffer's early theological interest in the theme of the secular was cut short by the beginning of the church struggle.[1] But in spite of an instinctive 'concern for the earth and its creatures', it must be acknowledged that a preoccupation with secularism and history and a validation of these *as primary areas of investigation for a theory of revelation* are decidedly new elements in Bonhoeffer's theological development. This investigation of history and secularism is linked with his past concerns through his use of a particular Christological perspective. Here, Bonhoeffer was involved in a choice between elements of his Christology which were now shown to be incompatable, and he chose those which enabled him to affirm his new discoveries and to illuminate them theologically.

In this section of our study we shall trace the development of the theme of the secular in Bonhoeffer's thought (Chapter 11) and clarify it by examining his criticism of Karl Barth, the theologian with whom he had always been closely identified, which appears first in the prison letters (Chapter 12). In a concluding chapter (13) we will set Bonhoeffer's analysis of history alongside the explorations of two men who seem closest to Bonhoeffer's new interest: *Ernst Troeltsch* and *Friedrich Gogarten*.

The Emergence of the Theme of Secularism

Bonhoeffer's attitude towards the historical question as a theological interest was one of indifference, even hostility, prior to 1940. *Sanctorum Communio* and *Act and Being* ignored the question, raised by Troeltsch among others, whether it is possible in a world which thinks of itself as involved in and determined by its history to seek the answer to the problem of revelation in an ecclesiology. Bonhoeffer circumvented Troeltsch's question and presupposed, as did Seeberg, a special relationship between the church and the revelation in Christ.[2] His indifference became outright rejection during the church struggle; in *The Cost of Discipleship* and numerous essays Bonhoeffer strengthened his ecclesiological position and burned any bridges which could have led to a theological interest in worldly life.[3] He dismissed the historical question, even in the persuasive form in which it was being urged upon the Confessing Church by Confessing Churchmen, as the attempt by modern man to dissolve the central scandal of the Christian faith into an 'essence', which might then be manipulated and distorted in accordance with one's own purposes.[4] We are finally left with only two sources from which we may gather evidence for Bonhoeffer's understanding of history: the *Ethics* and the *Letters and Papers from Prison*.

Two essays in the *Ethics* introduce Bonhoeffer's view of history and the historical question. For the first time, Bonhoeffer sees the present situation of Christianity as one which can be understood only when one has first analyzed the relationship between church and world during the course of history. In 'Inheritance and Decay',[5] Bonhoeffer calls the new phenomenon in Western culture 'secularism' and the process which brought it into being 'secularization'. This initial study, which dates from 1940, needs to be examined closely.

Bonhoeffer defines history as a conception possible only in the West, for it presupposes a unity in Jesus Christ. It is the Christian message, 'linked with the consciousness of temporality and opposed to all mythologization', which has made possible the idea of history, because 'only where thought is consciously or unconsciously governed by the entry of God into history at a definite point of time, that is to say, by the incarnation of God in Jesus Christ', is history conceivable.[6] Only through the life and death of Jesus Christ does history become truly temporal. The history of the West can then be understood as a movement in Christ, 'in its nearness to Christ and in its opposition to him.' 'Jesus Christ has made of the west a historical unit. . . . The unity of the West is not an idea but a historical reality, of which the sole foundation is Christ.'[7] Therefore, the history of the West may be traced as a continuous battle between forces which, however divided, are none the less dedicated to an ideal of unity in Christ.

The Reformation destroyed this historical unity, breaking the *corpus christianum* into its true constituents, the *corpus Christi* and the world. Schism became 'the fate and inheritance of the Western world.'[8] The result was the existence side by side of two kingdoms which could neither be mixed nor torn asunder – the Word and the sword, the church and the world. Yet both Protestant and Catholic, by calling upon the name of Christ and confessing guilt for this visible disunity, preserved the unity of the West and the Lordship of Christ.

But at this juncture, through a misunderstanding of the

Reformation, 'the great process of secularization' set in, 'at the end of which we are standing today.' The world thought herself emancipated and sanctified in and of herself, and insisted upon her 'right' to independence. 'The emancipation of man in his conscience, his reason, and his culture, and the justification of the secular as such' was celebrated as the message of the Reformation. Faith in God was lost in a rationalized and mechanized world. Mastery rather than service became the goal of science and technology, man proclaimed his 'innate rights', and mass movements and nationalism became the inheritance of the Western world. 'The people deemed that they had now come of age, that they were now capable of taking in hand the direction of their own internal and external history.'[9]

The unity in Christ was replaced by a new unity, founded upon godlessness which 'already bears in itself the seeds of decay'. This unity based upon godlessness is no theoretical denial of God's existence, but rather is itself a religion. Because it is Western, it turns upon God yet assumes the form of a religion.[10] Its God is the New Man – man worshipped in the form of Christ. Having lost the unity which Western history possessed in Christ, 'everything established is threatened with annihilation'. Secularism is godlessness – Christian godlessness – which 'involves the dissolution of all values, and achieves its goal only in final self-destruction';

The master of the machine becomes its slave. The machine becomes the enemy of man. The creature turns against its creator in a strange re-enactment of the Fall. The emancipation of the masses leads to the reign of terror of the guillotine. Nationalism leads inevitably to war. The liberation of man as an absolute ideal leads only to man's self-destruction. At the end of the path which was first trodden in the French revolution there is nihilism.

The new unity which the French revolution brought to Europe – and what we are experiencing today is the crisis of this unity – is therefore Western godlessness.[11]

Is the outcome of this situation the inevitable warfare between the *corpus Christi* and the secularized world, with the first fighting for the restoration of the unity in' Christ and the second seeking to complete the revolution? Bonhoeffer himself does not appear to have decided precisely what the significance of his historical analysis ought to be.[12] It is at this point that we must turn to another of his essays from the *Ethics* and the warning against 'thinking in terms of two spheres'. In this essay, Bonhoeffer's purpose is to expose the falsity of viewing reality as divisible into two juxtaposed and conflicting spheres, 'the one divine, holy, supernatural, and Christian, and the other worldly, profane, natural, and un-Christian'.[13] If in his essay on inheritance and decay he wished to point to the tragic and inevitable hostility between the two constituents of the broken *corpus christianum*, he now uses a Christology to assert the basic unity of the sacred and secular:

There are, therefore, not two spheres, but only the one sphere of the realization of Christ, in which the reality of God and the reality of the world are united. . . . There are not two spheres, standing side by side, competing with each other and attacking each other's frontiers. If that were so, this frontier dispute would always be the decisive problem of history. But the whole reality of the world is already drawn into Christ and bound together in him, and the movement of history consists solely in divergence and convergence in relation to this centre.[14]

Bonhoeffer seems unable to decide between an affirmation of secularism which would run the risk of lapsing into 'cheap grace',[15] and a condemnation of secularism as the anti-Christ which would lead him to the retrenchment and radicalism he wants to avoid. He is wrestling, in short, with the problem of what valuation one can place upon a secularism which one has described as 'godless'. To keep from thinking in two spheres he is unwilling to draw the conclusions which would logically follow from the picture of the *corpus Christi* confronting a hostile world. Although this picture is the result of his historical analysis, his Christology will not allow it to remain. Thus he cannot settle finally on a definition of secularism, worldliness, or godlessness.

In most instances in the *Ethics*, secularism has a pejorative sense. Secularism leads to the abyss and means, if its relentless march is not halted, the ultimate destruction of history. But Bonhoeffer can also recognize a 'better secularism'. 'When Christianity is employed as a polemical weapon against the secular,' he writes, 'this must be done in the name of a better

secularism and above all it must not lead back to a pre-
dominance of the spiritual sphere as an end in itself.' Realizing
her obligation to the future, the church unreservedly allies
herself with the secular forces of justice, truth, science, art,
humanity, culture, liberty, and patriotism.[16]

Bonhoeffer's refusal to condemn all 'godlessness' is even more
striking. He speaks suddenly (and all too briefly) of a 'promising
godlessness' which serves Christ against its will. By speaking
against the church this godlessness 'defends the heritage of a
genuine faith in God and of a genuine church'.[17]

These qualifications seem to make it possible for Bonhoeffer
to affirm a 'genuine worldliness' as the proper description of the
Christian life:

There is no real possibility of being a Christian outside the reality of the
world and there is no real worldly existence outside of the reality of Jesus
Christ. . . . (The worldliness of the Christian) does not divide him from
Christ, and his Christianity does not divide him from the world. Belonging
wholly to Christ, he stands at the same time wholly in the world.[18]

This worldliness means primarily that the Christian can and
should ally himself with a 'better secularism' and recognize the
value of a 'promising godlessness' as he moves into enemy
territory to conquer in the name of Christ.

Bonhoeffer's Christological vision which abolishes the possibility of 'two spheres', which makes the worldliness of the
Christian inescapable, calls at the same time for 'a Lordship of
triumph and completion'.[19] For the picture of Christ which
Bonhoeffer presents to us and upon which his *Ethics* is based
recalls the massive, mosaic *Christus Pantokrator* of the cloister at
Daphni, the triumphant Lord in whom the contradictions of
the world are reconciled:

The world is not divided between Christ and the devil but, whether it
recognizes it or not, it is solely and entirely the world of Christ. . . . The
dark and evil world must not be abandoned to the devil. It must be
claimed for him who has won it by his incarnation, his death and his
resurrection. Christ gives up nothing of what he has won. He holds it fast
in his hands. . . . This world has fallen under the sentence which God
passes on all enmity to Christ. It is engaged in a life-and-death struggle
with the church. And yet it is the task and the essential character of the

church that she shall impart to precisely this world its reconciliation with God and that she shall open its eyes to the reality of the love of God, against which it is blindly raging. In this way it is also, and indeed especially, the lost and sentenced world that is incessantly drawn in into the event of Christ.[20]

In the prison letters, the triumphant Lordship of Christ, the Reconciler will give way to a quite different view of Christ's Lordship. In the same way, the negative judgement of secularism and godlessness will give way to a picture of a world whose 'coming of age' can be *affirmed* through Christ; a world which may live *etsi deus non daretur,* as though God were not given – before God.

The Affirmation of the Historical in the Prison Letters

Bonhoeffer begins his analysis of the historical situation in his famous letter of 30th April 1944 with a meditation upon the possibility of what he terms a 'religionless' Christianity:

> The time when men could be told everything by means of words, whether theological or simply pious, is over, and so is the time of inwardness and conscience, which is to say the time of religion as such. We are proceeding towards a time of no religion at all: men as they are now simply cannot be religious any more. . . . Our whole nineteen-hundred-year-old Christian preaching and theology rests upon the 'religious premise' of man. What we call Christianity has always been a pattern – perhaps a true pattern – of religion. But if one day it becomes apparent that this *a priori* 'premise' simply does not exist, but was a historical and temporary form of human self-expression, i.e. if we reach the stage of being radically without religion . . . what does that mean for Christianity?[21]

'Being radically without religion', a stage at which man has arrived through the course of human history, calls into question the apologetical basis upon which Christian preaching and theology has been built. As we have seen, the *Ethics* identified secularism with godlessness, against which the church had to contend with all its strength and in the face of which found itself allied with a 'better secularism'. But here he is willing to explore 'a time of no religion at all' which the church must affirm as the outcome of the historical process, an age which she must redeem and serve and in which she must live. What does 'a time of no religion at all' mean for Christianity?

It means that the linchpin is removed from the whole structure of our Christianity to date, and the only people left for us to light on in the way of 'religion' are a few 'last survivals of the age of chivalry' or else one or two who are intellectually dishonest. Would they be the chosen few? Is it upon this dubious group and none other that we are to pounce, in fervour, pique, or indignation, in order to sell them the goods we have to offer? Are we to fall upon one or two unhappy people in their weakest moment and force upon them a sort of religious coercion?[22]

Two things should be noted here. First, one suspects that such pictures of a 'better secularism' as that which Bonhoeffer sketched in the *Ethics* have here been discarded as part of what is meant by 'religion'.[23] Christianity can no longer be content simply with allying herself with 'last survivals of the age of chivalry.' Secondly, Bonhoeffer is attacking the kind of apologetic which assumes that all men are innately religious – that it is the task of the apologist to expose and make articulate the 'religious basis' of the life of every man and of the world in which he lives. In the following chapter, we will compare this suggestion to contemporary approaches which make use of this kind of argument – for which Bonhoeffer himself certainly found room in his *Ethics*. But now Bonhoeffer wishes to speak of Christ *without* the presupposition that the man who is addressed is innately and unalterably religious. What he demands is a 'religionless' Christianity: 'How can Christ become the Lord even of those with no religion? If religion is no more than the garment of Christianity – and even that garment has had very different aspects at different periods – then what is a religionless Christianity?'[24]

An understanding and acceptance of the movement of history is behind the demand for religionless Christianity. The stage which the world is approaching – indeed, at which it has already arrived – is the stage of *religionlessness*. The world has 'come of age'; that is, it has reached such a level of maturity and in-dependence that a reassessment of the church and Christian faith and theology is called for. But how has the world reached this stage? Bonhoeffer describes a movement, beginning about the thirteenth century, towards the autonomy of man; a historical process through which men 'learned to cope with all questions of importance without recourse to God as a working hypothesis.'[25] As this 'great defection from God' gathered momentum, God was edged out of ethical, scientific, aesthetic, and eventually religious discourse. Man declared his emancipation from God, the church, and the pastor. The church protested and opposed this trend, but this only made it the more radical and relentless and forced it to think of itself as anti-Christian.[26]

Bonhoeffer sees signs that this movement has reached some kind of completion, and that God is rapidly becoming superfluous as a solution for unsolved problems.[27] He describes the situation in a letter dated 16th July 1944:

There is no longer any need for God as a working hypothesis, whether in morals, politics, or science. Nor is there any need for such a God in religion or philosophy (Feuerbach). In the name of intellectual honesty these working hypotheses should be dropped or dispensed with as far as possible. . . . The only way is that of Matthew 18. 3; i.e., through repentance, through ultimate honesty. And the only way to be honest is to recognize that we have to live in the world *etsi deus non daretur*.

And this is just what we do see – before God! So our coming of age forces us to a true recognition of our situation *vis-à-vis* God. God is teaching us that we must learn to live as men who can get along very well without him. The God who is with us is the God who forsakes us (Mark 15. 34). The God who makes us live in this world without using him as a working hypothesis is the God before whom we are ever standing. Before God and with him we live without God. God allows himself to be edged out of the world and on to the cross. God is weak and powerless in the world, and that is exactly the way, the only way, in which he can be with us and help us. Matthew 8. 17 makes it crystal-clear that it is not by his omnipotence that Christ helps us, but by his weakness and suffering.

. . . To this extent we may say that the process we have described by which the world came of age was an abandonment of a false conception of God, and a clearing of the decks for the God of the Bible, who conquers space in the world by his weakness. This must be the starting point for our 'worldly' interpretation.[28]

The *Ethics*, it should be remembered, deplored the defection from God and the growth of 'godless' secularism (except in so far as that secularism protested against a church whose essential idolatry was hidden under her piety and religiosity). There, Bonhoeffer attempted to impress upon the church the dangers of this growth in order that she, and the 'better secularism' allied with her, might halt this process by all means. But he is now prepared theologically to affirm this movement and even to help it to its conclusion: the historical process *must* be accepted if Christianity is to be honest intellectually and true to its message. Bonhoeffer seems to have resolved the difficulties of holding together the anti-secular argument of 'Inheritance and Decay' and the pro-worldly argument of 'Thinking in Terms of Two Spheres' by reinterpreting the former essay in the light of the latter. The effect is astonishing. As William Hamilton writes:

Bonhoeffer gives a particular reading of the intellectual history of the West since the middle ages that has rarely been characteristic of Christian theologians. The process of secularization has generally been treated as a calamity, or at least as a serious deviation that ought to be arrested. But in this historical survey Bonhoeffer tries to reclaim the heritage of the Renaissance and the Enlightenment as good, desirable, and necessary to the Christian.

The process of secularizing is affirmed, not reluctantly, sadly, or for the sake of relevance or realism. The coming of age of the world means the secularization of all life, even the religious life of man . . .[29]

The world come of age, which is the world without God, is the world redeemed by Christ and reconciled with him. It is *this* world over which he assumes his Lordship. It is clear from these sentences that one can only understand the meaning of the phrase 'the world come of age' by speaking at the same time of 'the end of the time of religion' and of the increasingly explicit Christology which underlies all of Bonhoeffer's meditations.[30] In coming chapters we will examine more closely the meaning of 'religionlessness'. We must now take a preliminary look at the Christological vision which makes acceptance of the world come of age possible and imperative.

Bonhoeffer appears to have moved from the 'Lordship of triumph and completion' which formed the Christological basis of the *Ethics* to a humiliated, suffering Christ very like that of his 1933 Christology lectures, and has described this Christ in terms of his new acceptance of worldliness. In the prison letters, this vision of Christ will become much clearer and more insistent. What this means for Bonhoeffer's affirmation of worldliness and how it relates to his past can best be clarified by turning to his unexpected attack on the position of his teacher, Karl Barth.

CHAPTER 12

'Positivism of Revelation'

Bonhoeffer's analysis of 'a world come of age', with its theological interest in secularism and new perspectives for Christian faith and existence, made Karl Barth's reading of the prison letters an uneasy one.[1] Since Bonhoeffer's theological path had, until 1940, been charted along lines described by Barth's protest against Liberalism and his subsequent positive dogmatic-exegetical emphasis, the latter's uneasiness can well serve us to illuminate the decisive change in Bonhoeffer's thought which the letters represent.

Barth's attitude towards the letters has been, for the most part, one of bewilderment. He seems now to have recognized, sadly and reluctantly, that the new direction indicated by his student is one which he cannot himself follow. Bonhoeffer suspected for his part that his discoveries would not meet with Barth's approval. Consequently, important sections of the prison letters criticize explicitly certain fundamental characteristics of Barth's theology. These, in turn, direct one to basic divergent tendencies present from the beginnings of the theological careers of the two men.

The evidence of the prison letters

Regin Prenter has expressed the view that the characterization of Barth's theology as 'positivism of revelation' was not intended as criticism of a side issue in Barth's thinking. Bonhoeffer 'wished without doubt to characterize a feature which *runs throughout* the thought of Karl Barth'.[2] It is certain that this phrase 'positivism of revelation' occurs at a crucial point in the first letter in which Bonhoeffer speaks of his new concern. Following the question concerning the possibility of a 'religionless' Christianity, he turns to Barth (and his past association with Barth) for clarification:

How can Christ be the Lord of the religionless as well? Are there religionless Christians? If religion is only the garment of Christianity – and even this garment has looked very different at different times – what then is a religionless Christianity? Barth, who is the only one to have begun to think in this direction, still has not carried it through and thought it through: but has ended with a positivism of revelation, which in the last analysis is really a restoration. For the religionless worker or mankind in general nothing decisive has been accomplished by that. The questions needing to be answered would indeed be: what do a church, a congregation, sermon, liturgy, a Christian life mean in a religionless world? How do we speak of God without religion – i.e. without the temporally influenced presuppositions of metaphysics, inwardness, etc., etc.? How do we speak (but perhaps one cannot simply 'speak' of them as formerly) in a 'worldly' manner about 'God'? In what way are we 'religionless-worldly' Christians, in what way are we the *ek-klesia,* those who are called forth, without conceiving of ourselves as religiously favoured but much more as belonging wholly to the world? Then Christ is no longer the object of religion, but something entirely different, really the Lord of the world. But what does that mean? What do the cult and prayer mean in a religionless time? Do the secret discipline or the difference (which you have met with me before) between ultimate and penultimate take on new significance?[3]

There is much to be examined in this passage, but we shall focus upon the phrase 'positivism of revelation'. A second letter opposes Barth's position to what has come to be called 'this-worldly' transcendence, an understanding of the 'otherness' of revelation which will recognize, accept, and serve the matured world:

It is not with the next world that we are concerned, but with this world as created and preserved and set subject to laws and atoned for and made new. What is above the world is, in the Gospel, intended to exist *for* this world – I mean that not in the anthropocentric sense of liberal, pietistic, ethical theology, but in the Bible sense of the creation and of the incarnation, crucifixion, and resurrection of Jesus Christ.

Barth was the first theologian – and this remains his truly great service – to begin the criticism of religion, but then he set in its place a positivist doctrine of revelation which asks one to 'take it or leave it'; Virgin Birth, Trinity or whatever, each an equally significant and necessary part of the whole, which just has to be swallowed as a whole or not at all. That is not biblical. There are degrees of perception and degrees of significance; i.e. a secret discipline must be established once more, by means of which the *secrets* of Christian faith may be protected against profanation. Positivism of revelation makes it too easy for itself, in so far as it sets up in the last analysis, a law of faith and thus mutilates what is a gift for us – through the incarnation of Christ! In the place of religion there now stands the church – that is in itself biblical, but the world is to a certain extent made to depend upon itself and left to its own devices, and that is a mistake.[4]

Barth's positivism, then, violates the world's maturity; Christologically expressed, it incorrectly describes the manner of Christ's Lordship over the mature world. The last piece of literary evidence needed for this final appraisal of Barth's theology is the letter of 8th June 1944. Bonhoeffer is discussing the attempts of several contemporaries (Tillich, Althaus, Heim) to make 'a completely fresh start based on a consideration of the Bible and Reformation fundamentals of the faith', following the collapse of Liberal theology. Against all these attempts, Bonhoeffer champions Barth's line of attack:

Barth was the first to realize the mistake that all these efforts (which were all unintentionally sailing in the channel of liberal theology) were making in having as their objective the clearing of a space of religion in the world or against the world.

He called the God of Jesus Christ into the lists against religion, '*pneuma* against *sarx*'. That was and is his greatest service (the second edition of his *Epistle to the Romans*, in spite of all its neo-Kantian shavings). Through his later dogmatics, he enabled the church to effect this distinction in principle all along the line. It was not that he subsequently, as is often claimed, failed in ethics, for his ethical observations – so far as he has made any – are just as significant as his dogmatic ones; it was that he gave no concrete guidance, either in dogmatics or in ethics, on the non-religious interpretation of theological concepts. There lies his limitation, and because of it his theology of revelation becomes positivist, a 'positivism of revelation', as I put it.[5]

'By "positivism of revelation",' Prenter tells us, 'Bonhoeffer means a proclamation of the revelation of God which presents its truth as postulates, without being capable of making clear their relationship to the life of man in the world come of age.' 'The unrelatedness of the propositions of faith is meant, in so far as they must simply be taken as crude data ("*posita*") without any other foundation.'[6] The positivist sets a 'law of faith, in consequence of which the "truths" of revelation must merely be introduced, all in the same groundless fashion'.[7] Positivism, as Bonhoeffer uses the term, means the blatant disregard of the relationship of God to the world as Creator to creation which robs God of his Lordship and the world of its maturity. Against this view, he wishes to present a conception of revelation 'which will, above all, express the relationship of the revelation of *God* to the *world come of age'*.[8] Given an affirmation of the world as essentially historical and of Christ as Lord of a humanity freed for life in this world, the positivist view of revelation is simply not tenable.

Bonhoeffer's appreciation of Barth

It is important that we see in Bonhoeffer's assessment of Barth the appreciation of the achievement of his teacher which introduces each passage. He has no brief for that common criticism which charges Barth with 'failure in ethics'. Indeed, he imagines himself to be taking Barth's revolution to its logical conclusion – and by this he means the protest against religion which began with the *Epistle to the Romans* and carried into the *Church Dogmatics*.[9] This is a revolution which Barth himself has not concluded, and it is because Barth has refused to carry out the programme with which he began that his theology has become positivist. Bonhoeffer finds the position of the later works of Barth determined by reaction to Liberal theology and the desire to provide a positive alternative based on the content of orthodox biblical thought and the Reformation. The real questions of Liberal theology cannot be taken up and answered and the movement itself overcome by adopting this attitude. Therefore, Bonhoeffer wishes to move beyond Barth on the basis of Barth's early presuppositions, by taking up the questions Barth chose to neglect. Honesty leads him to do this 'as one who, though a modern theologian, is still aware of the debt we owe to Liberal theology'.[10] In his way, Bonhoeffer is seeking to rescue Barth from well-meaning Barthians and interpreters who have 'to a great extent forgotten all about the Barthian approach, and lapsed from positivism into conservative restoration'.[11] Unless we keep the affirmative side of Bonhoeffer's criticism before us throughout our inquiry, we will fail to understand his concern.

Criticism of Barth in Bonhoeffer's earliest works

Regin Prenter suggests that the differences between the two men may be discerned in works as early as *Act and Being* and the *Epistle to the Romans*. There, Bonhoeffer and Barth appear to be in disagreement over the seriousness with which history and man's earthly nature should be taken. For this reason, they also differ on what ought to be the Christological presuppositions with which one begins constructing a doctrine of revelation. First, let us turn to an examination of the respective doctrines of revelation with which Barth and Bonhoeffer began their definitions of the theological task prior to 1932.

There is a wealth of material in Bonhoeffer's work which suggests that his uneasiness with Barth's view of revelation was as strong and consistent a factor in his theological development as was his appreciation of Barth's attack upon 'religion', and further, that this uneasiness was the result of the conviction that Barth was not taking seriously man's earthly nature. Bonhoeffer's instinctive defence of 'the world and its creatures' should by now be well known.[12] He could never feel fully at home with Barth's strident polemic against *'das Bestehende . . . the organized rebellion against God, which man expresses in the structures of society, particularly in those which he endows with moral and spiritual authority!'* Against his eager acceptance of the Barthian attack on 'religion' one must set Bonhoeffer's 'loving participation in all the ethical and spiritual richness of Prussian tradition which was the expression of his life'.[13] There is thus something of the intuitive revealed in his early, odd footnote concerning Barth in *Sanctorum Communio*:

. . . love really loves the other man, and not the One in him – who perhaps does not exist (double predestination! Barth, p. 452) – and it is precisely this love for the other man as the other man by which 'God . . . must be honoured' (p. 453). What authority has Barth for saying that the other 'in himself is trivial and temporal' (p. 452) when this is the very man that

God commands us to love? God has made our neighbour 'of supreme significance' in himself, and for us there is no other way in which he is important 'in himself'. The other man is not only a 'parable of the Wholly Other . . . the emissary' of the unknown God; but he is of supreme significance in himself, because God considers him significant (ibid.) . . . Is not the other man as a real man to receive his rights infinitely through God's command? . . . We can apprehend the will of God in all earnestness only as it is manifested in the concrete form of the other man.[14]

And if Bonhoeffer's dissertation has the character of a declaration of independence from his Liberal teachers and his affirmation of the Barthian revolution of the nineteen-twenties, we should nevertheless remember that the formula 'Christ existing as the church' is as much a protest against the ambiguity of the dialectical method. Bonhoeffer felt that Barth was in danger of reducing God to a formal construction, a negative. To say that the church is sinful, human, and inadequate has no bearing upon the fact that she is – precisely in this! – the 'community of revelation'. Barth, in his early writings, had characterized the church as an institution in which 'human indifference, misunderstanding, and opposition attain their most sublime and their most naïve form.'[15] Bonhoeffer agreed, but added his characteristic *nevertheless*:

[In the *communio sanctorum*] the old ontic relationships are not radically annulled, every empirical formation will necessarily be subject to the ambiguity inherent in all human actions. . . . In this we can perceive a special will of God which it is not open to us to belie by condemning everything that has taken on a form as the handiwork of man.[16]

This incipient dissatisfaction with the dialectical method and the presentation of earthly life as a 'parable' of the Wholly Other takes more definite shape in *Act and Being*. Theology, we are told, should not begin with a conception of the freedom of God, but rather with a doctrine of the church to which God has given himself. Christ is free, but he is also visible and tangible in the community of persons who comprise the church. Bonhoeffer is thus openly critical of Barth's 1927 *Christliche Dogmatik*, with its radical assertion of the boundless freedom of God. 'God can give and withdraw himself absolutely according to his pleasure', Barth wrote. 'In either action he remains free. He is never at man's discretion; it is his honour and glory to remain utterly free and unconditional in relation to everything bound and conditional.'[17] Bonhoeffer reacted to this at once from his Lutheran heritage, calling to mind one of the Reformer's famous – and to Barth, notorious – statements on the nature of the sacrament:

It is to the honour and glory of our God . . . however, that, giving himself for our sakes in deepest condescension, he passes into the flesh, the bread, our hearts, mouths, entrails, and suffers also for our sake that he be dishonourably . . . handled, on the altar as on the cross.[18]

The Humanity and 'Haveability' of God

Such a picture of the incarnation became as basic to Bonhoeffer's doctrine of revelation as it became foreign to Barth's. For the former, Christology and ecclesiology were based upon God's availability:

In revelation it is a question less of God's freedom on the far side of us, i.e. his eternal isolation and aseity, than of his forth-proceeding, his *given* Word, his bond in which he has bound himself, of his freedom as it is most strongly attested in his having freely bound himself to historical man, having placed himself at man's disposal. God is not free *of* man but *for* man. Christ is the Word of his freedom. God *is there*, which is to say: not in eternal non-objectivity but (looking ahead for the moment) 'haveable', graspable in his Word within the church.[19]

Thurneysen, the lifelong associate and friend of Barth, has argued that much of Bonhoeffer's continuing concern for the world which found its way into the prison letters and there assumed such radical form can be attributed to the influence of Barth's early emphasis on the solidarity of the church with the world and religious man's solidarity with secular man in sin and under grace.[20] But one must certainly add to the characteristics of Bonhoeffer's early theology a Lutheran Christology of condescension which Barth did not share. What the implications of this refusal were for Barth's further development we shall see shortly. Let us look first at Barth's progress to the *Church Dogmatics*.

Karl Barth's victory over the difficulty introduced by his consistent denial of natural theology and his assertion of God's majesty and freedom from earthly structures proceeded by stages.[21] It is generally acknowledged that the first major shift in his theology occurred with his rejection of the first volume of his *Christliche Dogmatik* and the fresh start upon what has been his masterwork, the *Church Dogmatics,* following his study of Anselm. What Barth discovered in Anselm was not the incorrectness of his own conception of God's freedom, however, but rather a better way of expressing it. The dearly-bought freedom which the dialectical method provided now gave place to the theological supplication of *fides quaerens intellectum* and *credo ut intelligam.* Since the publication of his book on Anselm, students of Barth's development have watched the *Church Dogmatics* focus more and more sharply upon Christology as the proper solution to the early and formalistic insistence upon God's otherness. Now Barth could confidently affirm that in Christ, the relationship between God and man is covenanted and God and man become dialogical partners. Christ is really man, and takes mankind up with himself in his exaltation to the right hand of God. This has been the theme of the fourth part of the *Church Dogmatics,* the high water mark of what has been called 'the triumph of grace' in Barth's theology: the doctrine of reconciliation.[22]

Soon after his students and critics began to speak of a 'new Barth', [23] Barth himself seemed to recognize a change of attitude in his theology. He announced it in a lecture in 1956 on the 'Humanity of God', and in the course of his argument provided what he seems to regard as an answer to Bonhoeffer's charge of 'positivism'. 'Surely I do not deceive myself,' Barth writes with his magnificent self-assurance, 'when I assume that our theme today should suggest a change of direction (*Wendung*) in the thinking of evangelical theology.'[24] This essay deserves careful study, for it represents not only Barth's understanding of his own past, but also the consequences for the future of theology, of his latest change in direction.

Barth begins with a restatement of his earliest concerns, which we have already encountered through the eyes of Bonhoeffer. 'What began forcibly to press itself upon us about forty years ago,' Barth says, 'was not so much the humanity of God as his *deity* – a God absolutely unique in his relation to man and the world, overpoweringly lofty and distant, strange, yes even wholly other' (p. 37).

... It must now quite frankly be granted that we were at that time only partially in the right, even in reference to the theology which we inherited and from which we had to disengage ourselves – partially right in the same sense in which all preponderantly critical-polemic movements, attitudes and positions, however meaningful they may be, are usually only partially in the right. What expressions we used – in part taken over and in part newly invented! – above all, the famous 'wholly other' breaking in upon us 'perpendicularly from above', the no less famous 'infinite qualitative distinction' between God and man, the vacuum, the mathematical point, and the tangent in which alone they must meet (p. 42).

... Did not the whole thing frequently seem more like the report of an enormous execution than the message of the Resurrection, which was its real aim? . . . We viewed this 'wholly other' in isolation, abstracted and absolutized, and set it over against man, this miserable wretch – not to say boxed his ears with it – in such fashion that it continually showed greater similarity to the deity of the God of the philosophers than to the deity of the God of Abraham, Isaac, and Jacob (pp. 43, 45).

Undoubtedly, Barth means to question the capacity of his own theology, in its earliest statement, to take account of the *humanity* of God. 'Who and what *God* is – this is what in particular we have to learn better and with more precision in the new change of direction in the thinking and speaking of evangelical theology, which has become necessary in the light of the earlier change' (p. 47). One never should have, and certainly can no longer 'deal with God in the abstract, not with one who in his deity exists only separated from man, distant and strange and thus a non-human if not indeed an inhuman God' (p. 46).

Where, then, can Barth correct the misunderstandings arising from a view of God which admits he was once his own? Within Christology, where God and man encounter one another:

In Jesus Christ there is no isolation of man from God or of God from man. Rather, in him we encounter the history, the dialogue, in which God and man meet together and are together, the reality of the covenant *mutually* contracted, preserved, and fulfilled by them. Jesus Christ is in his one person, as true *God, man's* loyal partner, and as true *man, God's* (p. 46). We do not need to engage in a free-ranging investigation to seek out and construct who and what God truly is, but only to read the truth about both where it resides, namely, in the fullness of their togetherness, their covenant which proclaims itself in Jesus Christ (p. 47). . . . It is when we look at Jesus Christ that we know decisively that God's deity does not exclude, but includes his *humanity* (p. 49). No, God requires no exclusion of humanity, no non-humanity, in order to be truly God. But we may and must, however, look further and recognize the fact that actually his deity *encloses humanity in itself* (p. 50).

'A little non-religious language'

When the theme of the humanity of God is properly set forth within Christology (and, as we shall soon see, Barth constructs his Christology in such a way that the direction *always* remains that of above to below, divine to human), certain theological possibilities emerge. 'The statement regarding God's humanity, the Immanuel, to which we have advanced as a first step from the Christological centre, cannot but have the most far-reaching consequences' (p. 52). The third of the consequences which Barth discusses concerns us particularly. 'God's humanity and the knowledge of it,' Barth writes, 'calls for a definite *attitude* and *alignment* of Christian theological thinking and speaking. It can never approach its subject matter in a vacuum, never in mere theory. Theology cannot fix upon, consider, or put into words any truths which rest on or are moved by themselves. . . . It can never verify, reflect, or report in a monologue' (p. 57). Having said this, Barth is ready to consider how much sympathy he feels for those who have raised questions concerning the capacity of his own theology really to speak to man in his secular situation. His reply is addressed obviously to Bonhoeffer, and he shows that he considers this interest no different from that which he has encountered in Bultmann, Gogarten, and Tillich:

The question of *language,* about which one must speak in reference to the so-called 'outsiders', is not so burning today as is asserted in various quarters. This is true in the first place because, again thinking in terms of the humanity of God, we cannot at all reckon in a serious way with *real* 'outsiders', with a 'world come of age', but only with a world which *regards* itself as of age (and proves daily that it is precisely not that). Thus

the so-called 'outsiders' are really only 'insiders' who have not yet understood and apprehended themselves as such. On the other hand, even the
most persuaded Christian, in the final analysis, must and will recognize
himself ever and again as an 'outsider'. So there must then be no particular language for insiders and outsiders. Both are contemporary men-of-
the-world – all of us are. A little 'non-religious' language from the street,
the newspaper, literature, and, if one is ambitious, from the philosopher
may thus, for the sake of communication, occasionally be in order.
However, we should not be particularly concerned about this. A little of
the language of Canaan, a little 'positivism of revelation', can also be a
good thing in addressing us all and, according to my experience, in which
I am certainly not alone, will often, though not always, be still better
understood even by the oddest strangers (pp. 58–59).

We shall have to return to the question of whether or not
Bonhoeffer, in his letters, is thinking primarily of what has
come to be called the 'hermeneutical problem' when he speaks
of a 'religionless Christianity'.[25] Here we should begin by saying
that others, have considered Bonhoeffer's question a probing of
a much more fundamental theological problem than Barth is
willing to concede. The reason for Barth's inability to recognize
this question is hinted at in the above citation: his doctrine
of election does not allow him to take 'secular' man seriously.
There are not and can be no 'outsiders'. 'On the basis of
the eternal will of God,' he writes, 'we have to think of every
human being, even the oddest, most villainous, or miserable, as
one to whom Jesus Christ is Brother and God is Father, and we
have to deal with him on this assumption. If the other person
knows that already, then we have to strengthen him in the
knowledge. If he does not know it or no longer knows it, our
business is to transmit this knowledge to him.'[26] With this
understanding, Barth can shrug off any characterization of his
theology as 'positivist' as merely a useful protest against the
dangers of theological imperialism, and 'non-religious language'
(like demythologization) as an occasionally useful apologetical
weapon.[27]

The Church and Historical Consciousness

If this were Barth's last word on the subject, we would be
obliged to end our conversation at this point. But there are still

several nagging, unanswered questions which lead us, in spite of Barth's intransigence, to seek to continue it. In the first place, we have Bonhoeffer's insistence that he is seeking to carry forward some basic Barthian themes (an appreciation of Barth which some of Barth's followers have taken to mean that Barth is now, in the fourth volume of his *Dogmatics*, carrying forward some basic Bonhoefferian themes). Secondly, we have argued that Bonhoeffer's position is directly related to his historical assessment, and we would wish to have from Barth a more direct encounter with the problem of history. Thirdly, we have spoken of basic Christological divergencies which, if examined, may provide us with invaluable clues to the understanding of the prison letters.

Barth has addressed himself quite pointedly to the second of our questions. In a long footnote in Volume iv/3 of the *Church Dogmatics*, he has outlined and criticized an interpretation of history which is unquestionably indebted to Bonhoeffer's prison letters.[28] The argument occurs directly following the introduction of the 'third problem' of the doctrine of reconciliation, that of the prophetic office of Christ.

In the history of the last four hundred and fifty years, Barth writes, a shadow has been cast upon the question of the relationship between the church and human culture and history. The combined forces of the Renaissance and the Reformation broke apart the basic unity which the *corpus christianum* represented. The church was separated from the world and, proleptically, the world was provided with the means by which she could justify her developing autonomy and rejoice in her emancipation. 'Intimations of many kinds were not lacking in the later and early Middle Ages. But the modern epoch is distinguished from those which preceded by the fact that certain tendencies which were previously latent, isolated, and in the main suppressed have now become increasingly patent, general, and dominating.'[29] The problem which becomes so pressing is 'secularism'. It is this phenomenon which makes the modern age different from those which came before. Man has arrived at an understanding of himself and his world which has not found the church congenial or even tolerable, and the church has consequently found itself pushed into a ghetto of indifference or hostility.

Given this situation, Barth continues, what alternative courses of action are available for the church? It may ally itself with reactionary forces to fight this movement. It may retreat into piety, liturgics, or dogmatics and accept its banishment. 'Or it might accept the increasing secularism on an optimistic interpretation, taking it up into its own self-understanding, working away so critically at the Bible, tradition, and the creeds that it appears to be in harmony with the progressive spirit of the age, to justify modern man and to offer to the adult world (*der mündig gewordenen Welt*) a suitably adult form of Christianity, thus exposing all the more obviously and palpably the alienation of the life of man from that of the church and vice-versa.'[30]

It is this latter alternative that Barth especially dislikes, and his rejection combines elements of his dismissal of Troeltsch and Bultmann and Seeberg's 'modern positivism'. He reminds us that each generation has thought itself the discoverer of this 'lamentable' situation, and that each has, in turn, failed to recognize the *positive* character of the gulf between the church and the world. The break-up of the *corpus christianum* resulted in a relationship between church and world more in keeping with the Gospel and a true understanding of the nature of revelation. The reconciliation of the world is achieved by the recognition that the church is the church and the world is the world. If the church is to serve the world, she must remain the church – this is the basis for Barth's contention that the doctrine of reconciliation must pay special attention to the classic *munus Christi propheticum*, the prophetic office of Christ. The church can move into the world only when she is certain of her boundaries. Her position in the world is therefore that of a prophet.

Barth's description of the situation and the consequent positive view of the gap between church and world reminds one strongly of Bonhoeffer's development of this theme in the *Ethics*. The *Church Dogmatics* dismisses those (nameless) theologians who develop the theme of 'a world come of age' as wistfully longing for some restoration of the pre-Reformation *corpus christianum*, having failed to see the positive significance of the irreconcilability of church and world which the Reformation exposed. If Barth believes this to be Bonhoeffer's picture of the effect of the Reformation he is certainly mistaken. 'It was the Reformation,' the latter wrote, 'that broke asunder the unity of the faith. . . . The unity of the church can only lie in Jesus Christ as he lives in his word and sacrament. . . . Only a Pope who submitted unreservedly to the word of the Bible could be the shepherd of a united Christendom. But the Pope . . . was incapable of this submission, and that is why the unity of Christendom was destroyed. *The corpus christianum is resolved into its true constituents, the corpus Christi and the world.* . . . There are two kingdoms which, so long as the world continues, must neither be mixed together nor yet be torn asunder. . . .'[31] In destroying the *corpus christianum*, the Reformation exposed the situation as it really was and remains. No sentimental yearning for the unity of the middle ages on these terms instructs Bonhoeffer's thinking.

Nor has Barth understood that the phrase 'world come of age' does not suggest for Bonhoeffer a sort of emotional or moral maturity to which the world may or may not daily prove its right. He is speaking primarily of the impossibility of articulating the traditional idea of God in the contemporary world because the mind of western man has simply outgrown it; of 'a psychological stage of development in which religion and its attempt to keep man in strings is dismissed as childish.'[32] The true unity of the West is in no *corpus christianum,* but rather in the *corpus Christi.*[33] It is *this* unity which must be demonstrated even as church and world are kept separate. But it must be declared in such a way that the maturity of the world, her independence of a traditional way of speaking of God, is respected.

The enemy, for Barth, is still *Kulturprotestantismus;* under which heading he places all demands for a synthesis of worldly forms of life, thinking, and action on the one hand and the church and her doctrine on the other. Clearly, he believes that Bonhoeffer resurrected these demands. And those who find the 'new Barth' more receptive than the 'old' to questions concerning the relationship between historical process and revelation have but to ponder sections of the *Church Dogmatics* published twenty years before Bonhoeffer's question was raised where Barth used the same arguments we have just presented against an array of Liberal opponents.[34]

Whatever the much discussed 'change of attitude' in Barth's theology might mean, it surely does not suggest that he is now prepared to discuss the theological meaning of history with nineteenth-century theologians who made this their special concern. The concern itself remains for Barth a 'blind alley'.[35] The historical question and the reality of secularism do not concern the Christian theologian. If 'positivism of revelation' means nothing else, it is at least a judgement of any theology which refuses to give more than a passing glance to man in his secular condition and to the question of relating the revelation which entered history in the culture, thought forms, and language of the Middle East in the first century to this man. Unless this problem is confronted, Christianity can scarcely free itself of ideological overtones, imperialism, possessiveness, and ultimate trust in theological expressions rather than in the God to whom they direct us.

The genus majestaticum

But the basic underlying difference between Bonhoeffer and Barth, which leads the one to take seriously the question of history and secularism and the other to disregard it, remains a Christological one. Perhaps the best way to understand how antagonistic the interest of the prison letters is to Barth's theological outlook is to examine that part of the *Church Dogmatics* where Barth takes up and rejects a Lutheran tradition concerning the human nature of Christ. In volume IV/2, Barth introduces a discussion of the *genus majestaticum*, a characteristically Lutheran development in Protestant scholasticism which originated in Luther's thinking on the sacrament. As Barth outlines it, the central concern for Lutheran scholastic Christology was that 'the divine triumph over the distinction and antithesis between God and man took place directly, and is a fact, in the humanity of Jesus Christ'.[36] The mutual participation between the two natures enclosed within Jesus Christ (known as the *communio idiomatum* or *communicatio naturarum*) had to be, and was, developed by both Lutheran and Reformed dogmaticians. But the Lutherans entered into an area of discussion which the Reformed scholastics had closed off from themselves, arguing that one cannot speak of the participation of the divine nature in the human without also speaking of the communication of the properties of the divine to the human nature. The purpose of the Lutherans was to show that 'the Godhead can be seen and grasped and experienced and directly known in the humanity of Jesus Christ'. By means of the so-called 'second *genus*' of the *communicatio idiomatum* – the *genus majestaticum* – the human nature 'experiences the additional development (beyond its humanity) of acquiring and having as such all the marks of divinity, of participating directly in the majesty of God, of enjoying in its creatureliness every perfection of the uncreated essence of God'.[37]

The purpose of the doctrine was to complete the explication of the inseparability of the union of the two natures of Christ and, to this end, it was developed with precision and with the safe-guards necessary to prevent misunderstandings. Barth hardly blames the Lutheran dogmaticians themselves for what followed from this notion. But he feels, as the Reformed contemporaries of the originators of this notion felt, that the difficulties raised by this idea prove insurmountable:

... How are we to guard against a deduction [Barth writes] which is very near the surface, which once it is seen is extremely tempting, and once accepted very easy to draw, but which can compromise at a single stroke nothing less than the whole of Christology? For after all, is not the humanity of Jesus Christ, by definition, that of all men? And even if it said only of him, does that not mean that the essence of all men, human essence as such, is capable of divinization? If it can be said in relation to him, why not to all men? But this means that in Christology a door is left wide open, not this time by a secular philosophy which has entered in with subtlety, but in fulfilment of the strictest theological discussion and osten-sibly from the very heart of the Christian faith. And through this door it is basically free for anyone to wander right away from Christology. . . . And where does this door lead? It obviously leads smoothly and directly to anthropology. . . . If the supreme achievement of Christology, its final word, is the apotheosized flesh of Jesus Christ, omnipotent, omnipresent, and omniscient, deserving of our worship, is it not merely a hard shell which conceals the sweet kernel of the divinity of humanity as a whole and as such, a shell which we can confidently discard and throw away once it has performed this service?[38]

Barth sees this as the door through which came Hegel, professing to be a good Lutheran; Feuerbach, referring his identification of divine with human essence to Luther; and Idealism and Liberalism on Lutheran soil. We have already cited in this chapter Bonhoeffer's willing use of Luther's view of the sacrament in support of his ecclesiological theory of revelation. The Lutheran Christology of condescension, the conviction that after all has been said, *finitum capax infiniti*, remained the central strand of Bonhoeffer's theology throughout his lifetime.[39] Bonhoeffer accepted the Lutheran tradition with all its risks, certain that the alternative cannot but lead to 'positivism of revelation'. The Word became flesh; nothing less than a complete incarnation will do. 'The fullness of God is to be found in that limited, weak, and humiliated man Jesus, who took the risk of utter human concreteness.'[40]

There is a check upon the distortion of this humiliated Christ, and we shall be dealing with this at a future time. Here we conclude our considerations by stating quite simply: Bonhoeffer recognizes that the recovery of Christ for us today will begin by taking seriously the question of history, accepting man in his secular condition and, in the light of the incarnation itself, turning away from the certainty of 'positivism of revelation' to the uncertainty of searching for Christian existence in a world come of age.

CHAPTER 13

Letting the World be the World

It is obvious from the preceding chapter that Bonhoeffer is not the only Protestant theologian in this century to have considered vital the question of the relationship between revelation and secularism and historical consciousness. For our purposes, the two most useful analyses of the theological meaning of history undertaken since 1900 have been those of Ernst Troeltsch and Friedrich Gogarten. In order to sharpen our focus on the historical question which Bonhoeffer raises in the *Ethics* and prison letters, we will pause to examine and compare the contributions of these two men.

Ernst Troeltsch and the Problem of Historical Relativity

One of the peculiar aspects of *Sanctorum Communio*, we argued,[1] was Bonhoeffer's avoidance of a direct encounter with the historical problem and a consideration of its importance for constructing any ecclesiology. A major weakness of Bonhoeffer's dissertation was its failure really to confront the contribution of Ernst Troeltsch. For, as Gogarten writes, 'It is no doubt Troeltsch who, as a theologican troubled by the immensely difficult problem of the relation between faith and history, has studied the problem of history in its most comprehensive aspects.'[2] Troeltsch had undertaken this study in order to illuminate what he saw as the single most important problem confronting any theologian who attempted to describe revelation and the nature and function of the church in the modern world.

Yet Bonhoeffer passed Troeltsch by and developed his argument within the framework provided by his teacher, Seeberg,
and Albrecht Ritschl.

Many years later, in his prison cell, Bonhoeffer reflected on
the Liberal theology of his student days in Berlin and became
keenly aware of 'the debt we owe'. In a passage which expresses
his ambivalent feelings towards this heritage, he singled out
Troeltsch for a special appreciation:

> But first a word or two on the historical situation. The question is, Christ
> and the world come of age. It was the weak point of Liberal theology that
> it allowed the world the right to assign Christ his place in that world: in
> the dispute between the church and the world it accepted the compara-
> tively clement peace dictated by the world. It was its strong point that it
> did not seek to put back the clock, and genuinely accepted the battle
> (Troeltsch), even though this came to an end with its overthrow.[3]

Let us examine the battle which Troeltsch accepted, and the
weapons with which he sought to fight it.

Troeltsch's understanding of the movement of history and his
desire to converse with secular disciplines such as philosophy
and sociology led him to refuse to begin any ecclesiological
discussion from the standpoint of traditional dogmatics. The
language of a dogmatics whose authority came from the divine
revelation embodied within it is hardly serviceable for a modern
world. Indeed, the modern world is modern to the extent to
which this divine authority has disappeared. And Troeltsch
located three interwoven strands of history leading up to
modern civilization: the rise of secularism, the development of
Protestantism, and the destruction of the *corpus christianum*.

The beginning of the modern age coincided with the destruction of the absolute authority which had been embodied in the
medieval church; the great period of civilization in which
divine revelation was immediate and absolute:

> This was an age of authority, directing men to the other and higher world
> with ordered and organized functions. It was based on an elastic union of
> the ascetic and natural life. Nothing of importance took place outside of
> this sacerdotal structure. The compromise was dominated by its ascetic,
> world-renouncing side, and outside influence generally complemented
> church civilization.[4]

The Reformation had the unintentional effect of shattering the *corpus christianum* and the authority embodied within its structure. This authority was soon replaced by a doctrine of scriptural inspiration which, for a time, restored unity, order, and ecclesiastical authority within Protestant churches. Closer to Troeltsch's own time, however, ecclesiastical and dogmatic authority founded upon a conception of verbal inspiration was shaken by the historical criticism of the Scriptures. Therefore: 'With the nineteenth century, church history entered upon a new phase of existence. . . . It has since then no longer possessed a fixed and objective ideal of unity.'[5]

Without this ideal of unity fixed in an infallible Bible, dogma, or a church hierarchy there can no longer be a fixed and objective form for the church. Her authority and her structure are no longer imposed from outside, but reside in her membership. Men no longer live in 'a strictly ecclesiastical supernaturalistic civilization, resting on an immediate authority with a strictly defined sphere, distinct from the world and all its interests',[6] and the church must find for herself a form and purpose which affirm 'the duty of historico-philological principles, the organization of churches formed by voluntary association, independent of the state, and *the doctrine of revelation by inner personal conviction and illumination*'.[7] It is the peculiar gift of Protestantism, and the primary reason why it remains suited to the modern world, that she is capable of doing just this. For Protestantism has grown with the modern world; she has often, in spite of herself, directly aided in the development of secularism through constant reference to her basic metaphysic of absolute personality. Having 'consciously and definitely' formulated this as its principle, 'loosed it from its connection with a hierarchic, world-dominating institution, and made it capable of freely combining with all the interests and factors of life',[8] Protestantism alone is capable of serving this new world. 'Taking it all in all,' Troeltsch concluded, 'we may fairly say that the religion of personal conviction and conscience, basing itself upon history, but not petrifying history into dogma, is the form of religion which is homogeneous with and adapted to modern individualistic civilization.'[9]

When he came to the writing of his massive *Social Teachings of the Christian Churches*, Troeltsch's method was to elicit from Christian history those ethical principles still valuable for an individualized, fully secularized civilization. He saw the contemporary problem of the church to be that of discovering a form proper to her new role: harmonizing with the structures of 'modern *bourgeois* capitalistic society and militaristic states', so that together they would form a unity of civilization.[10] Troeltsch himself did not know what this form would be. He compared the task of writing his *Social Teachings* to that of sorting out the materials of a destroyed house out of which a new building, of a form yet to be determined, is to be built. But the function of the church was at least clear: she is to 'lead forth Christian social and ethical ideals and continually produce them afresh'.[11] He did not – probably could not – seek a solution to the problem of history in an ecclesiology. The ruined house was the church which had formerly embodied revelation.

The sphere of 'revelation' (if, indeed, the term could still be used) was the world itself. Troeltsch operated with a religious notion of 'the essential and individual identity of finite minds with the infinite mind, and, precisely through this, their intuitive participation in its concrete contents and its motivated vital unity'.[12] It would appear that whatever the historical process removed by destroying the absolute authority embodied in the church was returned in the form of a generalized religious view of man. Troeltsch, following Dilthey, saw in historical criticism a force for the recovery and purification of human religion, a quest which 'endeavours to go back beyond the traditional formulations, histories, and dogmas to something humanly divine which is always and everywhere active in the soul and of which all these particular manifestations of religious life are products'.[13] Although 'revelation' is not possible, 'religion' *is*. The more revelation is erased by the growing historical consciousness of modern man, the more religion – 'the essential and individual identity of finite minds with the infinite mind' – is disclosed. Man – *secular* man! – is *homo religiosus*, and the stripping away of ecclesiastical trappings reveals rather than disproves this fact.

It is at this point that Gogarten accuses Troeltsch of 'departing from history and seeking refuge in metaphysics'. The world celebrates her emancipation from the supernatural only to be asked to acknowledge a metaphysical foundation and a religious dynamism said to be manifested in all her history. The authoritative, supernatural power of revelation embodied in the church, scripture, or dogma is replaced by a metaphysically conceived God-consciousness which is thought not to violate the modernity of the world. But is it in fact true that a religious understanding of the world is more acceptable, more congenial than a concept of revelation to a world which has become historically conscious? Bonhoeffer, accepting Barth's revolution, held that *revelation*, not religion, is the proper way to speak of the word of God – precisely because it violates, and does not deny that it violates, the structures of the world. His disagreement both with Barth and with Troeltsch begins when one begins to consider how this 'violation' is to be conceived. He remains eager to defend Barth's revolution: no inwardness, metaphysics, or conscience can serve as a substitute in order to avoid the 'embarrassment' of revelation. This embarrassment is necessary and indispensable. But how is one to *state* this embarrassment? Until the theology of revelation criticizes itself with the questions Troeltsch raised concerning the fact of history, it cannot begin to answer *this* question. It stands in danger of being simply an anachronism, an attempt simply to turn back the clock. In spite of its protest, Bonhoeffer tells us in his prison letters, revelation will only commend itself as another form of 'religion', a metaphysical sphere. It cannot turn its back on the problem of the modern conscience.

Friedrich Gogarten: The Incarnation and Verweltlichung

One contemporary theologian who has refused to shrug off the questions raised by Troeltsch is Friedrich Gogarten. He believes, with his teacher, that the nineteenth-century rise of the historical sciences completed a revolution in man's self-understanding which cannot now be reversed or denied:

There can be no doubt that in history, as it is understood in the light of this historical method which modern historiography has elaborated, man occupies a position different from that which was previously adjudged to him in the general context of the world. It is not an overstatement to say that his position has become so central that this history is now his own, the history of man. And this idea, the idea that it is his own history, means in its deepest sense that he, man, is responsible for history.[14]

Were Gogarten to use the phrase 'the coming of age of the world' (he prefers the term *Verweltlichung*, the secularizing or 'making worldly' of the world), he would mean by it that the world has become completely historical, and that this fact must now be accepted by men who, at the same time, bear the responsibility to take up and shape this history. Secularism is considered as the opponent of Christian faith, which in turn regards secularism as the disintegration of the genuine heritage of a 'Christian' past. Neither Christianity nor secularism have here been understood as historical, in the proper sense of that word. Gogarten therefore sets out to show that 'the reality of man just as the reality of his world has become historical', that secularism is the legitimate consequence of the Incarnation, and that Christian faith, by finding her way back to her own historical nature, can assist secularism towards a recovery and understanding of the real foundation and hope of the modern world.[15]

Gogarten illuminates the problem by means of an analysis of Western history. Within the *corpus christianum* of the Middle Ages, historical life was organized theologically – so completely that man had no historical existence apart from the theological presuppositions provided for him by the church.[16] But these assumptions were based upon the metaphysics of a pre-scientific era, derived as they were from church councils, the Church Fathers, and Roman sacramentalism. The Reformation and the Renaissance shattered the *corpus christianum* and signalled the end of pre-scientific metaphysics. Troeltsch, following Dilthey, recognized that the primary task in the modern age was to acknowledge this revolution in man's understanding of himself (which had resulted from the marriage of historical awareness to the scientific method) and to sweep away any left-overs from a pre-scientific view of man and the world. But (as we have seen)

Troeltsch and Dilthey replaced a particular supernatural revelation with a universal and unquestionable religious view of man, which was then defended as 'scientific'. This ultimately set Liberal theology in opposition to any secular view which might assert the *absolute* independence of man from any metaphysical world view and from the supposed universality of the religious 'inner life'.

Whereas Troeltsch envisaged a Protestantism which would expose and undergird the 'innate religious nature' of secular man, Gogarten claims that this metaphysical foundation is necessary neither for secular man nor for the Christian faith. It is, in fact, an affront to both. Men are freed from metaphysics for history, and this freedom can only have come about through the events and experiences of the Christian revelation. If Bonhoeffer sees the beginning of this claim to autonomy in the Renaissance and provides it with a Christological justification, Gogarten describes this freedom as the meaning of the Incarnation itself, which freed the world from any bondage to the 'powers of this world', that is, from the worship of or control by natural or supernatural deities:

If, however, secularization can and may be viewed in the theological sense, such that it has its foundation in Christian faith . . . then that means, in so far as it is grounded in Christian faith, making the world into the world [*Verweltlichung der Welt*]. Making the world into the world: that means that under all conditions and in every respect and in everything which belongs to it, it is and remains what it is – sheer world.[17]

R. Gregor Smith, following Gogarten, has put the position simply and more clearly:

I should say, first of all, what happens with the coming of Christianity is that the old gods are expelled from the world. The world is de-divinized. In the early generations of Christianity the Christians were called the atheists; the point was simply that the world was freed of the old fears and the old gods; the world became independent of God, autonomous. Then, at the same time, man himself was set free from these fears and became responsible for his own history.[18]

The remarkable thing about the growth of secularism, then, is that 'the independence of man in the radical sense, which he possesses in the modern world, could only have been won through the experiences and perceptions made accessible in Christian faith'.[19] The Christian faith allows for, indeed, demands this kind of freedom for the secular world to be secular. In such a world, the content of the Christian faith will have at its centre a proclamation of the freedom of man from the 'powers of the world', a freedom granted with the recognition of his creaturehood and sonship to God the Father – which is, at the same time, freedom to exercise responsibility for history. Man's historical self-awareness can only point to and illuminate the fact that the Christian faith is radically historical. For 'this historical approach, at least in so far as it grasps the actual essential nature of history brings to the forefront once more 'the genuinely Christian view of human existence and of its world as a historical world'.[20]

It is not difficult to see why Gogarten's view allies him with Rudolf Bultmann. Both men are advocating a way of speaking about the events upon which Christianity is founded which demonstrates, in complete accordance with the Christian message, the essential freedom of the *kerygma from* those events. Although the *kerygma* was (and could only have been) set down in the language and concepts of first-century Asia Minor, at its heart is the proclamation that the Word has been made flesh for all men in all cultures throughout history. For men *in history*! The Incarnation itself is a proclamation of freedom from all time-bound language and concepts. Therefore 'making worldly' and de-divinizing are not unlike demythologizing, and the arguments of Gogarten logically complement those of Bultmann. Once the issue has been defined by the meaning of the Incarnation, Bonhoeffer too may be drawn into conversation.

Gogarten's description of the de-divinizing of the world through the Incarnation makes the necessary connection Bonhoeffer failed to make between his historical analysis (which he began with the Renaissance) and his suggestions concerning 'religion' and Paul's teaching on circumcision.[21] With Gogarten as mediator, he would have found himself closer to Bultmann's programme than he imagined. Where Bonhoeffer differs from these theologians will become clear in our final chapters.[22] Certainly, and in spite of the fact that all three men agree as to the point of departure for such thinking, Bonhoeffer is the more radically and insistently Christological. His concentration upon the Lordship of Christ will not allow him to be at ease with too blindly optimistic an appreciation of autonomous man, an exuberant worldliness, or a radical sweeping away of distinctively Christian forms and structures. The historically conscious world can neither be affirmed nor denied except in the historical consciousness made possible in the Incarnation. The Christian who lives in such a historically conscious world affirms its history, its independence, its joys and pleasures only as he participates in the weakness and suffering of the God who allows himself to be 'edged out' of such a world. '*Christ* and the *world come of age*' is the question: always together and at the same time.

We have watched Bonhoeffer wrestle with the theme of the secular as he determined to turn from 'thinking in terms of two spheres' to a consideration of the meaning of the historical development of the Western world away from God and the church. We discovered the Christological basis for his thinking in a Lutheran Christology of condescension newly freed from ecclesiological restrictions, and allowed Barth to comment on this historical and Christological problem of secularism. We then developed and clarified Bonhoeffer's thoughts with the aid of Ernst Troeltsch and Friedrich Gogarten. Our final task is to examine the future course of Bonhoeffer's theology from this foundation of a Christ who affirms a world come of age. For, as Hammelsbeck comments, 'We cannot speak theologically of the world come of age without asking at the same time how Christ the Lord accepts or rejects such a world. What is involved is how the world is laid claim to by Christ.'[23]

THIS-WORLDLY
TRANSCENDENCE

Jesus did not call men to a new 'religion', but to life.
18th July 1944. Letters, pp. 123–4

CHAPTER 14

Christ, the Wordly Man

Three central theological ideas take shape following the Christological affirmation of 'the world come of age' which Bonhoeffer makes in his prison letters. Although several themes weave in and out of Bonhoeffer's letters beginning with the letter of 30th April 1944, his scattered thoughts may be collected and set in order beneath these three headings: 'this-worldly transcendence', 'the non-religious interpretation of biblical concepts', and 'sharing in the sufferings of God at the hands of a godless world'. These phrases are closely dependent upon one another, with the third perhaps representing the final unification of Bonhoeffer's vision and incorporating a corrective to certain dangers to which the other two notions, taken by themselves, are susceptible. In this concluding section, we shall examine each of these in turn.

We have suggested that these conceptions are products of the impact of Bonhoeffer's *new* Christological affirmation of the secular as a theological theme upon his *earlier* Christology and doctrine of revelation. The limited 'space' of revelation which Bonhoeffer located in the church as 'the community of revelation' or as 'Christ existing as the church' has become the boundless 'world come of age'. In *this* world, the church and the traditional 'content' of Christian faith (biblical-dogmatic concepts, the doctrines of God and the church, devotional and communal Christian activity) become 'hidden' or 'secret'; Christian faith is seen to be a dialectical process uniting Christology, transcendence, and discipleship in such a way that the Christian is freed for life in a secular, godless world.

The phrase 'this-worldly transcendence' reflects Bonhoeffer's rejection of the traditional Christian doctrine of God and his replacement of this with an understanding of transcendence which is focused upon the worldly humanity of Christ and the participation of the disciple, through him, in the life of the mature world. 'The non-religious interpretation of biblical concepts' explores the consequences of this motion for theology and the faith and mission of the church. Finally, a view of discipleship which attempts to recover a worldly form of *imitatio Christi* as the centre of a theology of revelation is described as 'sharing in the sufferings of God at the hands of a godless world'. We shall be concerned in this chapter with 'this-worldly transcendence' and with the Christology with which Bonhoeffer defended it.

Loving God in this World

We have already made some preliminary investigations into the nature of Bonhoeffer's protest against 'religion',[1] and we have had much more to say about the development of secularism as a theological theme. The prison letters are filled with passages which express fascination with what Bonhoeffer now calls, exclusively, 'worldliness' and a corresponding dislike of 'religion' and 'religiosity'. Frequent meditations on the goodness of *bourgeois* life, on history and psychology, memory, travel, friendship, the meaning of 'time' and 'shame', and especially on art and music are punctuated with 'a suspicion and horror of "religiosity"', 'forcing religion down one's throat', or a refusal to 'utter the name of God'.[2] Bonhoeffer brought his love for the worldly and his growing uneasiness about religion into a letter which related the two as 'ultimate' and 'penultimate' matters:

It is only when one loves life and the earth so much that without them everything would be gone, that one can believe in the resurrection and a new world. It is only when one submits to the law that one may speak of grace, and only when one sees the anger and wrath of God hanging like grim realities over the heads of one's enemies that one can know something of what it means to love them and forgive them. I don't think it is Christian to want to get to the New Testament too soon and too directly. . . . You cannot and must not speak the last word before you have spoken the next-to-last. We live on the next-to-last word and believe on the last, don't we? Lutherans (so-called) and pietists would be shocked by such an idea, but it is true all the same. In my *Cost of Discipleship* I just hinted at this (in Chapter 1), but did not carry it any further. I must do so some day. The consequences are far-reaching, e.g. for the problem of Catholicism, for the doctrine of the ministry, for the use of the Bible, and above all for ethics.[3]

These comments are followed by an appreciation of the worldliness of the life of the Old Testament as opposed to the New. The emphasis falls upon the 'penultimate', the 'this-worldliness' of the Christian life as the means of witnessing to the 'ultimate', and we notice that Bonhoeffer recognizes that his theme is at some remove from certain traditional Lutheran tendencies.[4] One must turn first, he argues, to *this* world if one is to understand the meaning of the Christian life of faith.

The next development in Bonhoeffer's thinking comes within a few days, one week before Christmas, 1943. He reasserts the goodness of life and the love of the world, but now there is a real tension between this world and what he calls, for the first time, 'the transcendent';

And on the Christian aspect of the matter, there are some lines which say:
> . . . *that we remember, what we would fain forget,*
> *That this poor earth is not our home*

– a very important sentiment, though one which can only come right at the end; for I am sure we ought to love God in our *lives* and in all the blessings he sends us. We should trust him in our lives, so that when the time comes, but not before, we may go to him in love and trust and joy. But, speaking frankly, to long for the transcendent when you are in your wife's arms is, to put it mildly, a lack of taste, and it is certainly not what God expects of us. We ought to find God and love him in the blessings he sends us. If he pleases to grant us some overwhelming earthly bliss, we ought not to try and spoil that bliss by our presumption and arrogance; we should be letting our religious fantasies run riot and refusing to be satisfied with what he gives us. Once a man has found God in his earthly bliss and has thanked him for it, there will be plenty of opportunities for him to remind himself that these earthly pleasures are only transitory, and that it is good for him to accustom himself to the idea of eternity, and there will be many hours in which he can say with all sincerity, 'I would that I were home.' But everything in its season . . .[5]

At least part of what Bonhoeffer means by 'religion' is taken up in the meaning of the word 'transcendence', and he indicates that his is not simply the conventional protest against religiosity and piety. Transcendence *is* necessary, but it has a proper place and a proper time. There *is* in the Christian life an element of other-worldliness, longing for the eternal, desire for what is not revealed in this world. But this world can also serve as the way to the other, and the love of the earth is said to be a proper way of expressing one's love for God – even though the time will come when the believer will be required to turn away from the world towards his true home. Later, Bonhoeffer lessened the tension between other-worldly and this-worldly by comparing it to polyphonic form in music:

What I mean is that God requires that we should love him eternally with our whole hearts, yet not so as to compromise or diminish our earthly affections, but as a kind of *cantus firmus* to which the other melodies of life provide the counterpoint. Earthly affection is one of these contrapuntal themes, a theme which enjoys an autonomy of its own.[6]

Bonhoeffer is searching for a genuine transcendence, one which allows the Christian to bear witness to God in Christ in his life in *this* world. There is a false kind of transcendence in view of which the believer thinks it possible to escape the cares and longings of this world, 'renouncing a full life and all its joys in order to escape pain'. Genuine transcendence 'accepts the life God gives us with all its blessings, loving it and drinking it to the full, grieving deeply and sincerely when we have belittled or thrown away any of the precious things of life...'[7] Bonhoeffer finally brings together in one letter the false and proper views of transcendence:

The religious speak of God when human perception (often just from laziness) has reached its limit or when human powers give out – it is really always the *deus ex machina* they parade about, either as the apparent solution to insoluble problems or as a support for human failure – thus always to help out human weakness or human limitations. Of necessity, that can only go on until men can, by their own strength, push those borders out a little farther so that God becomes superfluous as a *deus ex machina*. Talk of human boundaries has become altogether questionable for me (is even death today, which men scarcely fear and sin, which they can scarcely grasp, still a genuine boundary?) It is always seems to me as though we are trying anxiously in this way to reserve some space for God; and I should like to speak of God not on the borderlines, but in the middle, not in the weaknesses, but in strength, thus not in sin and death but in life and goodness. . . . The beyond of God is not the beyond of our perceptive faculties. The transcendence of epistemological theory has nothing to do with the transcendence of God. God is the beyond in the midst of our life. The church stands not where human powers give out, on the borders, but in the centre of the village. That is the way it is in the Old Testament, and in this sense we still read the New Testament far too little on the basis of the Old. The outward aspect of this religionless Christianity, the form it takes, is something to which I am giving much thought . . .[8]

'Religionless Christianity', then, is Christianity which has had the proper meaning of transcendence and witness to the Transcendent restored to it. It does not turn man's back upon his life in the world and his face towards God, but rather directs him towards God and the world at one and the same time. God, the Transcendent, is active in this world. Therefore the Christian can and may and must live in this world and, by doing so, bear witness to God in this world.

When the notion of a 'world come of age' enters into Bonhoeffer's thinking (within the letter from which we have just quoted), the question of 'this-worldly transcendence' takes on still another meaning and becomes much more urgent. For now, he argues, men no longer believe in a transcendent realm where their longings will be fulfilled. A radical adjustment therefore becomes necessary, both in the way in which God is spoken of (if and when he is spoken of at all) and in the understanding of Christ as the centre of the Gospel message.

God Edged Out of the World

A radical theological position is presently taking shape, largely in America, which announces without apology that God is 'dead', that at least some Christian theologians today do not know, worship, or believe in God as they once could and did. They claim that the admission of this fact need not be a disaster for Christian theology; indeed, it may represent its rebirth. In their writings, whether explicitly or implicitly, they recall the remark Bonhoeffer made in his prison cell: 'The only way to be honest is to recognize that we have to live in the world *etsi deus non daretur* . . . God is teaching us that we must live as men who can get along very well without him.'

The radical theologians distinguish their position from one which is also indebted to the prison letters (represented by the writings of J. A. T. Robinson and Harvey Cox, among others) which holds that the traditional Christian *concept* of God, 'a certain way of speaking about God and on his behalf', is outmoded or inadequate. The radical theologians refuse to distinguish between the reality of God and the way in which that reality is conceptualized; between the symbol and the thing symbolized. For them, it is God himself who cannot be experienced or believed in. Therefore, the problem of unbelief cannot be dealt with by describing God – as do Robinson and Cox – as 'absent' from or 'hidden' or 'obscured' within the secular world come of age because we cannot find the language to depict God in secular terms. For the radical theologians, theology must begin with the statement: the coming of age of the world directly involves an acceptance of the death of God as an historical event.[9]

It is not our purpose to place Bonhoeffer in one camp or the other; his thinking in his prison letters was in such a state that either side can find quotations sufficient to support their claims that Bonhoeffer anticipated their thinking. Probably Bonhoeffer ended his life and work with a position similar to that of the latter group, although he made it impossible that the other position should not have developed his thoughts further in the radical direction. At its lowest estimate, 'this worldly transcendence' opposes a traditional way of speaking about God which involves an 'abstract belief in his omnipotence', 'a religious relationship to a supreme being absolute in power and goodness', 'a concentration upon tasks beyond our scope and power', 'the absolute, metaphysical, infinite', etc.[10] There may have been a time when this way of speaking about God's transcendence was the correct way, but it is no longer acceptable in a world which has come of age. From the perspective of the worldly man, the man who accepts and participates in the maturity of the world, God has been withdrawn from one area after another as the maturing world moved into and occupied spheres and began to exercise powers formerly ascribed to him. God is relegated to the unexplored territories of our experiential and intellectual maps. The problem is not whether there will still remain some 'spaces for God' for a long time to come, but whether these *ought* to remain, and whether God ought to be thought of as inhabiting them. God belongs in the midst of the world, in the world made up, for the most part, of those spaces from which he has been withdrawn. He exercises his Lordship over the world which has come of age and which has taken control of its own affairs. But thus far, the church has not seemed to recognize that there can be a difference between believing in God and fighting a battle to prove his existence. R. Gregor Smith has put it this way:

We have been all too ready, especially since the great breakthrough of the Renaissance, to fight a kind of battle against the world on behalf of God. Here too the church has desired, as it were, to rescue God from the consequences of his own recklessness first in creating and then in saving his world. God's liberating action in his Word – which . . . can be seen as truly liberating only when it is seen more than as an isolated occurrence in history – has been disallowed by the common sense of Christian people as altogether too dashing, too audacious and foolhardy. So when the breakthrough of man's spirit beat back the Christian warrior from one entrenched position after another, the Christian response in recent centuries has varied little. Before the advancing battalions of intelligence and reason and scepticism, as one area after another was captured for technology, or science, or psychology, God has been rescued by too willing hands. The children of light have been happily engaged in drawing God back into the darkness, beyond the frontiers of assured life, into the region which is euphemistically called the mystery of God. The mystery of God has been equated with a kind of *terra incognita*, as an as-yet unknowable rather than a truly ineffable mystery, which is to say a *present* mystery whose mystery is an actual, encountered, lived experience of an incomprehensible but not inapprehensible gift. The consequences of this series of retreats have been distortion of the understanding of God, confusion among the ranks of both sides, and dishonour of God's name.[11]

Transcendence as an 'as-yet unknowable' area of human life is, then, not the transcendence of God. Is there then a way in which a man can think about God and witness to him without sacrificing his own worldliness on the one hand or God's genuine transcendence of the world on the other?

Bonhoeffer suggests several times that the proper description of God will not only take account of his 'removal' from the world but that this removal is, at the same time, a positive revelation of him. In the past few decades of theological thought, we have become accustomed to the phrase 'God is known by his absence'. Bonhoeffer would have liked this, and he would have referred to the basis of this odd phrase in what the New Testament has to say about weakness, powerlessness, suffering, and forsakenness. At one point, he wrote:

And the only way to be honest is to recognize that we have to live in the world *etsi deus non daretur*. And this is just what we *do* see – before God! So our coming of age forces us to a true recognition of our situation *vis-à-vis* God. God is teaching us that we must live as men who can get along very well without him. The God who is with us is the God who forsakes us (Mark 15. 34). The God who makes us live in this world without using him as a working hypothesis is the God before whom we are ever standing. Before God and with him we live without God. God allows himself to be edged out of the world and on to the cross. God is weak and powerless in the world, and that is exactly the way, the only way in which he can be with us and help us. Matthew 8. 17 makes it crystal-clear that it is not by his omnipotence that Christ helps us, but by his weakness and suffering. This is the decisive difference between Christianity and all religions. Man's religiosity makes him look in his distress to the power of God in the world; he uses God as a *deus ex machina*. The Bible, however, directs him to the powerlessness and suffering of God; only a suffering God can help. To this extent we may say that the process we have described by which the world came of age was an abandonment of a false conception of God and a clearing of the decks for the God of the Bible, who conquers space and power in the world by his weakness.[12]

There is reason to doubt that Bonhoeffer has done full justice to 'the God of the Bible' by referring simply to weakness and suffering; certainly one would want to say more especially about the record of the Old Testament. Certainly, he wishes to focus on the element of powerlessness which is very much present in both the Old Testament and the New. One must speak of God's transcendence without speaking of 'God' at all, without turning to a 'doctrine' of God. God throws over all descriptions of himself which proceed from a 'doctrine' of God in order to allow the world to be itself. In this much, Christians can justifiably be called 'atheists'. But Bonhoeffer is also describing the cross as the solution to the problem of how one speaks of God, laying the groundwork for a *theologia crucis* as the centre of his own meditations. The cross proclaims the disappearance of God from the world. But the cross remains *in* the world, and this means that one should look to Christ – to his weakness and suffering and forsakenness and powerlessness – for those things for which one formerly looked to God. For if God has disappeared, Christ is very much at hand, and 'all that we rightly expect from God and pray for is to be found in Jesus Christ'.[13]

The God of Jesus Christ has nothing to do with all that we, in our human way, think he can and ought to do. We must persevere in quiet meditation on the life, sayings, deeds, sufferings, and death of Jesus in order to learn what God promises and what he fulfils. One thing is certain: we must always live close to the presence of God, for that is newness of life . . .[14]

'This-worldly transcendence' will thus be grounded in Christology.

The Man for Others

The Christology of the prison letters, like the Christology of 1933, concentrates on the person and work of Christ and sets aside for the moment – permanently, as fate was to decide – any consideration of the church as the *Body of Christ*. We find ourselves back in the realm of the *theologia crucis,* of the humiliated Christ, and of the Lutheran Christology of condescension which causes Barth such uneasiness. Bonhoeffer uses such a Christology in order to defend his thoughts on the 'world come of age' which, he argues, is grounded in the revelation of God in Christ. 'The world's coming of age is . . . really understood better than it understands itself, namely on the basis of the Gospel, and in the light of Christ.'[15] He also turns to Christology in order to define 'this-worldly transcendence' and to guard his idea against possible misinterpretations:

It is not with this next world that we are concerned but with this world as created and preserved and set subject to laws and atoned for and made new. What is above the world is, in the Gospel, intended to exist *for* this world – I mean that not in the anthropomorphic sense of liberal, pietistic, ethical theology, but in the Bible sense of the creation and the incarnation, crucifixion, and resurrection of Jesus Christ.[16]

William Hamilton, in his ordering of the material in the prison letters, suggests that Bonhoeffer moves forward from a general, rather blurred Christological view of his discoveries along two lines which become increasingly distinct.[17] Bonhoeffer does not at first seem to recognize the tension between them and therefore makes no attempt to reconcile them. On the one hand there is the Christ who 'drinks the earthly cup to the lees' and suffers upon the cross. On the other, we have described for us the worldly man who 'never throws doubt on a man's health, vigour, and fortune', who 'claims for himself and the Kingdom of God the whole of human life in all its manifestations'.[18] The tension between these two perspectives, Hamilton suggests, may be regarded as the tension between the Christology lectures of 1933, where Bonhoeffer adhered closely to a Lutheran humiliation Christology, and the emphasis on the worldly life and activity of Jesus expressed in *The Cost of Discipleship* and the *Ethics*. Only at the end of the prison letters do we find these conflicting Christological views reconciled.

There is good evidence for this view of the development of Bonhoeffer's Christology in the prison letters. His determination to demonstrate that revelation is concrete, graspable and haveable in Christ led him in the past to draw upon traditions which were not always compatible. The Lutheran Christology of condescension stressed the humble givenness of God in Christ in the Incarnation, and Bonhoeffer found this useful for combatting the abstract and distant God of the dialecticians. But this tradition also included the hiddenness and submission of Christ. Bonhoeffer managed to accept the tradition in its entirety for his 1933 lectures, by making the humiliated Christ that which is actually seen in the revelation – both in the sacrament and in the church as the Body of Christ.[19]

We know that the date of these lectures was also, however, the time when a direction in his thinking came to an end. Bonhoeffer now became occupied with the possibility of a positive and vigorous protest *against* the world. The new problem of concretion was solved when Bonhoeffer became a champion of the Confessing Church and called it into battle against the world. The Lordship of Christ became a Lordship of triumph which remained, even when the ecclesiological container for his idea was removed in order to allow him to develop his *Ethics*.

But the prison letters return to the older stress on the humiliation and submission of Christ and, at least for a time, carry this theme alongside of the newer one.

At first, and throughout most of the prison letters, the stress falls upon the theme of 'Christ, the triumphant Lord'. Jesus Christ rules the world and our lives. He is the bridge back to the worldliness of the Old Testament, and as Lord of both books of the Bible, he cannot be divorced from the Old Testament in order to be interpreted in the light of the salvation myths – i.e. as the answer to man's unfulfilled longings and desires.[20] 'Christ is in the centre of life, and in no sense did he come to answer our unsolved problems.' At the same time, one apprehends Jesus as the Lord of life by recognizing him to be 'a man, pure and simple', who calls children, the Wise Men, shepherds, Joseph of Arimathea and the women at the tomb to come to him. Jesus' life on earth makes our lives on earth worth living.[21]

But with increasing insistence and boldness, Bonhoeffer supports his contention that Christianity has primarily to do with this world by directing us once more to Jesus' cross, humiliation and suffering. 'Matthew 8. 17 makes it crystal clear that it is not by his omnipotence that Christ helps us, but by his suffering and weakness.' We are to 'stand by God in his hour of grieving', to 'watch with Christ in Gethsemane'.[22] This real presence of Christ in his weakness and suffering is strongly flavoured with the Christological emphasis of the 1933 lectures. One recalls, for example, such passages as: 'If Jesus Christ is to be described as God, then one must speak not about his divine essence, but only about this weak man among sinners, about his cradle and his cross. If we are speaking about the divinity of Jesus we must speak especially of his weakness.'[23]

Now Bonhoeffer makes use of this stress on the humiliation of Jesus as the basis of his plea for a this-worldly understanding of transcendence. As Hanfried Müller writes, 'The entry of God into the man Jesus Christ in the world is the ground of the this-worldliness of Christianity. To this this-worldliness corresponds the suffering of God in the world.'[24] Jesus is the man in whom God reveals himself, and he reveals himself by absenting himself in his power and glory. In this way, God reveals to us the this-worldly nature of his transcendence. Jesus is the man who is 'lonely and forsaken (and) without transcendent escape. . . . He, though longing for him, does not experience the *deus ex machina*.'[25]

Two final formulas overcome what tension remains between this-worldliness based upon the cross and this-worldliness based upon Jesus' life. The first of these, 'sharing in the sufferings of God at the hands of a godless world', describes a faith which involves one directly in the being of Jesus, in his life and in his forsakenness. Men 'must live worldly lives and so participate in the sufferings of God'.[26] Bonhoeffer has taken such care to keep this from being interpreted as simply the expression of a pessimistic world view that it is deeply disappointing to find Barth dismissing the letters as one more chapter in the history of 'the melancholy theology of the north German plains'.[27] The Old Testament blessing, Bonhoeffer reminds us, may not be set against the cross – blessing and cross are not mutually exclusive and contradictory. Kierkegaard failed to realize this, and as a result he made the cross into a principle of the structure and life of the world.[28] This-sidedness, the penultimate, stands under the cross, but this in no way negates or denies the world:

. . . God comes into the world, not as God, but rather as man; not in power, but in powerlessness; not in activity, but in suffering. In *this* suffering – but not in the suffering of the world – God is to be found; and therefore Bonhoeffer, unlike Kierkegaard, can see the world positively, optimistically, affirmatively, happy in itself. At the same time he finds God in his sufferings in the affirmed, mature world – so that his theology is to this extent ever more governed by the cross. In this way, his theology is *optimistically* this-worldly.[29]

The other formula is 'Jesus, the man for others'. This characterization is carefully and deliberately unfolded as the Christological basis for this-worldly transcendence. It occurs in a passage (to which we shall have to return in our last chapter and examine from another perspective) in the 'Outline for a Book', where it serves as the sketch for a part of the projected second chapter:

(a) Worldliness and God.
(b) What is God? Not in the first place a general belief in God's omnipotence, etc. That is not a genuine experience of God, but rather a piece of prolonged world. Encounter with Jesus. The experience that here there is a reversal of all human existence, in that Jesus is there solely 'for others'. This 'being-there-for-others' of Jesus is the experience of transcendence! Out of the freedom from self, out of 'being-there-for-others' to the point of death emerges omnipotence, omniscience, omnipresence. Faith is participation in this being of Jesus. (Incarnation, cross, resurrection). Our relationship to God is not a 'religious' one to a highest, most powerful, best nature conceivable – that is not genuine transcendence – rather our relationship to God is new life in 'being-there-for-others', in participation in the being of Jesus. Transcendence is not in eternal and unattainable tasks, but in the already given and attainable fellow man. God in human form! not, as in oriental religions, in animal form as monstrous, chaotic, distant, awesome, etc. – but also not in god-man form of 'man in himself' but rather 'the man for others!' and therefore the crucified. Man living out of the transcendent.[30]

The 'haveability' of Christ, his being *'pro-me'* his 'taking form in the world' – all of Bonhoeffer's previous Christological formulations which stressed the real presence and availability of Christ to faith – have culminated in the formula: Christ, the man for others. Encounter with the 'being of Jesus for others' is the experience of transcendence – *this-worldly* transcendence. There can be no doubt that Bonhoeffer finally has committed himself wholeheartedly to the kind of Lutheran development Barth deplored, with all its risks. The finite world *is* capable of the infinite; this world bears the other world, and it does so in Christ's absolute givenness 'for others'.

In any event Bonhoeffer retains an important check on the misinterpretation of his formula – the 'secret discipline', which supports and witnesses to that hope and love which *cannot* be stated in terms of this world, in and of itself; simply because there is nothing in the world which might serve as an analogy.[31] This too is given in Jesus Christ; given for all men, but it is kept and protected as a treasure for those who 'have ears to hear'. Could Bonhoeffer have constructed a complete Christology from this basis? Is it possible, even retaining some sort of secret discipline, to reduce the Christian to 'the man for others'?

Bonhoeffer did not seem concerned with the vulnerability of his position. He knew only that the recovery of this-worldly transcendence was essential if Christianity was to have something to do with the man who has come of age, and that this transcendence could be located in Jesus' being for others, through 'meditation on the life, sayings, deeds, sufferings, and death of Jesus' and thus learning what God promises and what he fulfils.[31] What would come later he did not know and did not live to say, and we must content ourselves with that profound poetic summary of his thought:

> For Christians, heathens alike he hangeth dead:
> And both alike forgiving.[33]

CHAPTER 15

Religionless Christianity

Of all of the original ideas and notions which Bonhoeffer developed during his lifetime, one has been the object of more interest, the cause of more concern, and the target for more criticism than any other. The full title of this notion is 'the non-religious interpretation of biblical concepts', but this has usually been made the pivotal phrase for Bonhoeffer's later theology in a shortened form: 'religionless Christianity'. It is certain that in speaking of 'the non-religious interpretation of biblical concepts', Bonhoeffer wished to examine more closely the implications of 'this-worldly transcendence' for traditional Christian theology. He found himself responding to the questions raised by his contemporaries and directing their attention to the questions he wished to raise. His interpreters, coming upon his attempts to clarify his thoughts and set them in order as a trained theologian, have made these attempts the focal point of the prison letters and have subjected all the ideas which appear there to the possibility or impossibility of a 'religionless Christianity'.

Whether Bonhoeffer would have wanted to see *this* phrase (which has by this time become something of a slogan)[1] used to characterize the whole of his thinking in the prison letters is a question well worth raising. It has certainly remained the most elusive and most problematic of his ideas, the one he defended most inadequately, and consequently the one most easily misunderstood and dismissed. It is unfortunate that 'this worldly transcendence' and 'sharing in the sufferings of God' have been ignored or forgotten in this; separated from its conceptual partners, 'non-religious Christianity' loses its Christological foundation.

199

Checked and interpreted by the other two, however, this notion can serve as the way into the difficult technical problems following from Bonhoeffer's discoveries, and enable one to see what his concern is in the light of what other theologians are thinking. Several questions are suddenly thrown into sharp relief by the meditation on 'non-religious Christianity': What does Bonhoeffer mean by 'religion'? How is 'religion' related to the essential Christian proclamation? Can the *kerygma* be interpreted 'non-religiously'? Can a demand to interpret the *kerygma* in such a way be defended exegetically? How does Bonhoeffer's thinking relate to that of other theologians – especially Bultmann and Tillich – who would seem to share his interests? And what corrections would he make in the courses of the theological currents which today most imagine themselves to be reflecting Bonhoeffer's concern: the interest in the hermeneutical problem in the West, and adherence to the revolutionary spirit if not the content of Marxist socialism in the East?

Non-religious Christianity is not all that Bonhoeffer has to say, but it is an important part of his statement. We must therefore examine this phrase, and the questions it raises, very closely.

The Religious a Priori

The attack upon religion made in the prison letters has its roots far back in Bonhoeffer's thinking. The effort to give shape and direction to this attack begins in the *Ethics*, where 'thinking in terms of two spheres' is rejected and worldliness and 'promising godlessness' are affirmed.[2] The protest against religion which presupposed this rejection and defence became explicit for the first time in the letter Bonhoeffer wrote to Bethge from the Munich train in June 1942. Henceforth, Bonhoeffer's disapproval of 'the religious' and 'otherworldliness' went hand in hand with a defence of 'loving God in the blessings he sends us'. Gradually, in the prison letters, Bonhoeffer sharpened the more positive side of his discovery into 'this-worldly transcendence' and provided it with a Christological foundation. His uneasiness with 'the religious' took a decisive turn in his letter of 30th April 1944:

The time when men could be told everything by means of words – be they theological or pious – is over, and so is the time of inwardness and conscience, which is to say the time of religion altogether. We are proceeding towards a completely religionless time; men simply, in the condition they are now in, cannot be religious any more. Even those who honestly describe themselves as 'religious' do not in the least act up to it, and so when they say 'religious' they evidently mean something wholly different. Our whole nineteen-hundred-year-old Christian proclamation and theology rest upon the 'religious *a priori*' of mankind. Christianity has always been a form – perhaps the true form – of 'religion'. But if one day it becomes obvious that this '*a priori*' just doesn't exist but was a historically conditioned human form of self-expression, if therefore man becomes radically religionless (and I think that is more or less the case already, else how is it, for example, that this war in contrast to all those which have gone before is not calling forth a 'religious' reaction) – what does this mean for 'Christianity'?

If we don't want to do that, if our final judgement must be that the western form of Christianity also was a preliminary stage to a completely religionless time, what kind of a situation emerges for us, for the church? How can Christ be the Lord of the religionless as well? Are there religionless Christians? If religion is only the garment of Christianity – and even this garment has looked very different at different times – what then is a religionless Christianity?[3]

These paragraphs will occupy us in the next two sections of this chapter.

Our first impression is that Bonhoeffer has rejected afresh the Liberal theology of his teachers, in line with the denial of 'religion' which he made from the time of his earliest theological writings.[4] Interestingly, the touchstone in Bonhoeffer's past is not the doctrine of the church outlined in *Sanctorum Communio*, which criticized the understanding of the church as a 'religious community'; Bonhoeffer speaks rather of the disappearance of the 'religious *a priori*', of the end of 'inwardness' and 'conscience'. We thus find ourselves back in the pages of *Act and Being*, where Bonhoeffer dismissed the 'religious spaces' of his teachers, Reinhold Seeberg and Karl Holl.[5]

In his *Habilitationsschrift*, we recall that Bonhoeffer introduced Seeberg's metaphysical notion of a 'religious *a priori*' as an example of the apologetic method of many nineteenth-century protestant theologians. The clarity and precision of Seeberg's *Dogmatics* made his formulation of this widely-used concept a useful foil for Bonhoeffer's argument. According to Seeberg (and as we have developed at length in the fifth chapter of this study), the *a priori* was 'the intrinsic capacity . . . for becoming aware of the being and activity of the supramundane God, and accordingly for the receiving of the content of his revelation, as divine, into the soul'.[16] Bonhoeffer found fault with this notion on the grounds of the Reformation: only the Word can mediate the contact between God and man; there can be posited neither immediacy nor a prerequisite mental form, by means of which God's Word is heard and received. Revelation creates its own reception when and where and if it occurs, and it commends itself only as 'opposed to every human being, to human experience of value and of good'.[7] To propose a divine-human continuum in this way is to circumvent the whole problem of revelation.

In like manner, Bonhoeffer rejected Holl's picture of the human conscience, whereby God encountered man and could be apprehended and comprehended by him. Aligning himself with the protest of Karl Barth's *Epistle to the Romans* Bonhoeffer countered: 'There is no point in man where God can win space in him; indeed, it belongs to his essence to be *incapax infiniti*.'[8] *God* can enter the consciousness as a reality, as *self*-revelation, only when he shatters all human forms, desires, and presuppositions concerning himself – in short, only when he destroys *religion*.

In part, then, Bonhoeffer is recalling a controversy in which he engaged fifteen years before his meditations in his prison cell. Is he still concerned primarily with 'retrieving from the smothering arms of the religious subjectivity of liberal theology the concern of traditional theology for God's work in Jesus Christ?'[9] Here it would be well to review Bonhoeffer's dependence upon Barth's critique of religion, and we can be helped greatly by the treatment of this relationship in Daniel Jenkins's *Beyond Religion*.[10]

In 'The Revelation of God as the Abolition of Religion' (*Church Dogmatics*, 1/2, pp. 280–361), Barth systematizes some of the thinking which found such violent expression in his *Epistle to the Romans*. Once more, he defines faith as the response to a revelation in which the initiative rests solely with God, and indicates that the primary concern of theology is to reflect upon and protect God's freedom of action. But religion is man's quest for God. Had religion sufficed as the description of man's relationship to God, revelation need never have occurred. But revelation *did* occur, and this means that the status of religion must be investigated from the point of view of revelation and man's faithful response. From this point of view, religion can only be adjudged to be 'unbelief': the expression of the effort of godless man to make up for the absence of God in his life on his own terms, and therefore the attempt to seize and manipulate God. At the same time, Jenkins writes:

Revelation does not merely indict religion as unbelief; it also vindicates one kind of religion as pleasing in God's sight, that Christian religion which knows that it is possible to speak of 'true religion' only in the same way that it is possible to speak of a 'justified sinner'. The Christian religion becomes 'true' only as it is formed and sustained by divine revelation.[11]

The truth of Christian faith is to be found in God's grace alone, as it is manifested in Jesus Christ. 'Where it tries to create an animating principle of its own,' Jenkins writes, 'the church ceases to be the church of Jesus Christ and becomes an organ of that religion which is the enemy of faith.'[12] Jenkins therefore summarizes (and approves) Barth's findings as follows:

Man's religion provides him with the final and most closely guarded citadel in which he can defend himself against the divine grace. Religion fulfils the positive function of making man aware of the inadequacy of his own resources and ready to lift up his eyes towards God, but of itself it cannot save man. Faith working through love which transcends religion and yet produces more religion and transcends religion once more is alone that which justifies men in God's sight.[13]

In the light of Barth's contribution, Jenkins reads Bonhoeffer's critique of religion. He makes use of the summary list of the characteristics of religion in the prison letters which Bethge has provided, noting:

'First, [religion] is individualistic. The religious man is preoccupied with himself and his interior states in such a way as to forget his neighbour, even though this individualism may take ascetic and apparently self-sacrificial forms. Secondly, it is metaphysical. God is brought into complete, as the supernatural, a fundamentally man-centred view of reality. Thirdly, the religious interest becomes more and more one department of life only. Scientific discovery and other forces push it more and more into insignificant areas of life. And fourthly, the God of religion is a *deus ex machina*, one who comes in from outside to help his children when they are in trouble. He is not the one at the centre of life, who controls and directs it and meets and sustains us in our strength as well as our weakness.'[14]

Jenkins concludes that Bonhoeffer has followed fully in Barth's train of thought, calling upon Christianity once more to prune, purify, and re-examine the relationship between faith and religion in order to free the Christian for the life of faith in the world:

It may be that there is a dimension of meaning in Bonhoeffer's thought to which we have failed to penetrate, but it is hard to resist the conclusion that his plea for a 'religionless Christianity' in this context means primarily a plea for a redefinition of the church, of faith and of the religion of faith. It starts from a fresh insight into the nature of Christian maturity as freedom to serve with Christ in the real life of the world, and it seeks to abolish much which passes for 'the life of the church' but which, in its tired flabbiness, is no more than a quasi-religious conformity to this world which passes away.[15]

Thus Bonhoeffer points primarily to 'the permanent protest against its own religious forms and expressions'[16] which Christianity bears within it and of which it seems ever prone to lose sight. Only when Christianity recalls this protest can she reflect true faith, moving again and again 'beyond religion'.

We are one step farther on the way to an understanding of 'non-religious Christianity', but we may not have taken the last step. *Is* there a 'dimension of meaning in Bonhoeffer's thought' to which Jenkins has 'failed to penetrate?'

Religion and 'Ultimate Questions'

In the letter of 30th April 1944, Bonhoeffer is attacking 'religion' and 'the religious *a priori*' as the basis not only of the Liberal understanding of Christianity, but of 'the whole nineteen-hundred-year-old Christian proclamation and theology'.[17] Christianity has always assumed that its necessity is given in man's weakness and in man's desire to overcome his weakness. It has therefore depended upon a religious *a priori*, a religious attitude in man towards himself and his problems – and, thus far, it has always found man willing to grant his own religious need. Albrecht Schönherr defines the religious *a priori* of the prison letters as follows:

It is the tacit, all-embracing presupposition carried through the centuries that man *needs* the concept of God in order to develop himself, solve his problems, perceive his world. . . . The hallmark of such a 'religious inter-pretation', Bonhoeffer holds, is that it is in essence metaphysically and individualistically determined. Individualistically – that means that in the centre stand the personal problems of man: his distress, guilt, birth and death, spiritual welfare. Metaphysical – that means that God's action appears as the prolongation of our questions and distresses into the beyond; God is the helper in need, the *deus ex machina*, the solution of our 'ultimate questions'. In this way, the beyond is understood to be that which temporally and materially 'comes afterward'. This is the same concept of 'religion' against which Karl Barth's *Epistle to the Romans* had previously spoken. Man stands in the centre, God is the answer to his questions, the helper in his needs, the guarantor of his peace, the watch-man on the boundaries of his possibilities. The biblical proclamation of the Kingdom of God provides the complementary antithesis.[18]

The religious *a priori* is apologetically useful not only for theologians who were consciously a part of the Liberal move-ment, therefore, but also for those who as consciously opposed it. Bonhoeffer mentions especially Heim, Althaus and Tillich – all of whom were at one time identified with the 'theology of revelation' which overthrew Liberal theology. Ultimately, his criticism touches Barth as well, in so far as Barth's theology is dependent upon its own special 'religious' presuppositions. Any of these four roads – those of Heim, Althaus, Tillich, or Barth – could be followed to clarify *this* meaning of the term 'religious' as it is used in the prison letters; perhaps the most serviceable and interesting passes through the theology of Paul Tillich.[19] Bonhoeffer's characterization of Tillich in the prison letters is anything but clear, and when we have clarified it by alluding to Bonhoeffer's earlier writings, we will wish to correct it. Possibly, Bonhoeffer has painted Tillich with a brush he might have used for Karl Heim, with whose theology he was better acquainted.[20] We may assume that Bonhoeffer lost touch with Tillich's theology when the latter emigrated to America in 1933, and that he still thought of him, even in the prison letters, as the 'religious socialist' of the nineteen twenties. Still, contemporary Bonhoeffer interpretations have linked Tillich's notion of God as 'Being Itself' or the 'depth of existence' with Bonhoeffer's programme.[21] It remains impossible to criticize this identification on biographical grounds because Bonhoeffer simply did not read and respond to the later writings of his contemporary. There are, however, some comments which might be made concerning the relationship between the two men – comments which, if they are unfair to Tillich, will at least give us a clearer picture of Bonhoeffer's concern.

In his *Act and Being*, Bonhoeffer had occasion to respond to Tillich's *Religiöse Verwirklichung*,[22] where Tillich proposed the identification of theological with philosophical anthropology and asked that both be guided by the insights of existentialism. Both disciplines could well characterize man as 'being at risk in the ultimate sense'; and in so far as they did so, philosophical and theological anthropology dealt with the same subject matter. Bonhoeffer found this proposal unacceptable, replying that 'from the standpoint of revelation, the existence of man is seen by a theological anthropology as determined essentially either by guilt or by grace – and not merely as "being at risk in the unconditional sense. . .!".'[23] He set Tillich's endeavour alongside the interests of Gogarten and Bultmann, and saw all three attempting to locate a point at which theology could be related positively to philosophy on the question of man's basic situation, the state to which revelation comes. Bonhoeffer followed Kurt Löwith in rejecting any attempt to make theological use of existentialist categories, arguing that when the question of existence is asked without recourse to revelation, a 'preformed ideal of man' is inevitably posited which limits the freedom of God's self-revealing. 'If revelation is essentially an event brought about by the free act of God,' Bonhoeffer concluded, 'it outbids and supersedes the existential-ontological possibilities of existence.'[24] In other words, Bonhoeffer is certain that such a methodology puts revelation in the position of being an 'answer' presupposed by the question asked by 'man', out of his supposedly universal situation of existential estrangement and apart from revelation.[25] Revelation, he encounters, must itself ask the question which it answers without 'outside help'.

Bonhoeffer's understanding of Tillich and his implicit criticism of him are developed in his description in the introductory lecture in Berlin in 1930, 'Man in Contemporary Philosophy and Theology'. He writes:

> That man asks about himself, that he remains essentially questionable – this defines his nature. . . . Tillich . . . sees man, in the last resort, as characterized by his failure to arrive at his essence because there is for him no certain, unified basis from which his self-understanding might be posited. . . . Man first comes to himself when, standing on the boundary, he experiences the inbreaking of the eternal. Here he understands himself in 'living through the boundary situation', the 'threat in the unconditional sense'. . . . The absolute boundary is the inbreaking of the Absolute Itself; the unconditional No is, at the same time, the absolute Yes.[26]

This characterization seems to have remained in Bonhoeffer's mind even at the time of the prison letters, almost fifteen years later (and we should again remind ourselves that in the intervening years, Tillich refined his theme considerably and departed from what must have seemed too slavish a dependence upon existentialist terminology). To picture man as the questioning and questionable creature, Bonhoeffer is saying, is to picture him as essentially *religious*:

> Tillich undertook it to depict the development of the world – against its will – as religious; to give it its form through religion. That was very brave of him, but the world unseated him and ran on alone; he too wanted to understand the world better than it understood itself, but the world felt utterly misunderstood and rejected such allegations.[27]

To this explicit criticism we should add the vigorous attack upon any apologetic which calls upon God for the 'solving of insoluble problems or as support in human failure' and which, in this way, tries to 'make room for God'.[28] Here, men are concerned with the borders of experience, rather than with God in the centre of life. God is relegated to outstanding problems, for which, however, it is possible to find answers more conclusive or more compelling than the Christian ones. 'The Christian, unlike the devotees of the salvation myths, does not need a last refuge in the eternal from earthly tasks and difficulties.'[29] Although this kind of apologetic accepts the movement of the world towards autonomy in almost every area of life, it withholds for itself the 'ultimate' or 'last' questions:

Even though there has been surrender on all secular problems, there still remain the so-called 'ultimate' questions – death, guilt – on which only God can furnish an answer, and which are the reason why God and the church and the pastor are needed. But what if one day . . . they no longer exist as such, if they too can be answered without God?[30]

Christian theology, however, accepted such an apologetic in order to survive. It asked for (and, in most cases, received) 'space' for God within the realm of outstanding questions – distress, despair, the fear of death, the unknown or unknowable which manifests itself in situations of crisis. Christianity became the answer to these problems, and the world was convinced that it cannot live without the tutelage of 'religion' or 'God':

God thus became the answer to life's problems, the solution of its distresses and conflicts. As a result, if anyone had no such difficulties, if he refused to identify himself in sympathy with those who had, it was no good trying to win him for God. The only way of getting at him was to show that he had all these problems, needs, and conflicts without being aware of it or owning up to it. Existentialist philosophy and psychology have both been pretty clever at this sort of thing. It is then possible to talk to a man about God, and methodism can celebrate its triumph. If however it does not come off, if a man won't see that his happiness is really damnation, his health sickness, his vigour and vitality despair; if he won't call them what they are, the theologian is at his wit's end.[31]

The 'weaknesses' of man are thereby exploited 'for purposes alien to him', and the maturity of man is disregarded by 'thrusting him back into the midst of problems which are in fact not problems for him any more'.[32]

Tillich today bases his position upon given ontological truths, so basic as to seem unquestionable, e.g.: 'Although man is actually separated from the infinite, he could not be aware of it if he did not participate in it potentially. This is expressed in the state of being ultimately concerned, a state which is universally human, whatever the content of the concern may be.'[33] Here, 'ultimate concern' surely does not mean (just as 'the boundary situation' never meant) a concentration upon 'borderline questions' or 'unsolved problems'. Ultimate concern underlies *every human activity*; it is central to any definition of man. Similarly universal and seemingly impregnable is Tillich's definition of the human condition which is open to revelation. The conceptual expression of man's existential status is 'the dialectical situation'. 'It is the condition for man's religious existence and for his ability to receive revelation.'[34] Tillich has never tired of insisting that neither this nor any other universal description of the human situation can be used as a demonstration of the *inevitability of* or the *necessity for* a Christian 'answer'. This represents, one would think, a pointed response to criticism from Bonhoeffer (and others) that in his system, revelation has been made *dependent* upon a secular condition.

Ironically, it has been Tillich who, more than any other theologian in our time, has directed the attention of theology to secular culture and worldly life as its legitimate concerns. Has Bonhoeffer's project no affinities, then, with Tillich's major interest? And were we finally to clarify Bonhoeffer's position as incompatible with the general lines of Tillich's theology of culture, should it be because we characterize the latter's interpretation of the world as one in which 'men are seen, in their acts and in their despair, unconsciously longing for God and in their negations of God unconsciously witnessing to him?'[35]

Bonhoeffer's point is still elusive, and to pursue the argument further it is necessary to retrace our steps and view the question from another perspective. Bonhoeffer seems to be attacking a theological attitude of over-confidence, a certain assurance with which theologians relate themselves to the world and justify their work.[36] He finds such over-confidence in Tillich's offer to demonstrate to protesting secular man that regardless of any arguments to the contrary, all men are nevertheless in the state of ultimate concern and therefore open to the religious question. He finds it also in Barth's 'positivism', based as his theology is upon an unquestionable assurance given in his doctrine of election. What is behind this protest against dogmatic certainty and existentialist self-assurance? Some highly interesting work by some of Bonhoeffer's interpreters has suggested that it is the demand for a new understanding of the relationship between Law and Gospel.

Religion, Law and Gospel

Without following in the direction indicated, Bonhoeffer suggested that the problem of religionless Christianity would involve a reinterpretation of the relationship between Law and Gospel or, more exactly, between circumcision and justification. 'The Pauline question, whether the *peritome* is a condition of salvation,' he wrote, 'really means today whether religion is a condition of salvation.' He recalled the analogy later, in the context of a discussion of Bultmann's demythologization programme: 'Biblical concepts must be interpreted in such a fashion that religion is not set forth as a precondition of faith (compare the *peritome* in St. Paul).'[37] The question of setting aside religious preconditions which offend the maturity of the world come of age is thus identified with the Pauline problem of relating circumcision to justification in such a manner that the former is not a requirement for obtaining the latter.

What we have before us in Bonhoeffer's criticism of religion is, then, a fundamental concern for the proper understanding of the Law and its relationship to the proclamation of the Gospel. This sets his programme against the theologies of his contemporaries. For Barth's confidence is founded upon the assumption that all men, whether conscious of the fact or not, stand under the Law. Tillich's 'ultimate concern' attempts to win for apologetics a universal category, 'estrangement', which will demonstrate to contemporary man that all men are subject to the Law. Bultmann's views, however, 'unorthodox', take for granted the fact that 'the possibility of understanding' is given to man under the Law 'in the very fact that he is a sinner, that he is in death'.[38] But Bonhoeffer wishes to interpret the Law and relate it to the Gospel in such a fashion that the knowledge that man is, under the Law, a sinner and in death will not offend the maturity of the world by being used as a *presupposition* of Christian apologetics. Is this at all possible or desirable? Can Christianity do without a theological anthropology (whether set forth in traditional dogmatic terms or in the form of ontological or existential truths) which so describes man's condition under the Law that Christianity is made to seem the only reasonable choice of the man who cannot but wish to be free from his plight? Can a refusal to make any apologetical use of such an understanding of man's condition be given a theological and exegetical basis in the New Testament?

In attempting to make theological sense out of Bonhoeffer's radical question (and we shall see shortly just how radical a question it is), we must acknowledge the convenience of two helplul essays which have recently appeared. The first is an investigation of Bonhoeffer's 'non-religious interpretation of biblical concepts' in the light of the Law–Gospel distinction, written in 1955 by Gerhard Ebeling.[39] The second, an exegetical study completed in 1961 by Krister Stendahl, raises independently of the above the question whether the traditional protestant interpretation of Paul as 'a hero of the introspective conscience' and the Pauline letters as 'documents of human consciousness' can still be maintained.[40] Our first task is to make clear the direction of Bonhoeffer's thinking, and here we may turn directly to Ebeling's summary.

The preaching of the Law and the preaching of the Gospel, Ebeling reminds us, are closely bound together in Paul's letters. God's Law is the reality of man's existence, universally apprehensible and applicable, under which and before God all men, Jew and Greek, stand.[41] It is preached for the sake of the Gospel, to enable it to speak to man in his concrete reality. Christianity therefore has no interest in simply doing away with the Law – for this would mean that the Gospel itself has become nothing more than a *nova lex*. Without the Law, the Gospel cannot be preached. Christian preaching must, however, preach the Law in such a way that the Law is not presented as the means of attaining salvation.

Ebeling underlines the fact that Bonhoeffer does not equate

religion with Law, but with circumcision. 'An identification of religion and Law would rest ... on the mistaken idea that non-religiousness is lawlessness, which of course is not at all what Bonhoeffer means.'[42] The Gospel is not lawlessness, but rather freedom from the Law. So also, non-religious interpretation distinguishes Law and Gospel and demonstrates freedom from legalistic, religious interpretation. That the Law exists, that *religion* exists is not the problem. In the light of Paul's use of the Law for the sake of the Gospel and not as its precondition, however, one must find a non-religious interpretation which shows the Gospel to be free from religious preconditions.

The traditional exposition of the Law cannot do this if left to itself, because it simply is not understandable and binding for modern, non-religious man. It does not speak of his reality, which is a world in which he has learned to do without God, metaphysics, and inwardness. Religious interpretation of the Law can only 'add on and hold over against him a Law which is not verifiable as the Law under which the modern, non-religious man *de facto* stands'.[43] Therefore, and for the sake of the Gospel, 'the task is precisely to ask ourselves anew in view of modern non-religious man what it means to take the Law that belongs inseparably to the existence of man, and is in fact his very reality, and testify to it as God's Law'.[44] The traditional interpretation of the Law is not this reality, but an additional one, bordering on the existence of man. To ask him to accept this additional reality as the only means through which he may hear the Gospel is to ask him to agree to a religious precondition.

The decisive question therefore is: how do we preach the Gospel to the non-religious man as freedom from the Law – and that means, Jesus Christ as the fulfilment and end of the Law – without laying on him beforehand a Law that is strange to him and does not concern him? How does the Law get home to the non-religious man? What is it that unconditionally concerns him? How do we bring to expression the Law under which he stands *de facto*?[45]

The problem is to interpret the content and significance of the Law 'non-religiously', and that means to describe the reality of modern man – to *proclaim* the reality of modern man – in such fashion that he may recognize himself in that reality and hear the Law preached for the sake of the Gospel.

Here Ebeling ends his inquiry. Has he in fact located 'the decisive question' posed by Bonhoeffer? One notices that his conclusion provides an excellent point of departure for a defence of Bultmann's demythologizing programme, and it is worth remembering that Ebeling is, as a theologian, heavily indebted to Bultmann, his teacher. Ebeling sees the problem to be that of demythologizing the Law, of describing its reality and significance apart from the thought forms and patterns of a past age. Taken for granted (and here one touches upon Tillich's concern for a 'method of correlation') is that non-religious man *still has* an 'unconditional concern'. Ebeling assumes that any denial that this unconditional concern exists within man's *de facto* reality must mean the end of the Gospel altogether. There must, then, be something in the Law and something in man's 'reality' upon which the Gospel depends for its existence. The conclusion one must draw is that the most honest, most realistic and non-religious appraisal of the human situation, which demythologization will help us accomplish, will inevitably disclose the unconditional concern that is the *sine qua non* of Christian apologetics.

It is at this point that one questions whether Bonhoeffer's concern is reflected in its entirety. *Not only the mythological clothing of the Law is 'religious', but also the traditional use of the statement 'all men are under the Law' in Christian apologetics.* In so far as the first word of the *kerygma* is spoken out of the knowledge that all men are under the Law, that they exhibit an ultimate or unconditional concern to be free of the Law – that there, and as the first step towards faith, a man is 'utterly convicted in his conscience' – Christian apologetics is based upon a religious *a priori*. Here, however subtly, the central claim of Christianity becomes its availability or inevitability as an answer to the basic human question posed by the Law. In this way, Christianity becomes the completion of reality by means of God; the religious answer to the universal religious question.

It would indeed seem that Bonhoeffer has breached the law of contradiction and made the Gospel superfluous. As Ebeling says, if the Law is man's reality, it makes no sense to say that this reality may not exist. But the question is not the *existence* of the Law. It is rather the *use* Christianity makes of its understanding of the Law and, secondly, whether the realization that the *kerygma* is dependent upon one's understanding of the Law does not lead the Christian to describe the human situation in such a way that the Gospel comes as an answer or solution to man's predicament. Still, one cannot but be uneasy with a request to break this kind of link between Law and Gospel and to hold our peace concerning the inadequacy of the Law to save us. Given Paul's use of the Law in the New Testament and the dependence of protestant theology upon this use since the time of Luther, have we any alternative to the traditional interpretation?

An imaginative and persuasive essay which has recently appeared suggests a possible affirmative answer to that question. In 'The Apostle Paul and the Introspective Conscience of the West,' Krister Stendahl questions whether this use of the Law is at all Pauline. He suspects that the Western psychological condition has read the Pauline letters as 'documents of human consciousness' and has hailed Paul as 'the hero of the introspective conscience'.[46] In this way a far different understanding of the meaning of the Law than Paul ever intended has become a foundation stone of Christian apologetics.

For Paul the problem was, quite simply, what should be said about the Law (the Mosaic Law)[47] since the coming of the Messiah – an event which, according to Judaic thought, would bring to an end the custodial role of the Old Covenant (Gal. 3. 24). For the relationship between Jew and Gentile, this event meant that there was no reason to impose a no-longer-valid Law upon those who did not understand themselves to be included in the Old Covenant. Paul, as a righteous Jew, had no difficulty in fulfilling the Law – and certainly never assumed that keeping the Law would end inevitably in despair, hence in the arms of Christ.[48] In any event (and as Paul surely knew), forgiveness and grace were available to the Jew who failed fully to keep the Law.

Augustine was the first of the Church Fathers to have located a 'deeper layer' in the thought of Paul, and he defined this as a universal human longing. But it remained for Luther, convicted by a medieval system of penance, to identify his terror with the damnation of man beneath the burden of the Law. Since that time, 'Paul's statements about justification by faith have been hailed as the answer to the problem which faces the ruthlessly honest man in his practice of introspection,'[49] and the Western problem of conscience has become the unchallenged and self-evident prerequisite for the proclamation of the Gospel. The meaning of the Law now is that 'nobody can attain a true faith in Christ unless his self-righteousness has been crushed by the Law'.[50] Since Luther, 'all men must come to Christ with consciences properly convicted by the Law and its insatiable requirements for righteousness'.[51]

Stendahl is interested simply in making less overpowering and confident the assumption that the only door into the church and the proper clue for the understanding of the gospels is 'an evermore introspective awareness of sin and guilt'.[52] Accordingly, he does not move very far into the question raised by his conclusion. The existential hermeneutical principle 'rests on the presupposition that man is essentially the same through the ages, and that this continuity in the human self-consciousness is the common denominator between the New Testament and any age of human history'.[53] Stendahl suggests that to question this assumption on exegetical grounds might prove damaging to the presuppositions with which these theologians, particularly Bultmann, operate. Let us now leave Stendahl in order to examine, briefly, the effect this new understanding of Paul's use of the Law–Gospel relationship might have upon the apologetical method of a contemporary theologian such as Bultmann.

Is it the purpose of the Law, as Paul understands it, to deliver the convicted sinner into the arms of Christ? Is contemporary theology therefore 'Pauline' when it attempts in a similar fashion to point modern man to his own reality (the 'Law') for the purpose of providing him with the evidence which will enable him to 'decide' for or against 'authentic existence'? This is the crux of the question, for one cannot be blamed for suspecting that the Christian theologian will have a vested interest in portraying reality as incapable of delivering the meaning of life to the man whose essence it is to search for it – in picturing man's reality as that from which he must be saved, and Christianity as the only ultimate means of salvation.

Bultmann is very careful to point out that there is neither necessity nor inevitability that man, regarding his situation under the Law, will turn to Christ for his salvation. 'The sinner who is in death is confronted by the Gospel when it reaches him with the decision whether or not he is willing to understand himself anew and to receive his life from the hand of God.'[54] The Gospel reaches the sinner in and through the Law, and offers to man the possibility of a new understanding of himself. But is there not, beneath this formula, the tacit and unquestioned restless conscience of Western man at work, driving him towards his decision? Bultmann stresses the importance for his own position of the fact that Pauline theology, as he sees it, is mainly anthropology. When Paul speaks of God, he does so only as God is significant for man and for his salvation. And Paul's Christology is always soteriology. Is it fair to say, then, that Bultmann's characterization of Pauline theology and his subsequent theological interests are based upon what Bonhoeffer calls a 'religious' view of man?

Demythologizing and the Non-Religious Interpretation of Biblical Concepts

It is clear from his comments in the prison letters that Bonhoeffer thinks it is fair to say this. But before we show how and in what way he wishes to make this criticism of Bultmann, we should first recall that Bonhoeffer spoke of Bultmann as the one who 'somehow recognized Barth's limitations'.[55] We are offered a clue to what Bonhoeffer meant by this statement when we read Bultmann's comments concerning that single work by Barth which Bonhoeffer found most instructive. Of the first edition of the *Epistle to the Romans,* Bultmann wrote:

The artificiality of a Catholicizing repristination of the ancient cult, as well as the orthodox transfiguration of Pauline myth and ecclesiastical dogma, are to be condemned from the outset. This applies also to the fanatical renewal of the Pauline myth in Barthian polish. As much as I welcome the religious criticism of culture in Barth's *Romans*, I cannot see, in what he presents positively, anything other than an arbitrary adaptation of the Pauline myth of Christ. The judgement Barth passes upon 'liberal theology' strikes Barth himself to the same extent.[56]

In what way does Barth's criticism of 'religion' strike himself as well? In that he has chosen to adopt the mythological language of Paul as the vehicle for his protest. This 'repristination' follows a refusal, in Bultmann's view, to go the whole distance. The gulf between the New Testament and the modern scientific age can hardly be overcome, in Bultmann's view, by condemning the latter and concentrating the attention of theology upon a restatement of the former. At the same time, Bultmann can see nothing wrong with a modern attempt to construct a religious *a priori*; he has faulted Barth simply for failing to understand what 'modern' means. In a passage which can only be astonishing to those who have followed what we have said thus far, Bultmann praised the *second* edition of the *Epistle to the Romans* as just such an attempt:

Although in the original form of a commentary, it falls in line with works such as Schleiermacher's *Speeches on Religion* and Otto's *Idea of the Holy*, with modern attempts to work out a religious *a priori*, and finally with Romans itself, whose radical antithesis between works and faith is really attempting to do the same thing. No matter how different these may be in details, all of them are attempts to express in language the awareness of the distinctiveness and absoluteness of religion.[57]

Clearly, Bultmann views a religious *a priori* as the *sine qua non* of theology, believing this to be fully in line with Pauline theology. But he cannot accept a formulation of this religious *a priori* in terms of the mythological structures of a pre-scientific age. Thus Bultmann is defining religion in two ways – one of which he wishes to assert as basic to theology and hence unquestionable and irreplaceable, the other synonymous with 'mythological' and therefore problematic. In rejecting 'religion' in this second sense, Bultmann once wrote:

Religion is man's yearning for something beyond the world, is the discovery of a sphere above the world in which only the soul can live, detached from worldly things. In religion man is alone with God, radiant with the power of a higher world of truth. And religion manifests itself not in the shaping of the life of the world but in the aimless action of the cultus.[58]

Barth declared that Christian theology stands opposed to 'religion' and meant by that the cultural and philosophical expression of man's attempts to grasp at God. He believed at the same time that to express the distinctiveness of God, theology must be bound to the language of the Bible and dogmatics. Bultmann, however, sees that *this language itself* constitutes the real difficulty. For the latter, the mythological language of the New Testament can hardly be used to proclaim the Gospel to men who no longer participate in that myth as their own reality; to attempt to do so is to direct attention towards a special, other-worldly sphere and 'the aimless action of the cultus'.

What of Bonhoeffer? We have seen that his criticism of Tillich did not reflect an understanding of the latter's real concern. It is also likely that Bonhoeffer did not fully understand Bultmann's intention in proposing the demythologizing of the New Testament. We know at least that Bonhoeffer read, appreciated, and wrestled with the famous essay which Bultmann wrote during the war.[59] It was on this contribution that he commented in two passages in the prison letters:

A few words about 'religionlessness'. I expect you remember the Bultmann essay about the demythologizing of the New Testament? My opinion today would be not that he went 'too far', as most people think, but that he did not go far enough. It is not only the 'mythological' concepts such as miracles, the ascension, etc. (which are really inseparable from the concepts God, faith, etc.), but also the 'religious' concepts which are problematic. You cannot, as Bultmann imagines, separate God from miracles, but you do have to be able to interpret and proclaim both of them in a non-religious sense. Bultmann's approach is really at bottom the Liberal one (i.e., abridging the Gospels) whereas I try to think theologically.

Bultmann would seem to have felt Barth's limitations in some way, but he misconstrues them in the light of liberal theology, and hence goes off into the typical Liberal reduction process (the 'mythological' elements of Christianity are dropped, and Christianity is reduced to its 'essence'). I am of the view that the full content, including the mythological concepts, must be maintained. The New Testament is not a mythological garbing of the universal truth; this mythology (resurrection and so on) is the thing itself – but the concepts must be reinterpreted in such a way as not to make religion a precondition of faith (cf. the *peritome* in St. Paul).[60]

Bonhoeffer attempted in these words to relate his programme not only to Barth's protest against religion but also to Bultmann's recognition of Barth's limitations. Once again, someone 'has not gone far enough'. Both Barth and Bultmann have, however, gone part of the distance, for each recognizes a sense in which Christianity may and must be spoken of as 'religionless'. Barth would speak of a 'religionless' Christianity as one which recognized the necessity for a continuous protest from within against its own tendencies to become one more means by which man can grasp at the majesty and freedom of God. God is free, and Christianity must be religionless in so far as it proceeds from God's free revelation of himself. Bultmann would affirm as properly 'religionless' a Christianity which could interpret for contemporaries a revelation which was necessarily expressed in the words and ways of thinking of first-century men. For modern men, these words and ways of thinking no longer express what they once did. To avoid 'religion', Barth would insist that Christianity turn the eyes of men away from their prideful search for God towards the Incarnation, in which God comes to them. *Any* religious *a priori* is a greater threat to the sovereignty of God than expressing oneself in what Bultmann would call 'mythological' (or 'religious'), but which is none the less biblical and traditional, terminology.

But Bultmann disagrees that a religious *a priori* can or should be avoided. It cannot be avoided if 'the distinctiveness and absoluteness' of Christianity is to be asserted and preserved. The attention of theology must rather be directed towards the interpretation of mythological language for contemporary man and, in this way, towards a Christianity freed from 'religion'. Christianity must be shown to be independent of the otherworldly and responsible to the man who lives in this world.

Bonhoeffer's 'non-religious interpretation' recognizes the contribution of both men. Like Bultmann, he realizes that the exclusive use of a special and historically dated language for expressing the *kerygma* and the demand that apologetics become dogmatics will inevitably require in the hearer some form of religious *a priori* – and he is grateful to Bultmann for having demonstrated this. But in keeping with Barth's intention (and regardless of the failure of the latter's attempt to carry this forward), Bonhoeffer believes that a theology based upon *any* religious *a priori* is no longer tenable in a world come of age – that is, a world which no longer feels itself threatened by the biblical Law, its own reality, its failure to find 'meaning' or 'authentic existence', its inability to locate or to realize its 'ultimate concern'. Bonhoeffer therefore reaffirms his trust in Barth's instinctive refusal to surrender the mythological world or language of the Bible. 'The full content' of the Bible, 'including the mythological concepts, must be maintained'; the cultus cannot be dismissed simply as 'purposeless action', whatever the risks of doing so. For the greater danger is to fall, as Bonhoeffer imagines Bultmann to have done, into the Liberal trap of supposing that underneath and independent of the historical form and setting of the New Testament proclamation, eternal and universal Christian 'truth' may be discovered. It is for this reason that the 'mysteries' must remain mysteries, retaining their own independent logic and linguistic peculiarity, their distinctiveness and other-worldliness. Is this refusal to give up what Bultmann believes he must simply an unwarranted, reactionary twinge of conservatism on Bonhoeffer's part?

At least one of Bonhoeffer's interpreters, J. A. T. Robinson, believes it possible that one can plead for 'the unemotional recognition of the validity of the myth in its own right' while insisting that one 'differentiate and assess the mythological positively for what it is' for the benefit of a world come of age.[61] This is a fair statement of Bonhoeffer's purpose. Demythologizing, while it is a part of this process of differentiation and assessment, has failed fully to reflect the concern of a non-religious interpretation not only because it frequently confuses interpretation with substitution, but also to the extent to which it has found comfort in the religious *a priori* of existentialism. The present-day concern for the hermeneutical problem, in order to correct itself, needs to question seriously its confidence in existentialist philosophy and, indeed, the existential concern of theology throughout the history of western Christendom.

But if Bonhoeffer insists that to disregard the independent validity of the biblical concepts would lead inevitably to the discovery of a universal religious truth separable from its historical/mythological setting, he is equally insistent that these concepts not be 'profaned'. By this he means to avoid presenting them to the world simply as they are, uninterpreted, asking the hearer to 'take or leave' them. To 'take' them thus would require a form of the religious *a priori* regardless of the ferocity of the theologian's denial. To 'leave them' in order to be true to a world come of age (which he thought would become increasingly the case) would demonstrate the failure of Christian proclamation to take seriously the secular condition of the hearer. Bonhoeffer therefore calls for an interpretation of biblical concepts which will take seriously that secular condition by proclaiming the gospel 'non-religiously'. Here many interpreters hail him as a champion of the concern for the problems of Christian speech and language which surround the study of hermeneutics. But this is the point at which Bonhoeffer eludes all of our attempts to capture him. The demand for the 'non-religious interpretation of biblical concepts' seems to be set aside, and in its place Bonhoeffer puts the phrase 'sharing in the sufferings of God at the hands of a godless world'. This includes, no doubt, the interest in a 'non-religious interpretation'. But increasingly, Bonhoeffer loses interest in problems of speech and apologetics, and speaks instead of a special kind of 'silence' and holding one's peace before such concerns. His Christological vision returns, and the mysterious 'secret discipline' comes into its own. 'Sharing in the sufferings of God' represents the consummation of Bonhoeffer's theology.

CHAPTER 16

Sharing in the Sufferings
of God

But in conclusion, I must say something 'spiritual'. You know of course the books of Bernanos? There, when the priests speak, their words mean something. This is because they come not out of some speech considera- tion or observation, but quite simply out of daily, personal correspondence with the crucified Jesus Christ. This is the depth out of which a word must come, if it is to mean something. One might also say it has to do with whether or not we judge ourselves daily with the picture of the crucified Jesus Christ himself, and allow ourselves to be called to repentance. Where the Word comes to us, so to speak, immediately from the cross of Jesus itself, where Christ is so contemporary for us that he speaks our words himself, only there can the terrible danger of spiritual chatter be banished. But who among us lives with this composure?

'An eine unbekannte Frau'. 1940(?). GS III, *p. 43.*

At the beginning of this century, Max Weber linked 'the radical elimination of magic from the world' with what he called 'the practice of worldly asceticism'.[1] The phrase 'worldly asceticism', *weltliche Askese,* was taken up by Ernst Troeltsch among others and elaborated as a particular style of life, suited to the self- consciousness of the modern world, which had been made possible by the growth to maturity of Protestant Christianity. Indeed, this life style was Protestantism's single most important contribution.

It is well known that most forms of the monastic asceticism to which this new style of life related itself historically saw as the supreme achievement of the monk the 'imitation of Christ' through contemplation on his virtues and their realization in one's life. But neither Troeltsch nor his fellow Liberal theologians

222

spoke of 'worldly asceticism' as an imitation of Christ. Turning away from the cloister and the chains of supernaturalism and meaningless piety, the nineteenth-century Liberal protestant 'undertook to remodel the world and to work out his ideals in the world'.[2] Christology (a treasury of just such traditional supernaturalism) underwent the most radical reshaping as the Jesus of history was pitted against the Christ of faith. The Christian life in the world was defined in terms of 'vocation' and an ethical activism which sought the realization of Christian 'ideals'. At its best, Liberal Christianity took these ideals from those 'ethical teachings' of Christ which were capable of realization in earthly society, fighting courageously against the brutality, greed and inhumanity of late nineteenth-century industrialism and nationalism with the religious principles to which the name 'social gospel' was affixed. At its worst, the dialectical nature of Christian existence in the world was lost sight of, and adherents of a tamed 'Liberalism' emptied it of its traditional Christian content and simply added a dash of piety to what had become essentially a capitulation to the economic, political, and social orders in which they lived.

'Worldly asceticism' thus described the nature and purpose of Christian discipleship in shaping the world and participating creatively in its forms and its life. But out of this participation, perhaps guided by presuppositions more Christological than the Liberal Christian would have cared to admit, a form and shape of Christian existence more intensive than 'activity' came to characterize the genuinely Liberal Christian. The nineteenth-century Liberal protestant was not, after all, simply the sum of his ethical and moral actions. What created his world far more than what he did was what he *was*.

Bonhoeffer loved the nineteenth century as the world of his youth and as his heritage. In his prison cell he meditated long hours on the grandeur, nobility, dedication, and real achievement which had shaped and which had been shaped by this style of life. Caught between his genuine appreciation for the integrity and accomplishment of nineteenth-century life and the realization that such life was no longer possible, he began to question whether it might not be necessary and proper for the twentieth-century Christian to recover the feeling, so strong in the nineteenth century, of being a human participant in everything which goes to make up the life of the world; to recover the lost consciousness of belonging to and dedicating oneself to a particular time and place in human history. Beginning with a faint suspicion, but with increasing boldness, he linked his theological meditation to his reflections on music and art, the nature of friendship, time and behaviour in an attempt to recover, for his own age, the meaning of 'the Christian life.'

Bonhoeffer rightly suspected that he had touched upon a concern of Liberal theology. But one element in his meditations differed radically from any Liberal discussion of the style of the Christian life: his astonishing and unashamed desire to establish a secular style of life upon a Christological foundation. The Christian can be a worldly man only because Jesus Christ was a worldly man; the Christian must participate in the life of the world because he must imitate the One who shared supremely in the life of the world.

The fragmentary, unsystematic *imitatio Christi* which comprised Bonhoeffer's final theological effort will, even in its incomplete form, disturb the peace of theologians for years to come. We simply have not sufficient evidence to enable us to say with certainty that we have understood this notion as Bonhoeffer would have wanted us to understand it. But there is enough of a pattern to the material we have at hand to allow us to place a certain interpretation upon it so that it may impress, startle, and move us more creatively. And at the very least, we may be certain that Bonhoeffer has found the realm of Christian existence a more promising field in which to explore the meaning of revelation than either ecclesiology or the concept of God; and his invitation to us to follow his lead is one of the more promising offers open to theologians in the present day.

Bonhoeffer proposed as the subject of inquiry what he came finally to call 'sharing in the sufferings of God at the hands of a godless world'. This phrase is a development of 'religionless Christianity' which establishes Christological guidelines to check the possible misunderstanding of that notion. We have

already seen (in Chapter 14) that Bonhoeffer wished to elabo-
rate the Lutheran Christology of condescension of his 1933
lectures as the theological basis of his new interest, the world
come of age. What now appears is a surprising reconstruction of
the tropological interpretation of Christology and discipleship
in which his efforts to proclaim the concretion of the revelation
culminated during the church struggle.[3] Discipleship is now
described as a profound dialectical, *lived* relationship relating
'sharing in the sufferings of God' to its conceptual partner, the
'secret discipline'.

To live this dialectical existence is to live the life of faith and,
as we have suggested, to imitate Christ. The Christian shares in
the sufferings of God by leading a worldly life, and in the secret
discipline by refusing the world any ultimate claims upon him.

Our first task is to attempt to determine the content and
nature of 'the secret discipline'. We may then move into an
examination of the meaning of 'sharing the sufferings of God at
the hands of a godless world'.

The Secret Discipline

One reads little, in the prison letters, concerning how one's faith
is to be distinguished from a stoic position about the world with
its growing disinterest in and independence from God and
religion. The safeguard Bonhoeffer proposed he called 'the
secret (or arcane) discipline'. He introduced the notion in a
rather offhand fashion, and his interest in elaborating upon this
introduction seems to have been subordinated to his determination to explore the phenomena of the coming of age of the world,
the disappearance of God and the religious *a priori*, the worldly
humanity of Christ and that of the Christian in Christ, and the
nature of the Lordship of God in Christ over a world defined in
terms of these realities.

Nevertheless, vague outlines of what Bonhoeffer was attempting to say may be discerned. The importance with which this
notion has been regarded by Bonhoeffer's interpreters as well as
the light they have been able to cast upon it – through analysis
of Bonhoeffer's previous writings and his treatment of related

ideas – lead one to state without reserve that the secret discipline is 'the heart of his thought'.[4] Among these interpretations there is considerable disagreement concerning which of Bonhoeffer's earlier notions can best serve to illuminate the meaning of the the secret discipline. Because the theme is not discussed at length in the prison letters yet can be related fruitfully to any number of earlier concepts, it is difficult to decide between these various treatments. We shall repeat and compare many of these findings in our discussion.

The secret discipline is referred to twice in the prison letters. The first mention occurs in the midst of Bonhoeffer's initial meditation on religionless Christianity; the second during the more technical elaboration of that theme in the discussion of the possibility of a non-religious interpretation of biblical concepts:

The questions needing to be answered would indeed be: what do a church, a congregation, sermon, liturgy, a Christian life mean in a religionless world? How do we speak of God without religion – i.e. without the temporally influenced presuppositions of metaphysics, inwardness, etc., etc.? How do we speak (but perhaps one cannot simply 'speak' of them as formerly) in a 'worldly' manner about 'God'? In what way are we 'religionless-worldly' Christians, in what way are we the *ek-klesia*, those who are called forth, without conceiving of ourselves as religiously favoured but much more as belonging wholly to the world? Then Christ is no longer the object of religion, but something entirely different, really the Lord of the world. But what does that mean? What do the cult and prayer mean in a religionless time? Do the secret discipline or the difference (which you have met with me before) between ultimate and penultimate take on new significance?

There are degrees of perception and degrees of significance; i.e. a secret discipline must be established once more, by means of which the *secrets* of Christian faith may be protected against profanation. Positivism of revelation makes it too easy for itself, in so far as it sets up in the last analysis, a law of faith and thus mutilates what is a gift for us – through the incarnation of Christ! In the place of religion there now stands the church – that is in itself biblical, but the world is to a certain extent made to depend upon itself and left to its own devices, and that is a mistake.[5]

According to this evidence, the secret discipline is integrally related to the process of non-religious interpretation. The 'secrets' – church, cult, prayer, dogmas, the life in Christ – are not circulated in public in their uninterpreted form. The traditional *content* of the Bible and the *faith* of the church must be 'protected', but in such a fashion that no special religious claims are made for them. Preaching, baptism, communion – these are part of the secret. Adherence to these, Hammelsbeck writes, is bondage to Christ as his chosen and elect, without however claiming any privileged status for the content of Christian tradition among the secular forms of the world, nor for oneself among one's neighbours.[6] The discipline consists in the refusal to betray the secret by profaning it or to disregard it by confusing it with or substituting for it inappropriate secular elements in the process of non-religious interpretation or this-sided existence.

Regin Prenter takes the secret discipline to mean that what one fails to interpret non-religiously must nevertheless remain 'as it is', for Christianity cannot be 'reduced' to a universal religious 'essence'.[7] What is uninterpreted (because it *cannot* be, and not because it *should not* be) is nevertheless retained. But it is held as a *secret*, since to expose it to the world in such a form is to violate the maturity of the world and to profane the concepts themselves. The traditional-biblical-dogmatic concepts in their irreducible and inevitably mythological forms are no less true if they cannot be interpreted. But because their form and logic is not the form and logic of the world, they will be 'for the world' in a way that will have to remain secret to the world. A certain initiation into these mysteries, and not the forced acceptance of them out of hand as 'the faith of the church', is called for. Prenter underscores the fact that this secrecy is not the selfish, jealous guarding of the knowledge of the elect but on the contrary, an act of penance on the part of the church for the sake of the world. In this respect, Bethge writes:

The church must not throw away its great terms 'creation', 'fall', 'atonement', 'repentance', 'last things', and so on. But if she cannot relate them to the secularized world in such a way that their essence can immediately be seen in worldly life, then the church had better keep silent. . . . And the adult church in a world come of age is not the church which exposes its secrets of faith cheaply, but that which exposes itself in its very existence.[8]

Bonhoeffer himself best explains this penitential, purgative secrecy in a passage that is undoubtedly related to our discussion:

But we too are once again being driven back to the beginnings of our understanding. Atonement and redemption, regeneration and the Holy Ghost, the love of our enemies, cross and resurrection, life in Christ and Christian discipleship – all these things have become so problematic and so remote that we hardly dare any more to speak of them. In the traditional words and acts we suspect there is something completely new and revolutionary, but we cannot conceive of it and utter it yet. That is our own fault. Our church, which has fought in the last years only for its self-preservation, as though that were an end in itself, is incapable of bearing the redeeming and saving word for men and for the world. Therefore our earlier words must become powerless and silent, and our Christian existence will be confined today to only two things: praying and acting justly among men. All thinking, speaking, and organizing of the things of Christianity must be born anew out of this praying and this acting. By the time you have grown up, the form of the church will have changed very much. We are not yet out of the melting pot, and any attempt to hasten matters to a new organizational show of force will only delay the churches' conversion and purgation. It is not for us to prophesy the day – but the day will come – when men will once again be called to utter the Word of God with such power that the world will be changed and renewed by it. It will be a new speech, perhaps wholly unreligious, but freeing and redeeming like the speech of Jesus, which will shock men and yet overcome them by its power; the language of a new righteousness and truth, which proclaims the peace of God with men and the advent of his kingdom. 'And they shall fear and tremble for all the good and for all the peace that I procure unto it' (Jer. 33. 9). Until then the Christian cause will be silent and a hidden affair, but there will be those who pray and do justly and wait for God's own time. [9]

An inability to speak, groping for something which cannot yet be uttered, the powerlessness and silence of traditional language, praying and doing right, conversion and purgation, a silent and hidden affair, and – out of this – a new language. Everything traditionally 'Christian' must steadfastly refuse to call attention to itself. It is difficult to see how this can be expressed positively, or how Bonhoeffer intended to relate this either to his past thinking or to the programme of 'non-religious interpretation'. Here, a historical excursus will be of some help.

1. The secret discipline has, first of all, an *ecclesiological* reference. In *The Cost of Discipleship* Bonhoeffer applauded the action of the post-Constantine church in protecting herself from 'cheap grace' by instituting the catechumenate and barring the

only outwardly Christian from the central cultic acts. Responding to the later threat of secularization, monasticism flowered.[10]
Here one must remember Bonhoeffer's consistently strong
ecclesiological concern and more especially the Finkenwalde
experiment and the book *Life Together*. Having spoken to his
friends of the necessity for a return to the cloister,[11] he sought
the content of a 'secret discipline' in actual corporate devotional
life. Through the worshipping community, the Christian prays
for and serves his neighbour. Through this communal service
and prayer life, a 'personal Christian engagement' without any
'signs of remoteness, of mania or mystification'[12] is made
possible. Hammelsbeck thus understands the secret discipline of
the prison letters as related especially to the communal life
described in *Life Together*:

'The secret discipline' . . . could serve as the subtitle for Bonhoeffer's
writing, *Life Together*. 'Remaining in Christ' requires a discipline, an
obedient attachment of oneself . . .
That I participate steadfastly in preaching, baptism, and the Lord's
Supper; that I pray, confess, and sing praises belongs to this secret. That
is and remains a secret to the world, a secret entrusted to me through the
prevenient grace of God. I adhere gratefully to this secret. The demand
and consolation of Christ meet me – this I cannot and may not conceal.
But I have no religious requirements to place before the world, which I
serve out of this secret.[13]

Hammelsbeck is equally certain that Bonhoeffer did not have
in mind a 'liturgical renewal' as a central factor in a communal
secret discipline. The identification of Bonhoeffer's secret discipline with a recovery of the meaning of liturgy has, however,
been widespread especially among those churches with a liturgical tradition, and even occasionally among those which historically have relegated liturgy to a secondary role. Typical of this
approach is an Anglican comment:

But 'being there for others', as Bonhoeffer means it, is a witness to God's
being there for us in Jesus Christ: and this will only be seen where the
church's being for others constantly springs from her own interior life in
which God is constantly 'there' for her as he was there in Christ, in the
word and sacraments. In other words, it needs liturgy – that point where
the church is being truly herself, the community for whom God in Christ

is there at the centre – for the kind of evangelism and social service that Bonhoeffer proposes. Otherwise it will become merely human and humanitarian.[14]

Bonhoeffer's letters were in fact keenly aware of the grandeur as well as the misery of the church, and there is a strong suggestion that he intended to relate the secret discipline to the place of the church in the world come of age. More often than not, he was sharply critical of the self-understanding of the church, particularly that of his own. As early as 1930, Bonhoeffer spoke of a necessity for 'silence', in order not to hide behind programmes, resolutions, and pious Christian principles.[15] In the *Ethics*, and especially in the prison letters, the reformation of the church (or rather, as he liked to put it, the preparing of the way for God's reformation), always lurked in the background.[16] When he turned to a direct treatment of this theme, however, Bonhoeffer was not very helpful in indicating how this reformation would be implemented. One thinks of the well-known, eccentric conclusion to his 'Outline for a Book': '. . . As a fresh start the church should give away all her endowments to the poor and needy. The clergy should live solely on the free-will offerings of their congregations, or possibly engage in some secular calling. She must take her part in the social life of the world . . .'[17]

There can be no doubt that in proposing a secret discipline and a non-religious Christianity Bonhoeffer had the renewal of the church somewhere in his mind and was committed to this task with no less than his whole heart. And yet, one is uneasy with too-confident and too-ready assertions that the realm of the secret discipline is ecclesiology, devotional life, and liturgy such as one finds elaborated in *Life Together*. Bonhoeffer simply raised too many questions which would seriously affect what was written in *Life Together* after the conclusion of the *Bruderhaus* experiment and his book. *Life Together* was closely identified with *The Cost of Discipleship* and therefore lies in the same strange shadow of the 'claim to space' with which Bonhoeffer chose to fight the church struggle. He suggested in his prison letters that *The Cost of Discipleship* needed to be rewritten in view of his affirmation of the coming of age of the world.[18] *Life*

Together would have had to await that revision, just as the original *had* to be preceded by *The Cost of Discipleship*. Any attempt to foreshorten or reverse the order of Bonhoeffer's thinking (or the thinking of any who wish to take up and carry forward Bonhoeffer's ideas) violates what Bonhoeffer called 'waiting on God's time'.

The important problem would have been, of course, what meaning might be attributed to such statements as 'Christ exists as the church', 'outside of the church there is no salvation' or 'the church is the community of revelation', once Christ has been affirmed as the Lord of a non-religious world come of age. Can even the secret discipline help us here, without leading us to the conservative restoration Bonhoeffer feared? The place and purpose of the church and her liturgy would have had to await the construction of a new ecclesiology which would deal with the problem of revelation – and Bonhoeffer has not left enough evidence behind to serve even as the roughest sketch of that ecclesiology. In his view, this problem had to wait while more pressing problems were considered. We too must wait, and press ahead with other matters. We will not be helped by seizing eagerly upon the notion of the secret discipline as an answer to questions we have not yet fully asked or understood; nor should we proceed with any illusions that with the best of intentions, Bonhoeffer's thoughts on non-religious Christianity represent no ultimate threat to the nature and structure of the church.

The theme of the church and its place in the religionless world directs us towards the concept Bonhoeffer suggested as a partner for the secret discipline: his distinction between ultimate and penultimate. Our discussion of this aspect of our problem is best carried out by reminding ourselves that the church is, after all, the church of the Word, of proclamation. In saying this we cannot help conversing with that all-pervading present day theological concern for the problem of *hermeneutics*.

2. '. . . Finding new, stammering words for the Word of God'; 'a groping rediscovery of what Christian faith really means' – this is how Gerhard Ebeling defines the hermeneutical endeavour which today has become in some quarters almost a

synonym for theology itself.[19] The problem of theology is *speech*:
what we shall say and how we shall say it, what has been said
and how it may again be said. Bonhoeffer's concern has undoubted affinities with the problem of hermeneutics. We shall
have to direct special attention to the question whether the
search for a 'new language' so closely resembles Bonhoeffer's
interrupted investigations that we may say that the hermeneutical concern is the legitimate – perhaps even the sole – heir
to his deliberations.

Early in his career, Bonhoeffer differentiated between 'qualified speech – the risk of unconditional, blind obedience to the
commandment of God', and 'qualified silence', waiting until
the time is ripe before speaking or, as he was later to speak of it,
'waiting upon God's time'.[20] The *Ethics* took a special interest
in qualified silence, just as *The Cost of Discipleship* was interested
especially in qualified speech. Qualified silence becomes the
question of the 'warrant for ethical discourse'. Each word,
Bonhoeffer wrote, does not belong in each mouth at every time.
'The ethical is tied to a definite time and place,' because everything in historical existence has its own time.[21] Not to understand and affirm this is 'to injure and destroy the creaturely
wholeness of life. To confine the ethical phenomenon to its
proper time and place is not to invalidate it; it is, on the contrary, to render it fully operative. Big guns are not the right
weapons for shooting sparrows.'[22] In certain circumstances the
better way to serve this 'qualitatively ultimate' concept may be
to refrain from treating it as a theme at all, 'because it goes
without saying'.[23] Bonhoeffer really did wish to find room in
theology for 'going without saying' as regards ultimate matters –
for silence as a means of saying a great deal when to speak
would be to profane. Using an illustration from a pastoral
counselling situation, he asked:

. . . why it is that precisely in thoroughly grave situations, for instance
when I am with someone who has suffered a bereavement, I often decide
to adopt a 'penultimate' attitude, particularly when I am dealing with
Christians, remaining silent as a sign that I share in the bereaved man's
helplessness in the face of such a grievous event, and not speaking the
biblical words of comfort which are, in fact, known to me and available to

me. . . . Does one not, in some cases, by remaining deliberately in the penultimate perhaps point all the more genuinely to the ultimate, which God will speak in his own time . . .?[24]

Here we are confronted with Bonhoeffer's famous distinction between ultimate and penultimate and his appreciation of the penultimate as a genuine and forgotten sphere of theological investigation. It was this appreciation which led him to his affirmation of worldly life in the prison letters, and he referred specifically in the prison letters to 'the distinction (which you have met with me before) between ultimate and penultimate'[25] as a concept which could be related to the secret discipline. The ultimate must neither be confused with the penultimate nor forgotten altogether. But there is an appropriate time and place for silence as regards the ultimate, and the suggestion is that a world come of age is such a time. Unless it can be interpreted in the form of the penultimate – worldly life – the ultimate must 'go without saying'. Dogmatic theology with its religious language, apologetic theology with its religious *a priori*, ecclesiology and the cultus – these are relegated to the realm of silence and secrecy.

Of course, the dialectic of worldly life/secret discipline calls for speaking as well as for silence. No mystical quiescence or stoic submission is meant; the 'discipline' consists not in keeping the secret but in keeping it from profanation. Bold experimentation is necessary, as Daniel Jenkins reminds us[26] – bold speech which will risk *naïveté*, stammering speech which will be uncertain and incomplete, speech which will prove to be improper and which will therefore have to be discarded in favour of new experimentation. No doubt much more of Bultmann's demythologizing is called for than Bonhoeffer thought necessary. Theologians must speak in order to determine how far into the forms of the world come of age the church can and should go without losing sight of the ultimate, and to what extent she can take up the forms of worldliness without the religious *a priori* and without profaning the secrets she attempts to interpret. But above all, in Alec Vidler's words, 'Christians should restrain their spate of words, their pious and theological jargon, and keep quiet until they have proved in their commerce with the life of the world which of their words ring true.'[27]

With this there is suggested a corrective for the direction in which the hermeneutical discussion seems headed at the present time. The search for 'principles of interpretation' should include a reverence and respect which has often been lacking in any confrontation with the Bible and biblical concepts. At least two contemporary theologians conversant with the problem of hermeneutics have recognized a tendency on the part of interpreters to speak before listening; a compulsive desire to begin interpreting before first having heard. Oscar Cullmann, while admitting the difficulty of his position (since it would seem to be impossible to approach the biblical texts *without* some hermeneutical principle) has reflected Bonhoeffer's concern for 'waiting to hear what God will say to us', for 'going without saying', in a passage introducing the third German edition of *Christ and Time*:

> . . . I regard the non-violation of the limits imposed on the New Testament scholar in studying New Testament texts as precisely a *theological* duty applicable to all, not only to the scholars: first, before all evaluation, all judging, perhaps even prior to all 'being addressed' in 'my understanding of existence', prior to all believing, simply to be obedient to what the men of the new covenant want to communicate to me as revelation, even if it is quite foreign to me. I am aware that I thereby stand in contradiction to a 'hermeneutical' trend widely prevalent today . . .[28]

Here is the awareness, however difficult to articulate and however unmodern and conservative it might seem, that the text in its original form is in some way 'the thing itself', that to understand it, one must be willing to do without the question of language for a time: to hear, and to wait. The ultimate is not some universal religious truth which is confronted with the *kerygma* only so that we might prove that the two are, after all, identical. However reactionary such a suggestion may seem, one confronts the Bible as the 'Word of God', and it is *this*, in its unchangeable form, one is seeking to understand and to interpret.

One needs also a certain sense of balance which ought to be but has not been presupposed in the present-day struggle for 'understanding'. What is in the Bible, no doubt because it is in some manner God's Word but also simply because it is foreign and past history, cannot be subjected to one's force and control. Ernst Käsemann has recognized the danger which comes of forgetting this in a recent remark:

The mistakes of historians and interpreters and the misunderstanding of the neighbour belong very much together, are not in the least merely the result of stupidity, and indeed prove that one is victim of a short circuit when one makes what is foreign in a contemporary or past history into something objective in the sense of being subject to our control. I regard the confusion of understanding and decision as no less dangerous. The assumed compulsion of having always to take a stand, rather than first hearing for once and waiting for what is given or taken by that which is foreign, is usually the death of understanding, the strangling of the real question, a chance missed to grow by learning. How many of our students still perceive that understanding is always a process of one's growth, and hence requires time and leisure even to the extent of self-forgetfulness; that only unripe fruit is shaken from the tree of knowledge by him who does not himself ripen in the handwork of the historian's trade? The cardinal virtue of the historian and the beginning of all meaningful hermeneutic is for me the practice of hearing, which begins simply by letting what is historically foreign maintain its validity and does not regard rape as the basic form of *engagement*.[29]

3. When Bonhoeffer speaks explicitly on the subject of the secret discipline in relation to the non-religious interpretation of biblical concepts, he seems to mean that the traditional and historical exposition of the Christian faith must be preserved – or at least respected – not in spite of but as an indispensable part of the interpretation itself. But if one looks at the prison letters in their entirety, a wider reference for the concept emerges. If certain related passages were to be extracted and assembled, one would be tempted to entitle the collection 'the secret discipline'. We are not speaking primarily of Bonhoeffer's reports of his devotional activity, nor of his meditations upon *Losungen* or biblical themes, although these would undoubtedly be included in the collection. What would appear as the central theme would be the description and affirmation of a particular style or attitude which one's life assumes in the midst of one's this-worldly existence. This style or attitude might be called a Christian 'way of life', although the word 'way' might better describe the secularity common to all men and 'style' the special marks those men who are also Christian would bear.

Jacques Ellul has put it in the spirit of Bonhoeffer though more traditionally: the Christian is 'the citizen of another kingdom, and it is thence that he derives his way of thinking, judging, and feeling'.[30] Certainly the Christian participates in the secular condition common to all men, but he receives it not on its own terms, but only as it is taken up and affirmed in Christ, his Lord. To preserve this sense of 'having received', a secret discipline is necessary, 'a kind of *cantus firmus* to which the other melodies of life provide the counterpoint'.[31] Although this is related to justification and sanctification and to a concept of revelation, it cannot finally be set into the framework of traditional theological discussion of these notions – nor of the cultus, nor of ecclesiology.

It is a kind of humorous, humble, self-effacing secrecy of devotion and hope, which finds no counterpart in the visible world, nothing in symbol or gesture by which it may be fully reflected and expressed; nothing in the cult or ritual which may presume to take its place. . . . Bonhoeffer was looking past these things to the form for his faith which could actually meet the world, actually be in it, without reserve, as Christ was in it. . . . That faith itself rested on the sketchy and strange tradition within Christianity of secrecy, exclusiveness, fastidiousness, which has never received great prominence. . . . It is the tradition whose origins lie in the same region as the origins of the doctrine of election; but it has a different bent and outcome. 'Cast not your pearls before swine'; 'shake off the dust of that city from your feet'; 'this is my body': these are all sayings which presuppose, indeed demand, a kind of initiation and secrecy which clearly forbids the intrusion of the curious or the self-certain. The words of Christ are for all, indeed, and the powerful strain of universalism has swept Christianity along many triumphant lines. Paul's equally powerful stress on the givenness, the gift, of God's grace, combines with this universalism to keep the idea of secrecy and exclusiveness from too great prominence in Christian history. Nevertheless it is there, and the simplicities of the Gospel, the call to be humble, and unostentatious in prayer, never using naked power, but always service, and sacrifice, are both its sustenance and its preservative.[32]

The secret discipline endeavours to preserve and give direction to a faith 'whose perfection consists in not professing itself, or rather, which confirms its reality not by assertion but by submission'.[33] To accomplish this kind of faith in the world come of age, a discipline is necessary, a steadfast determination not to belong to the world even as one lives in and for the world with all one's being and although one cannot speak except as a participant in the conditions of the world. Faith and life are affirmed anew each day, from outside of oneself – indeed, one must say it; from outside of the world and of one's neighbour – even though that affirmation will be delivered through what Luther called 'masks of God', the things of this world.

The basis for this discipline is, once again, Christological. The dialogue of faith between the secret discipline and worldly existence is 'the depth and inwardness of the affliction with which Christ was afflicted';[34] with which Christ loved the world at the same time that he wept over its sin and evil and hopelessness. The Christian affirms 'the secret of the humiliation of God'.[35]

The centre of the *arcanum*, the real 'secret', cannot be thought of otherwise than as the hiddenness of God in his sufferings. . . . What else could the contents of the *'secrets'* of Christian faith be, than the suffering of God in the world hidden in the revealed suffering of Jesus Christ? In other words: the *arcanum* has to do with the messianic secret of Jesus, that he who suffers in the world is Lord of the world.[36]

The source of strength which enables the Christian to live in and for the world come of age, to live a worldly life within that world and to share in Christ's Lordship over it, is hidden with God in Christ. It is real and positive. But it is manifested only indirectly, through powerlessness, submission, and the discipline and humility of holding one's peace.

With these words we have already begun discussion of 'sharing in the sufferings of God', the general description of the faith and life of the Christian in the world come of age.

Sharing in the Sufferings of God

Martin Luther once described the making of a theologian as 'living, nay rather dying and being damned . . . not understanding, reading, or speculating'.[37] The complement to this profound statement may well be the sentence which first appears in a letter in July 1944: 'Man is challenged to participate in the sufferings of God at the hands of a godless world.'

Not only the theologian, Bonhoeffer seems to be saying, but theology itself will be reconstructed by means of this participation in God's sufferings. Any 'non-religious interpretation' will have as its starting point an affirmation of the godless, religionless world and the suffering of God within such a world, and it will succeed to the extent to which the theologian and his theology participate in these sufferings. Indeed, an understanding of revelation itself, of the meaning of Christ for us today, will take shape as one shares in the sufferings of God in the life of the godless world.

Bonhoeffer evidently looked upon this formula as the consummation of his thinking in the prison letters. It embraces the this-sided nature of the Christian life of faith as well as the description of the mature world as 'godless'. Once more, a this-worldly life is made possible through adherence to Christ, who is described by means of a Christology in which his life with men and his suffering and death have at last 'merged into a single vision, both acting as signs of God's being for the world'.[38]

We should set the relevant passages before us, referring first to the conclusion of the lengthy letter of 16th July (quoted above in Chapter 14) and continuing below with major portions of the letters of 18th and 21st July:

Man is challenged to participate in the sufferings of God at the hands of a godless world. He must therefore really live in the godless world, without attempting to gloss over or explain its ungodliness in some religious way or other. He must live in a 'worldly' fashion and in just this way participate in the sufferings of God. He *may* live in a 'worldly' fashion, i.e. he is freed from false religious restrictions and bondage. To be a Christian does not mean to be religious in a particular way, to make something out of oneself (a sinner, penitent, or saint) on the basis of some method or other, but to be a man – not a type of man but the man Christ creates in us. It is not the religious act which makes a Christian, but participation in the sufferings of God in worldly life.

That is *metanoia*: not in meditation upon one's own problems, questions, anxiety, but by allowing oneself to be caught up on the way of Jesus Christ, in the messianic event, is Isaiah 53 fulfilled! . . . This being caught up in the messianic sufferings of God in Jesus Christ takes a variety of forms in the New Testament. . . . The one thing they have in common is participation in the sufferings of God in Christ. That is their 'faith'.

There is nothing of religious method here. The 'religious act' is always something partial; faith is something whole, an act of one's life. Jesus does not call men to a new religion, but to life. What does this life look like – this life of participation in the powerlessness of God in the world? I will write about that next time, I hope.

Just one more point for today. If one would speak in a 'non-religious' fashion of God, then one must speak of him in such a way that the godlessness of the world is not somehow glossed over, but indeed is just in this way exposed and a surprising light is thrown upon it. The world come of age is godless and therefore perhaps closer to God than the world which had not come of age.

During the last year or so I have come to know and understand the this-sidedness of Christianity as never before. The Christian is not a *homo religiosus*, but simply a man, like Jesus was a man, in distinction to John the Baptist. I don't mean the shallow and banal this-sidedness of the enlightened, the busy, the comfortable, or the lascivious, but a deep this-sidedness, which is cultivated and in which the knowledge of death and resurrection is ever present. I think that Luther lived such a this-sided existence.

I remember a conversation I had with a young French pastor at A. thirteen years ago. We asked ourselves, quite simply, the question what we really wanted to do with our lives. Then he said he wanted to become a saint (I think it possible he did become one). At the time I was very m pressed. Nevertheless, I argued with him and said something to the effect that I wished to learn to believe. For a long time I didn't understand the depth of our disagreement. I thought I could learn to believe by trying to live a holy life something like that. At the end of this path I wrote *The Cost of Discipleship*. Today I see clearly the dangers of this book – although, of course, I still stand by what I wrote as before.

Later I discovered and am still discovering up to this hour that it is only in the full this-sidedness of life that one learns to believe. When one has completely abandoned every attempt to make something of oneself, whether it be a saint, a converted sinner, a churchman (a so-called priestly type!), a righteous man or an unrighteous one, a sick man or a healthy one – and this is what I mean by this-sidedness: living to the full the duties and problems, successes and helplessness – then one throws oneself completely into the arms of God, then one takes seriously not his own sufferings but the sufferings of God in the world, then one watches with Christ in Gethsemane. And I think that is faith, that is *metanoia* and that is how one becomes a man and a Christian (cf. Jer. 45!). How can success make us arrogant or failure lead us astray when we participate in the sufferings of God in a this-sided life?[39]

It is Bonhoeffer's use of the term 'suffering' that led Barth to speak of this particular version of the theme of the imitation of Christ as indebted to 'the melancholy theology of the north

German plains'. Barth is not alone in finding in Bonhoeffer's picture of the Christian life, as in his Christology, a note of Kierkegaardian *tristitia*. In speaking of the ethic of sacrifice and living for others which Bonhoeffer left behind him as the culmination of his theology, W. W. Bartley questions whether he cannot be charged with the 'moral masochism' Karen Horney finds prevalent in the Christian consciousness of western man.[40] But we know enough about Bonhoeffer's mistrust of Kierkegaard, existentialism and introspection to know that there can hardly be a fascination with the morbid here, a refusal to participate in the full joys of life because of an obsession with sacrifice in any ascetic sense. Bonhoeffer has in mind an aesthetic-moral attitude of receiving and bearing one's world in freedom. To suffer means to forbear, to submit, to place one's cause, whether for blessing or for a cross, unreservedly and without anxiety in the hands of God.[41] Bonhoeffer would have liked Ellul's description of the Christian life as 'agonistic', with that word's original sense of 'contestant' or 'combative'. But unlike Ellul, he would have linked this to the Incarnation of God in Christ, pointing to Christ's own existence in the world as 'agonistic'. It is in the suffering of *God in Christ* that one participates, Christ's 'affliction'. At its lowest estimate, Bonhoeffer's phrase may be coupled with the words of H. Richard Niebuhr: 'The story of Jesus, and particularly of his passion, is the great illustration that enables us to say, "What we are now doing and suffering is like this."'[42] Bonhoeffer himself wrote, in August, that '. . . if the world was worthy of bearing the man Jesus Christ, if a man like Jesus lived, then and only then has our own life meaning. Had Jesus not lived, then in spite of all the other men whom we know, honour and love, our lives would be meaningless.'[43]

Is it sufficient simply to speak of Bonhoeffer's final comments on Jesus as indicative of the 'illustrative' meaning of Jesus for the Christian life? By referring to the relationship of the disciple to his Lord as a participation in the sufferings of God in Christ, Bonhoeffer may well have begun once more to describe an *imitatio Christi*, such as Barth found in the prison letters. That Bonhoeffer was moving in this direction, perhaps deliberately, cannot be doubted when one considers the projected second chapter of the 'Outline for a Book', which appeared in August and which we have cited previously.[44] Encounter with Jesus' 'being for others' as 'the reversal of all human being' is the experience of transcendence. 'Faith is the participation in this being of Jesus,' 'man living out of the transcendent'.

Bonhoeffer wished in 1930 to overcome the problem of act *versus* being in revelation 'in Christ', but in Christ who exists as the church. We saw how his Christology and the tropological formula of *The Cost of Discipleship* and *Life Together* produced a dynamic process rooted in meditation upon the scriptures, where Christ meets the believer and empowers him to fulfil his commands. But now one participates in Christ's being for others in the setting of worldly life. The 'space' of the church has been replaced by the archimedian point of the secret discipline which remains hidden and secret, while Christ is met and revelation is concrete in 'this-sidedness', the life of the world. By participating in Christ's being-for-others in worldly life, by encountering him there in the joys and sorrows, successes and failures of life in the world in which he lived and which he redeems through his incarnation, crucifixion, and resurrection, the Christian 'shares in the sufferings of God at the hands of a godless world'.

What form will this identification with Christ in the world come of age actually assume? First and foremost, it will take the form of a kind of identification with the *world*. A secret discipline may enable one to retrace one's steps when they have proved errant in order to begin afresh, but it cannot in and of itself recover the meaning of Christ in a world come of age. What is needed is an entry into the life of the world so complete that one's Christian presuppositions and answers, when they must be present, are powerless and tentative. 'Christ for us today' can be found only in the world, and the 'religious' barriers which keep one from one's neighbours must be broken down. This identification with the godless world must be a real one. Following Bonhoeffer, Daniel Jenkins writes:

The guiding principle for Christians in this realm is that of identification. They will recognize that they are part of the world Christ came to save and that they cannot participate in his saving act unless they do so at those

241

places in the world where they live alongside their fellows, whether their fellows bear a Christian name or not, and where they have to take those decisions which are most significant for their own lives and for the lives of others who depend upon them.

God must be obeyed not merely in what men call the church but also in what they call the world – in men's politics, business, industry and all the other spheres of human activity and association in which their lives are lived. And he must be obeyed not by considering how life in these spheres must be related to life in the institutions of the church, nor by turning the questions which confront men in their living experience into 'religious' questions, nor even by raising the 'Christian' issue in relation to them in a self-conscious way.[45]

'God must be obeyed' may and must read: 'Christ is to be found.' Finding Christ through this identification can only be accomplished through the cultivation of a this-worldly life which accepts full responsibility for the world's history, structures, laws, and influences; recognizing their power to destroy men but seeing in them a capacity to create as well. The Christian's first duty, Ellul reminds us, is to 'regard himself on the level of other men, with them subject to the same laws, to the same influences, to the same despair. . . . He ought to consider himself in this world, whose inner structure he perceives as involved in this civilization, moved by it, dependent on it, but also, perhaps, capable of altering it.'[46]

Here there can be no escape into the transcendent, no flight to the *deus ex machina* as the only solution to insoluble problems. It was the experience of this truth in his own involvement in the history of his country which led Bonhoeffer to make this responsibility axiomatic for any understanding of Christian faith and life:

It is only by refusing to allow any event to deprive us of our responsibility for history, because we know that is a responsibility laid upon us by God, that we shall achieve a relation to the events of history far more fruitful than criticism or opportunism. To talk about going down fighting like heroes in face of certain defeat is not really heroic at all, but a failure to face up to the future. The ultimate question the man of responsibility asks is not, How can I extricate myself from the affair? but, How is the coming generation to live?[47]

By speaking of 'identification with' and 'being responsible for' the world, it might be thought that what is required is more active Christian participation in secular, political, social, and economic life. No doubt this will have to occur. But it is only a part of the problem, and by no means the major part. Bonhoeffer hinted several times in the prison letters and throughout the *Ethics* that true identification and responsibility is the shaping of one's life in the tension between being fully in the world and deriving one's ways of thinking, judging, and feeling from another kingdom which claims one's ultimate allegiance. He would have applauded Ellul's remark that 'in a civilization which has lost the meaning of life, the most useful thing a Christian can do is to *live*, and life, understood from this point of view of faith, has an extraordinary force'.[48] Both Bonhoeffer and Ellul stress the 'apologetical' nature of the Christian life: the former speaks of 'the importance of human example' which gives the Word emphasis and power, the latter of living as a sign of the new covenant in Jesus Christ.[49] What is meant is not piety nor ethics, but a 'style' of life of such quality that it leads men to God:

Christians ought to try to create a style of life which does not differentiate them from others, but yet permits them to escape from the stifling pressure of our present form of civilization. . . . The only successful way to attack these features of our modern civilization is to 'give them the slip', to learn how to live on the edge of this totalitarian society, not simply rejecting it, but passing it through the sieve of God's judgement.[50]

In learning to live and in actually living such a life one allows for a confrontation between the secret discipline, which makes possible and obligatory an existence in the world, and the godless world come of age itself. This confrontation, this dialectical tension gives the Christian life its distinctiveness by moulding it into a particular shape and guiding it in a particular direction. The truth of the incarnation, crucifixion, and resurrection of Christ, the Lordship of Christ, is proclaimed by the living of such a life.

What this 'being in Christ' entails, what the content of this 'holy worldliness'[51] will be necessitates a great amount of involvement, reflection, and confession. Certainly it will mean different things to different people, and the comparing of 'notes' will be of the utmost importance as each Christian attempts to determine the degree to which his own life must be aesthetic or intellectual, simple or complex, meditative or occupied. Perhaps a new concept of 'Christ existing as the church' will emerge out of just this 'comparing of notes'. In any event, and although there were times when Bonhoeffer thought that the Christian life in this generation would have to remain fragmentary and strive simply to endure rather than to shape itself,[52] he found it possible to suggest certain marks of such a life upon which one could focus. Speaking to a circle of friends who shared his tradition and interests, he expressed his hope that a new, liberalized 'aristocracy' might emerge, one which would rediscover a sense of 'equality', of 'reserve between man and man':

Socially it implies the cessation of all place-hunting, of the cult of the star'; an open eye both upwards and downwards, especially in the choice of one's more intimate friends, and pleasure in private life as well as the courage of a public life. Culturally it means a return from the newspaper and the radio to the book, from feverish activity to unhurried leisure, from dissipation to recollection, from sensationalism to reflection, from virtuosity to art, from snobbery to modesty, from extravagance to moderation.[53]

Whatever the marks of such a Christian life, they will be determined by an encounter with Christ as 'the reversal of all human value'. One lives and learns to live by participating in the revelation which one has both received and has yet to receive; to find Christ in the world while one rejoices in the certainty that he already has been found and has found us there; to confess to and to identify with those who have not received, because Christ in his worldliness identifies with them even as he blesses those of us who have received.

From living and describing such lives lived in imitation of Christ, 'lives based on the transcendent', Bonhoeffer foresaw the renewal of theology and the church. A chapter in the book Bonhoeffer did not live to write was to deal with the nature of 'a life based upon the transcendent', a life for others. It was to be followed by: '(c) This as the starting point for the reinterpretation of bliblical terminology. (Creation, fall, atonement, repentance, faith, the new life, the last things.)'[54]

Upon the ability of Christian theology to rediscover what she can and may say about revelation in terms of the life Christ lives and to which he calls men, upon the ability of Christians really to *live* redeemed lives before men in this world, will depend the future shape of Christianity and its hope for the world.

We have followed the path of Bonhoeffer's theology from his early 'Christ existing as the church' to the breaking down of the limitations of his ecclesiological doctrine of revelation and of Christ in the *Ethics*, and to the final affirmation of the this-sidedness of Christ and the Christian life in a world come of age.

A systematization of his theological ideas would be the last thing Bonhoeffer would have wanted. His work is and must remain fragmentary – that is how he speaks and must speak to us, in 'fragments which must be fragments', which afford us but a glimpse of 'the way in which the whole was planned and conceived, and of what material he was building with or should have used had he lived'.[55] To have known that his work provided us with such a glimpse and has thus made a lasting contribution to the renewal of theology and the disclosure of 'Christ for us today' would have gratified him deeply. Our task is to strike our tents and to go forth into the region which he sketched crudely but did not live to enter. If we should have the courage to do so, that too will be due in great measure to the life and work of this astonishing, disturbing, and comforting man.

APPENDIX

Appendix

I. Translation of letters from Bonhoeffer concerning the 'demythologizing' controversy.

1. To Ernst Wolf, 24th March 1942. GS III, *pp.45–6.* . . . I am very happy about the new Bultmann volume. The intellectual honesty of his work always impresses me. I hear that a short time ago, D. took you and Bultmann apart in the Berlin circle in a pretty stupid fashion, and that the circle, as I hear it, came within a hair's breadth of protesting to you about Bultmann's theology! And that from the Berliners, of all people! I'd like to know whether any of them has worked through his commentary on John. The arrogant self-conceit that flourishes here – I think under the influence of some pompous asses – is a real pity for the Confessing Church . . .

*2. To a friend, 25th March 1942. Unpublished.** . . . Now about Bultmann: I am among those who hailed his writing – not because I agree with it, I regret his double point of departure

* . . . Nun zu Bultmann: ich gehöre zu denen, die seine Schrift begrüsst haben; nicht weil ich ihr zustimme, ich bedaure den doppelten Ansatz in ihr (das Argument von Joh. 1. 14 und vom Radio her sollte nicht vermischt werden, dabei halte ich auch das zweite für ein Argument, nur müsste die Trennung klarer sein), soweit bin ich also vielleicht noch ein Schuler Harnack's geblieben. Grob gesagt: Bultmann hat die Katze aus dem Sack gelassen, nicht nur für sich, sondern für sehr viele (die liberale Katze aus dem Bekenntnissack) und darüber freue ich mich. Er hat gewagt zu sagen, was viele in sich verdrängen (ich schliesse mich ein), ohne es überwunden zu haben. Er hat damit der intellektuellen Sauberkeit und Redlichkeit einen Dienst geleistet. Der Glaubenspharisäismus der nun dagegen von vielen Brüdern aufgeboten wird, ist mir fatal. Nun muss Rede und Antwort gestanden werden. Ich spräche gern mit Bultmann darüber und möchte mich der Zugluft, die von ihm kommt, gern aussetzen. Aber das Fenster muss dann auch wieder geschlossen werden. Sonst erkälten sich die Anfälligen zu leicht.

Wenn Du Bultmann siehst, grüsse ihn doch bitte von mir . . .

(the argument from John 1. 14 and from the radio ought not to be confused; I too, think the second is an argument, it's just that the separation must be clearer). In this much, I have perhaps remained a student of Harnack's. Putting it crudely: Bultmann has let the cat out of the bag, not only for himself, but for very many (i.e. the Liberal cat out of the Confessing Church bag), and I am happy about it. He has dared to say what many repress in themselves (I include myself), without having faced the issues. In this way he has done intellectual integrity and purity a service. The pharisaism of faith which, on the other hand, many of the brothers are calling upon, seems to me unfortunate. Speaking and answering are in order. I would gladly speak to Bultmann about it and set myself in the draught which blows from his direction. But then the window will have to be shut once more. Otherwise the susceptible will catch cold too easily.

If you see Bultmann, please give him my greetings. . . . Tell him that I would be glad to see him, and how I see things . . .

II. From a Letter of Karl Barth to Landessuperintendent P. W. Herrenbrück, 21st December 1952. MW I, *pp.121-2.*

. . . The letters, whatever one may make of their individual sentences (and I have let them work on me once again in their whole context since the beginning of your correspondence), are a particular thorn; to let them excite us can only do us all good – for, unlike 'demythologizing', this is unrest of a spiritual kind.

What an open and rich and at the same time deep and disturbing man stands before us – somehow shaming and comforting us at the same time. That is how I also personally remember him. An aristocratic Christian, one might say, who seemed to run on ahead in the most varied dimensions. That is why I always read his earlier writings, especially those which apparently or in reality said things which were not at once clear to me, with the thought that – when they were seen round some corner or other – he might be right. So too with these letters, parts of which of course astonish me too. One cannot read them without having the impression that there might be something in them. You are therefore certainly right to call your pastors' attention to them and to make some suggestions about their meaning.

But as always with Bonhoeffer one is faced by a peculiar difficulty. He was – how shall I put it? – an impulsive, visionary thinker who was suddenly seized by an idea to which he gave lively form, and then after a time he called a halt (one never knew whether it was final or temporary) with some provisional last point or other. Was this not the case with *The Cost of Discipleship*? Did he not also for a time have liturgical impulses – And how was it with the 'Mandates' of his *Ethics*, with which I tussled when I wrote [*Dogmatics*] III/4? Do we not always expect him to be clearer and more concise in some other context, either by withdrawing what he said, or by going even further? Now he has left us alone with the enigmatic utterances of his letters – at more than one point clearly showing that he sensed, without really knowing, how the story should continue – for example, what exactly he meant by the 'positivism of revelation' he found in me, and especially how the programme of an unreligious speech was to be realized.

As to the first, I have certainly been disturbed by the question of when and where I have asked anyone to 'take' or 'leave' the virgin birth, and by the question of what my neo-Calvinist well-wishers in Holland would think of me portrayed as a 'positivist of revelation'. But I am somewhat embarrassed by the thought that so sensible and well-meaning a man as Bonhoeffer somehow remembered my books (which he certainly did not have with him in his prison cell) in terms of this enigmatic expression. The hope remains that in heaven at least he has not reported about me to *all* the angels (including the church fathers, etc.) with just this expression. But perhaps I have indeed on occasion behaved and expressed myself 'positivistically', and if this is so then Bonhoeffer's recollections have brought it to light. Without being able to ask him personally, we shall have to make do with remaining behind, somewhat confused.

Similarly with the postulate of unreligious speech. I think that you have dealt rather too severely with him when (on your page 9) you tend to explain this in terms of existentialism, pre-understanding, etc. On the other hand you are right to indicate that he did not show any sign of putting the *kerygma* into 'other words', that is, doing what in practice Bultmann ends up with. Can he really have meant anything other than a warning against all unthought-out repetition of biblical and traditional images, phrases, and combinations of ideas, meaningless to the 'world' because the 'religious' speaker or writer does not think at all, or does not think properly, about what he is saying? But in the opinion that the stuff will somehow be God's Word he just lets fly – in much the same style as you will find happening about now – oh, I don't mean it in a bad sense, and how many of us really have the time and capacity to think things out in an orderly way? – under thousands of Christmas trees?

Certainly, Bonhoeffer has left us nothing tangible in this respect, and I almost think that it was not tangible to him either. What then remains for us but to take the best from him – in the way I have indicated or in some other way – without searching for a deeper meaning which he himself did not offer us, and perhaps had not even thought through himself? And what he says about sharing in the suffering of God, and so on, seems to me to be clearly a variation of the idea of *imitatio* which he rightly stressed. Why should one not allow onself to be addressed like this by a man of whom it was asked and to whom it was also given that he not only thought it and said it, but also lived it? It has long been clear to me that I will have to devote a lot of room to this matter in the *Church Dogmatics*. Was it Bonhoeffer's view that the whole of theology must be put on this basis? It is possible that in his cell he did at times think this. But again he has left us no clues about details and about how he regarded the questions which touch upon his thesis. Well, you understand that I do not want to dismiss him when I ascribe to him, 'more or less', as one so nicely puts it, what I call 'the melancholy theology of the North German plain'. I am thankful enough that I myself lived there for fifteen years, and that I have absorbed a good deal of this Lutheran melancholy. That is how I understand Bultmann, too. But it is not yet clear, and neither Bultmann nor Bonhoeffer has been successful in making it clear, that we have to look for the last word in this direction.

None of this is meant as criticism of your concern with Bonhoeffer. All you have said has to be pondered. A lessening of the offence he has provided for us would be the last thing I should wish . . .

NOTES

Notes

(Abbreviations are listed on p.298)

Chapter 1: Biography

1. Readers already acquainted with Bonhoeffer's life will find little that is new in this brief sketch, and are referred to Bethge, 'Challenge', *passim*; Godsey, *passim*; and G. Leibholz, 'Memoir', in CD; Ved Mehta, 'The New Theologian, III; Pastor Bonhoeffer', in *The New Yorker*, 27th November 1965, pp. 70-123. The primary source material is available in the five volumes of GS. Eberhard Bethge is presently preparing an extensive biography.

2. 22nd April 1944. *Letters*, p. 88.

3. *Sigmund Freud, Life and Work*. Vol. II, London, 1955. p. 279.

4. *Zeittafel*, GS II. Bonhoeffer could and did refer to his family connections in order to commend his own patriotism, especially when his movements were restricted in 1940 and again in 1943. Cf. GS II, pp. 363-6 and 'Report on Prison Life', *Letters*, p. 184.

5. Bonhoeffer's eldest brother, Walter, was killed in the First World War. Karl Friedrich became a biochemist and survived his brothers, dying in 1957. Klaus, a legal adviser to Lufthansa, was executed for his part in the resistance against Hitler, as were his brothers-in-law Hans von Dohnanyi (a lawyer who worked in various advisory capacities for the government) and Rüdiger Schleicher (a senior civil servant and legal adviser with the Air Ministry).

6. 'Challenge', p. 4. As Bethge remarks in his preface to GS III, Bonhoeffer never forgot his debt to Nietzsche and seemed particularly moved by the latter's use of the story of the giant Antaeus, who was invincible as long as his feet remained on the ground, drawing strength from the earth. In an early essay on Christian ethics, Bonhoeffer refers to the story, and he returned to it in one of his last writings, an uncompleted drama which he sketched in Tegel in 1943. Bonhoeffer's partners in conversation also stimulated his interest in sociology which concerned him so much in his dissertation a few years later.

7. 'Challenge', pp. 4, 7. Cf. also Bethge's interesting comparison of the backgrounds of Bonhoeffer and Paul Tillich as it reflected in their later work in *ibid.*, pp. 35-6, and H. C. von Hase, *Begriff und Wirklichkeit der Kirche in der Theologie Dietrich Bonhoeffers*, MW I, p. 27.

8. *Sanctorum Communio: eine dogmatische Untersuchung zur Soziologie der Kirche*. Berlin, 1930 (Eng. tr. = SC).

257

9. *Akt und Sein: Transzendentalphilosophie und Ontologie in der systematischen Theologie.* Gütersloh, 1931. 2d. ed., Munich, 1955 (Eng. tr. = AB).
10. GS I, pp. 51–111.
11. GS I, pp. 323–54.
12. 22nd April 1944. *Letters*, p. 88.
13. *Rede zum Gedächtnis Adolf von Harnacks*, GS III, pp. 59–61.
14. Cf. 'Letter to Winifred' in the appendix to this study.
15. GS I, pp. 17–22.
16. Bethge, 'Challenge', p. 7: 'But there is no doubt that as far as this independent and creative mind opened itself to contemporary influence Bonhoeffer sided with none more readily than with Karl Barth.' Cf. Bonhoeffer's article explaining Barth's theology to Americans in 1930 ('The Theology of Crisis', GS III, pp. 110–26). The powerful effect of Barth's personality upon the younger man is evident in his letter exchanges with Bonhoeffer in GS II, especially the first exchange, December 1932–February 1933 (pp. 39–41). The correspondence in its entirety provides a lively history of the important events in Bonhoeffer's life prior to the war. Barth's violent letter of 20th November 1933 (pp. 134–7) demanding Bonhoeffer's immediate return to Berlin from London was almost certainly in Bonhoeffer's mind when he debated a return to Germany from safety in America in 1939. For Barth's final assessment of Bonhoeffer, cf. 'Letter from Karl Barth to Landessuperintendent P. Herrenbrück'. (In the Appendix to this study).
17. 'Challenge', pp. 5–6.
18. *Schöpfung und Fall*, Munich, 1937 (Eng. tr. = CF). The early theological work, is in GS III. The Christology lectures have been published in translation as *Christ the Centre*, London and New York, 1966.
19. GS II, pp. 19–21, 22–38.
20. '. . . this law applied to two married relatives of Bonhoeffer.' 'Challenge', p. 14.
21. *Ibid.* Cf. GS II, pp. 44–53, 62–9.
22. *Ibid.*, pp. 77–119.
23. *Ibid.*, pp. 120–204.
24. GS I, pp. 182–278; GS II, pp. 120–204.
25. 'Challenge', p. 14.
26. GS I, pp. 279–354; GS II, pp. 347–62.
27. GS II, p. 362.
28. *Ethik*, Munich, 1949 (Eng. tr. = *Ethics*).
29. Bethge, 'Challenge', p. 27. The various parts of the resistance movement in Germany were very poorly co-ordinated. Bonhoeffer was in contact with the more active 'Kreisau Circle' which existed even before the war and which sought, at various times, to take Hitler's life. Much of the activity of this and other segments of the resistance was carried out under the cloak of the Military Intelligence Service,

headed by Admiral Canaris who died at Bonhoeffer's side in 1945. After the failure of the famous 20th July 1944 *coup d'état* adherents of various resistance groups were, to use Hitler's own phrase, 'exterminated mercilessly'. Cf. G. V. S. Gaevernitz, ed., in F. von Schlabrendorff, *Revolt Against Hitler*, London, 1948, p. xiii; Gerhard Ritter, *The German Resistance*, New York, 1958; H. Gollwitzer *et al.*, eds., *Dying We Live*, London, 1956.

The extent of Bonhoeffer's involvement in the activities of the Kreisau Circle is still unclear, and evidence is still coming to light. It is known that at the least, as a courier, he made two trips on behalf of the resistance and planned a third. Cf. *Revolt Against Hitler*, pp. 162–3; Eberhard Bethge, 'Dietrich Bonhoeffer', in *German Life and Letters*, Oxford, 1957, p. 128; 'Challenge', pp. 27–8; *Aus Bonhoeffers Konspirativen Reisen*, MW IV, pp. 109–39.

30. 'Challenge', p. 27.

31. Cf. W. A. Visser't Hooft, *Begegnung mit Dietrich Bonhoeffer*, in *Das Zeugnis Eines Boten*, Geneva, 1945.

32. Cf. G. K. A. Bell, 'The Background of the Hitler Plot' and 'The Church and the Resistance Movement', GS I, pp. 390–8, 399–413; and the various letter exchanges in GS I, pp. 355–89.

33. Munich, 1951, 6th enlarged ed., 1955. Eng. tr. London, 1953; Fontana ed., 1959 (= *Letters*).

34. Cf. 'The Last Days', *Letters*, pp. 176–82. Within one month Klaus Bonhoeffer, Hans von Dohnanyi, and Rüdiger Schleicher were executed as well.

Chapter 2 : Bonhoeffer as a Theologian

1. Selections from the *Gesammelte Schriften* are appearing in English translation. The first volume, covering the period 1928–36, is published under the title, *No Rusty Swords*, London and New York, 1965.

2. Selections from these four issues have recently been published under the title *World Come of Age*, London and New York, 1967.

3. CD, pp. 35–47. In so far as Bonhoeffer's name was widely known in Germany before the war, it was in connection with this phrase and this book.

4. Godsey, p. 264.

5. Müller, pp. 30–52. Müller sharpened this argument and repeated it at the fourth meeting of the Bonhoeffer 'circle' in East Berlin in 1961, arousing a great amount of controversy. Cf. *Zur Problematik der Rezeption und Interpretation Dietrich Bonhoeffers*, MW IV. pp. 52–78 and Bethge's review of his study, *Besprechung: Hanfried Müller, Von der Kirche zur Welt*, MW IV, pp. 169–74. A critical but appreciative examination of Müller's presuppositions and contribution which I

am tempted to reproduce is J. M. Lochman, 'From the Church to the World', *Communio Viatorum*, Prague, Winter 1962, pp. 279–86; reprinted in Martin E. Marty and Dean G. Peerman, eds., *New Theology No. 1*, New York, 1964, pp. 169–81.

6. Bethge, MW IV, p. 171.

7. Müller, pp. 244 ff. '. . . this way was really a detour; historically false – the right way was the later way with the Gospel and the world' (pp. 252–3). '*Life Together* is related to the later works of Bonhoeffer . . . as life under the Law to life under the Gospel' (p. 253).

8. Cf. 'Letter from Karl Barth to Landessuperintendent P. Herrenbrück' (Appendix).

9. 'His passion for human freedom sprang out of the whole of his life and it had a sense of joy about it. It sprang from a quite different dimension, and this he communicated to us in an irresistible way. . . . Anyone who enters into Bonhoeffer's ideas and thinks out his thoughts experiences an inner liberation'. Bethge, *German Life and Letters*, pp. 126, 130.

10. 9th March 1944. *Letters*, p. 77. Cf. also the comments on 'detachment' in the letter of 25th May 1944, *ibid.*, pp. 102 ff.

11. Godsey, p. 264. Cf. H. C. von Hase, *Begriff und Wirklichkeit der Kirche in der Theologie Dietrich Bonhoeffers*, MW I, pp. 26–46. Müller, pp. 9–14.

12. Godsey, pp. 264, cf. p. 17.

13. Godsey, p. 271.

14. 8th June 1944. *Letters*, p. 110.

15. Müller, MW IV, p. 53.

16. 30th April 1944. *Letters*, p. 92.

17. Bethge, MW IV, p. 172.

18. Müller, pp. 391 f.

19. Godsey, p. 264: 'The cohesive and elucidative element in the theology of Dietrich Bonhoeffer is his steadfast concentration upon the revelation of God in Jesus Christ'; Bethge, *German Life and Letters*, p. 129: 'Bonhoeffer cannot quite see what will happen to the traditional forms of the church, but he can fix the starting point for us. It has the figure of Christ as the centre. . .' Gerhard Ebeling, *Die nicht-religiöse Interpretation biblischer Begriffe*, MW II, p. 19: '. . . there can be no doubt of the intensity with which Bonhoeffer's thought is oriented on Jesus Christ.' Each of Bonhoeffer's major writings plunged fearlessly into a Christological theme, SC, p. 134: 'Christ exists as the church'; CF, p. 8: 'The Creation story should be read in church in the first place only from Christ . . . Christ is the beginning, the new, and the end of our world'; LT, p. 21: 'Christianity means community through Jesus Christ and in Jesus Christ'; *Ethics*, pp. 20, 166: 'The form of Jesus Christ takes form in man', 'Christ is the Mediator and sustainer of the Bible, the church, theology; humanity, reason, law, formation. To him must everything return, only in

him can there be life'; *Letters*, p. 90: 'The thing that keeps coming back to me is what is Christianity, and indeed, who is Christ for us today?'

20. 'Challenge', p. 7.
21. J. M. Lochman's complaint in reviewing Müller's study. Cf. *New Theology No. 1*, p. 175.
22. 'Letter from Karl Barth to Landessuperintendent P. Herrenbrück' (Appendix).

Chapter 3: Discovering God Anew

 1. *Ein Briefwechsel mit Adolf von Harnack*, in Karl Barth, *Theologische Fragen und Antworten*, Zurich, 1957, pp. 7–31.
 2. The phrase originated with R. G. Collingwood. In his *The Righteousness of God*, Gordon Rupp speaks of Luther's revolution as just such a crisis of vocabulary, stating that 'the changing pressures of social and political existence necessitate new adjustments of ideas and words, and eventually, though the element of novelty is always less than superficially appears, new ideas and words, so that every age of revolutionary new ferment brings with it a crisis of vocabulary' (London, 1953, p. 81).
 3. Adolf von Harnack, *The Essence of Christianity*, Eng. tr. London, 1901, p. 114.
 4. Karl Barth, *The Epistle to the Romans*, Eng. tr. of the 7th edition, London, 1937, p. 37.
 5. So Ernst Wolf, quoted in Rupp, *op. cit.*, p. 29.
 6. H. R. Mackintosh, *Types of Modern Theology*, London, 1937, pp. 181–3.
 7. Sidney Cave, *The Doctrine of the Person of Christ*, London, 1927, p. 214; Reinhold Seeberg, *Fundamental Truths of the Christian Religion*, Eng. tr. London, 1908, p. x.
 8. Richard R. Niebuhr, *Resurrection and Historical Reason*, New York, 1957, pp. 39 ff.
 9. Emil Brunner, *The Theology of Crisis*, New York, 1930, p. 7.
10. Cf. Mackintosh, *op. cit.*, p. 188.
11. Ernst Troeltsch, *Die Bedeutung der Geschichtlichkeit Jesus für den Glauben*, Tübingen, 1911, p. 6.
12. Ernst Troeltsch, *Protestantism and Progress*, Eng. tr. London, 1912, pp. 22–3.
13. *Ibid.*, pp. 78–9.
14. Ernst Troeltsch, *Social Teachings of the Christian Churches*, Vol. II, Eng. tr. London, 1931, p. 1006.
15. Troeltsch, *Protestantism and Progress*, *op. cit.*, pp. 11, 37.
16. Ernst Troeltsch, *Gesammelte Schriften* II, Tübingen, 1913, p. 516.
17. Hermann Diem, *Dogmatics*, Edinburgh, 1959, p. 8.
18. Troeltsch, *Bedeutung*, p. 9.
19. 'Challenge', p. 8.

20. Troeltsch, *Social Teachings,* p. 34.
21. So H. C. von Hase, MW I, pp. 27–8.
22. 'Challenge', p. 8.
23. Cf. Ernst Wolf, introduction to SC, pp. 5–6.
24. Brunner, *The Theology of Crisis, op. cit.,* p. 7.
25. 8th June 1944. *Letters,* p. 108.
26. Quoted in Rupp, *op. cit.,* p. 30.
27. *Ibid.,* p. 31.
28. *Ibid.,* p. 183.
29. Quoted *ibid.,* p. 183.
30. Cf. Wilhelm Pauck's foreword to Karl Holl, *The Cultural Significance of the Reformation,* Meridian ed., New York, 1959, p. 12.
31. Eng. tr. London, 1937, pp. 69–70.
32. *Ibid.,* p. 31.
33. *Ibid.,* p. 48.
34. 'Challenge', p. 4.
35. 30th April 1944. *Letters,* p. 91.
36. Cave, *op. cit.,* p. 214.
37. *Ibid.,* p. 212.
38. Seeberg, *Fundamental Truths,* pp. v–vi.
39. *Ibid.,* p. xi.
40. 'Challenge', p. 5.
41. Reinhold Seeberg, *Die christliche Dogmatik,* Erlangen, 1927, Vol. I, p. 200.
42. *Ibid.,* p. 104, quoted in AB, p. 46.
43. *Ibid.,* p. 74.
44. 'As the *logos* became flesh in Jesus, so the Holy Spirit becomes flesh in the church of Jesus Christ.' *Ibid.,* p. 154; cf. *Dogmatik* II pp. 357 ff.
45. Seeberg, *Fundamental Truths,* pp. 145–6.
46. *Ibid.,* p. 210.
47. *Ibid.,* p. 212.
48. Seeberg's influence upon his pupil was brief but, as we shall shortly see, distinctly visible. With the exception of Bethge, Bonhoeffer's interpreters tend to view Seeberg's influence as negligible (cf. Müller, p. 444, note 129).
49. GS II, p. 54. In a footnote in the *Church Dogmatics* (I/I), Barth has nothing but contempt for the programme of Seeberg and his followers: 'Had the modern positivist group . . . so much to reproach their liberal opponents with as they thought they had? . . . How many a one in their ranks could without special transformation waken up one morning a tolerably genuine religious philosopher, religious historian, or religious psychologist! How it further increased the confusion of points of view, especially in the sphere of exegesis, by a historism which was none the better because it was a supernatural

historism on friendly terms with tradition, without making the slightest impression on the enemy and without being able to prevent the frontiers between "Positive" and "Liberal" OT men, "Positive" and "Liberal" NT men, from being increasingly and finally altogether obliterated.' It is at least clear from this characterization what there was in Seeberg's theology that attracted Bonhoeffer: a positive witness to tradition which distinguished itself from Liberalism (however mild its reproach may have been), coupled with a keen awareness of the problem of Lessing.

50. R. R. Niebuhr, *op. cit.*, pp. 9–13.
51. Eng. tr. London, 1899, Vol. VII.
52. *Ibid.*, p. 226.
53. *Ibid.*, p. 274.
54. GS III, pp. 59–61.
55. 20th February, 1944. *Letters*, p. 38. Cf. *Letters* of 3rd March, 1944 and 23rd February 1944, pp. 38, 75 f.
56. 'Thoughts on Baptism'. *Letters*, p. 157.
57. *History of Dogma* VII, *op. cit.*, pp. 194–5.
58. 'Challenge', p. 8. Müller comments on the effect of Bonhoeffer's training upon his theology in a lengthy note (Müller, p. 444, n. 129). He stresses that 'apart from the strong impression which Harnack's personality made on the younger Bonhoeffer . . . one should not place too much value on the influence of his theological teachers.' He considers Seeberg's influence, 'apart from a certain formal dependence in SC', 'negligible'. Harnack affected Bonhoeffer's judgement of the place of hellenistic influence upon Christianity as well as his personal apprehension of the 'being' of Jesus. But for the most part, he concludes, Bonhoeffer was remarkably independent of his Liberal training.

Müller does not take into account Bonhoeffer's uneasiness, expressed in his letters, with Barth's theology – in spite of the undoubted impact Barth had upon his younger colleague. Bonhoeffer openly stated at several points in his prison letters that he was not nor had any desire to be wholly free of this heritage of intellectual honesty and willingness to enter battles, however poorly Liberalism might have fared in the ensuing struggle. We shall see in the following chapters that Seeberg had more of a hold upon Bonhoeffer than Müller will admit and that questions which bothered Bonhoeffer in his early writings, although they were set aside during the middle period of his theology, emerged once more with real power in his last years.

59. Charles West, *Communism and the Theologians*, London, 1958, p. 354.
60. C. W. Kegley and R. W. Bretall, *The Theology of Paul Tillich*, New York, 1952, p. 3.
61. 3rd March, 1944. *Letters*, pp. 38–9.

Chapter 4: Christ Exists as the Church

1. Cf. von Hase, MW I, pp. 27–8; 'Challenge', pp. 4–5, 7–8; Peter Berger, 'Sociology and Ecclesiology', in Marty, pp. 54–7. As Müller remarks (p. 35), Bonhoeffer seemed always in his thinking to anticipate the future movement of theological thought.

2. SC, p. 20. Cf. von Hase, MW I, p. 28: 'After dialectical theology had proscribed Troeltsch's sociological thought, this was a brave undertaking, which scarcely anyone has imitated up to now. He didn't allow himself to be frightened by the dangers of natural theology and historism, of which he certainly was conscious, but looked at pure sociological thought as a necessary help in interpreting the church theologically.' Cf. 'Challenge', pp. 7–8: 'It was a unique and unparalleled enterprise, in those days, to take into account both aspects, the *Offenbarungs-theologischen* (revelational) one and the sociological one. . . . He uses sociology for interpreting the shapes of this pretentious and mysterious body, the church. He brings together phenomenology and theology of revelation. But Bonhoeffer takes his stand within the church and rejects the possibility of grasping her sociological facts from outside. Thus he tries to overcome historico-sociological relativism.'

3. Godsey, p. 27.

4. 'When the book first appeared,' Bethge writes ('Challenge', p. 8), 'a friend pitied Bonhoeffer: "Not many will really grasp and accept your concern: neither the Barthians because of your sociology, nor the sociologists because of your Barth."' In keeping with the curious way in which, during his lifetime, Bonhoeffer called his earlier works into question without rejecting them (Cf. GS I, p. 26 on *Act and Being* and *Letters*, p. 125 (21st June 1944) on *The Cost of Discipleship*), Bonhoeffer remarked in the preface which he wrote for the published version of his dissertation that the three years which had elapsed since its completion revealed that conversation was being carried out in a quite different area, although his own approach remained 'the right and profitable one'. (SC, p. 11).

5. 'Sociology and Ecclesiology', Marty, pp. 58 ff. Upon its republication in 1954, *Sanctorum Communio* was praised in an introduction by Ernst Wolf; a tribute which has since been echoed by Karl Barth's footnote in *Church Dogmatics* IV/2, p. 261. It is difficult to know whether, without Bonhoeffer's later contribution, such interest in *Sanctorum Communio* would have arisen. The value of this peculiar work is greatly diminished for present-day theology because of the sociologists and theologians with whom Bonhoeffer chose to converse and those he neglected. As Berger shows, Bonhoeffer's sociology is outdated, and Müller's complaint that

Bonhoeffer shrugged off Marx seems to me fully justified. Among the theologians, Reinhold Seeberg has passed completely from theological discussion and the confrontation with Troeltsch, as I have argued below, never brought about a genuine conversation.

6. *Ibid.*, p. 58.

7. Peter Berger writes: 'Today there is some evidence that as neoorthodoxy has come to be something less than the latest vogue, there is renewed interest among theologians in the possible contribution to their task by the social scientists. If this interest should itself become a new fashion, Bonhoeffer's *Sanctorum Communio* would seem to be a natural choice for a legitimating classic' (*ibid.*, pp. 54–5).

8. *Ibid.*, p. 75.

9. SC, p. 112. As Müller remarks (p. 55), Bonhoeffer's methodology probably confused more than it clarified.

10. I cannot agree with many of Bonhoeffer's interpreters that the primary and direct encounter with Liberalism in the pages of *Sanctorum Communio* takes place in his confrontation with Troeltsch. Here again, Bonhoeffer's supporters are reading back into his early work what they would like Bonhoeffer to have written. It is certain that no contemporary interpretation of the church can afford to detour around Troeltsch's ecclesiology, or the lack of one, in the *Social Teachings*; it is also true that in the prison letters, Bonhoeffer begins to take up many of the problems with which Troeltsch was concerned. But it is not necessary to read these questions into Bonhoeffer's earliest work, nor do the facts warrant such an interpretation. Cf. Müller, pp. 64–7; von Hase, MW I, p. 28; Bethge, 'Challenge', p. 8.

11. Troeltsch, *Protestantism and Progress*, pp. 47–8.

12. Troeltsch, *Bedeutung*, pp. 29–30.

13. Seeberg, *Fundamental Truths*, p. 280.

14. Seeberg, *Dogmatik* II, p. 355.

15. *Ibid.*, I, p. 154.

16. *Ibid.*, II, p. 270.

17. *Ibid.*, I, p. 154; cf. *ibid.*, I, 385; II, 357 f.

18. SC, p. 89.

19. SC, note 32, p. 210, my translation. Cf. MW I, p. 28.

20. Cf. Hegel, *Encyclopedia*, Para. 483.

21. SC, p. 66.

22. Seeberg, *Dogmatik* I, *op. cit.*, p. 513, quoted in SC p. 56. Without this idea, Bonhoeffer argues (pp. 37–8), the ideas of the church and original sin cannot fully be understood.

23. Seeberg, *Fundamental Truths*, p. 267.

24. *Ibid.*, p. 270.

25. *Ibid.*, p. 272.

26. SC, p. 93.

27. *Ibid.*, p. 145, italics mine. The uniqueness of Bonhoeffer's work rested in the fact that he fearlessly took the next step, that of describing the empirical structure of the church with the use of sociological categories, however inadequate these last may have been. It is interesting to see how close Bonhoeffer is to later criticisms of liberal doctrines of the church which were made by his two older contemporaries, Karl Barth and Emil Brunner. In the fourth volume of his *Church Dogmatics*, Barth writes of the 'secret' of the church, 'its being in the third dimension, visible only to faith'. (IV/1, p. 660). He continues: 'Without this special visibility all that can be seen is the men united in it and their common activity, and this will be explained in terms of the categories which are regarded as the most appropriate for the understanding and appraisal of common human activities, with an attempt to subordinate it to some picture of the world and of history. On this view it can be understood as a religious society within human society generally and side by side with other organizations.' (p. 655). Further, in IV/2, p. 619, Barth writes: 'We can, of of course, see the members of the church, and its officials and constitutions and orders, its dogmatics and cultus, its organizations and societies, its leaders with their politics, and its laity . . . and all these in the context of its history. Where else is the church visible if not in these? If it is not visible in these it is obviously not visible at all. But is it really visible in these? . . . What is visible in all this may be only a religious society. . . . It will be always in the revelation of God that the true church is visible. And it will always be in faith awakened by this revelation that it is actually seen by men – at the place where without revelation and faith there is to be seen (perhaps in a very confusing and deceptive way) only this many-sided ecclesiastical quantity in all its ambiguity.' Brunner directly acknowledges the contribution of *Sanctorum Communio* in his *The Misunderstanding of the Church* (London, 1952): '(The church) is . . . unintelligible from a purely sociological view point. . . . For it is in fact intelligible only from the standpoint of the Christ who dwells within it and determines its life' (p. 12). Again, 'The fact that it is both *koinonia Christou* or *koinonia pneumatos* and "fellowship one with another", thus combining the vertical with the horizontal, divine with human communion – that fact constitutes its entire characteristic, its utterly unparalleled life' (p. 12).

28. SC, pp. 198 ff. (eschatology), 146 ff. (sanctification).

29. Godsey, p. 45. In the concluding sentence, the italics are mine.

30. 'Challenge', p. 8.

31. SC, p. 105.

32. SC, p. 198.

Chapter 5: Ecclesiology as the Ground of Revelation

1. AB, p. 12
2. AB, p. 16.
3. For a more complete look at the argument of *Act and Being*, cf. Müller, pp. 117–47; 'Challenge', pp. 9–10; and the essay by Franklin Sherman. 'Act and Being', in Marty, pp. 83–111. Some interesting but undeveloped remarks concerning Bonhoeffer's criticism of Barth in AB are to be found in Hans Urs von Balthasar, *Karl Barth: Darstellung und Deutung seiner Theologie*, Köln, 1951, pp. 306, 374, and 403.
4. This conception was not peculiar to Seeberg, although it may have reached its clearest formulation in his *Dogmatik*. 'In contrast to Enlightenment theology, the nineteenth-century theologians focused their attention on one particular point in relation to all the various world views of their time: man's supposedly innate and essential capacity to "sense and taste the infinite" as Schleiermacher said, or the *"religious a priori"* as later affirmed by Troeltsch. There was scarcely a theologian who did not also consider himself a professional philosopher. These philosophers of religion, more or less faithful or sophisticated advocates of one of the current world views, were busily working out a general epistemology, a system of ethics and metaphysics focusing on this very capacity. In these terms, they sought to validate the potential for religion, including the Christian faith' (Karl Barth, 'Evangelical Theology in the 19th Century', in *The Humanity of God*, Richmond, 1960, pp. 21–2).
5. AB, p. 47.
6. Seeberg, *Dogmatik* I, p. 91, quoted in AB, p. 46.
7. AB, p. 46.
8. Seeberg, *Dogmatik* I, p. 105, quoted in AB, p. 45. 'We now find in (Seeberg's) argument,' Bonhoeffer writes, 'bluntly juxtaposed statements which place the existence of the supramundane – and of concepts to boot – in the human mind alone, yet admit of no doubt as to an "objective being", i.e. a being of the supramundane which manifestly transcends consciousness' (p. 45). Bonhoeffer seems here to be expressing his exasperation with the whole of Seeberg's style in his *Dogmatik*, and, indeed, the programme of the Modern Positivists. The attention Seeberg paid to traditional dogmatics made him especially difficult to attack from this direction.
9. 'Nur dann kann Gott als Realität zum Bewusstsein kommen, wenn es in den Menschen ein Organ hierfür gibt!' *Dogmatik* I, p. 100.
10. *Ibid.*, pp. 81, 104, quoted in AB, p. 46.
11. AB, p. 47.
12. GS III, pp. 91–2, 6. Bonhoeffer's dismissal of Seeberg in 1930–1 seems complete. It meant, for the time being at least, a concentration on

dogmatics as Barth defined it as the proper subject matter for theology. Bonhoeffer's comment on Seeberg's theology in a letter which he wrote to his teacher in 1928 is worth recording, for it expresses Bonhoeffer's early suspicion that his teacher had given up the task of theology for something else: 'You once brought out the question of consciousness in a seminar; it should however be a theological, rather than psychological, undertaking.'

13. GS III, p. 102.
14. GS III, p. 75.
15. GS III, p. 76.
16. SC, p. 72.
17. AB, pp. 157–8. It should be noted, however, that Bonhoeffer is treating the question of conscience as he had the question of religious community. He removes its claims, as a human sphere, to embody the divine revelation *simpliciter*. 'It is the reflection on oneself (he writes) which is the farthest limit of Adam's penetration. Primarily it is not the voice of God but man's own voice' (AB, p. 177). Nevertheless, conscience, like religious community, remains a fact. Bonhoeffer speaks of it as 'the past as determinant of being in Christ' (AB, pp. 177–80). As reflection upon the self, conscience cannot be the faith intended purely towards Christ; yet it remains and possesses a form proper to itself. Now it no longer 'distracts my attention from Christ', but rather is taken up in faith. 'I see my sin,' Bonhoeffer states, 'in the context of my having been forgiven by Christ' (AB, p. 178).

Bonhoeffer thus carefully takes up conscience into the New Being of the Christian. In doing this, he is consciously developing the positive alternative to Barth's 'incomprehensible' picture of the new existence of the believer. Bonhoeffer criticizes Barth for refusing to take account of the *total* historical existence of the believer by cutting off his unbelieving past. He thus asks whether the new being posited by Barth does not remain a 'heavenly double' of the empirical 'total I' (AB, p. 102).

This valuation of 'pre-faith' existence lies behind several of Bonhoeffer's later ideas; the problem of 'The Pharisee' in the *Ethics*, and the concept of the 'penultimate' in *The Cost of Discipleship*, the *Ethics*, and the prison letters.

18. GS III, pp. 119–20. Cf. GS III, p. 101: 'Man after the fall refers everything to himself, puts himself at the centre of the world, does violence to reality, makes himself God, and God and the other man his creatures.'
19. AB, pp. 38–9.
20. AB, p. 22. On Barth's protest as the background to AB, cf. Sherman, in Marty, pp. 86–7.
21. AB, p. 41.

22. GS III, p. 109.
23. SC, p. 97. My translation.
24. *Op. cit.*, p. 418. H. R. Mackintosh wrote in 1937 his own impression of Barth's treatment of the church: 'More in sorrow than in anger, [Barth's] early work called attention to the fact that the concrete Church, the institution we know, belongs like all earthly things to the present age, the aeon of flesh and sin . . . ; like the world, of which as a visible undertaking it forms part, it stands in absolute opposition to God. . . . The Church, as we not only observe but share its life, is in itself utterly unworthy, and for that reason perpetually confronted with the possibility of rejection' (*Types of Modern Theology*, London, 1937, pp. 309–10).
25. SC, p. 87.
26. AB, p. 102.
27. AB, pp. 90–1. This is the summation of Bonhoeffer's position, carried from *Sanctorum Communio* into the pages of *Act and Being*. 'But how can I encounter God as a person in Christ? The phrase as it stands is too abstract for Bonhoeffer. With the aid of a concept developed in his doctoral dissertation *Sanctorum Communio* . . . he presses the notion of an encounter with God to its ultimate point of concreteness. I meet God in Christ; but I meet Christ in the church, for the church is the contemporary Christ – it is "Christ existing as community". . .' (Sherman, in Marty, p. 92). 'Bonhoeffer fully accepted and saw the great contribution of Barth in the uncompromising emphasis on the contingency of revelation, so that it might never become an object for our handling, in his interest in the *unverdingliche* ("not at our disposal") majesty of God. *But this interest Bonhoeffer sees safeguarded not in the beyond but in the Christ "existing as the community of men"*. There, in persons, the claim of God remains outside and does not come into our possession, its limits condemn and edify us, but it meets us continually *extra nos, pro nobis*. There Christ is and exists for other. . . . There is no God, Bonhoeffer emphasizes, other than the incarnated one known to us and meeting and claiming us in the "Christ existing as the community of men", the church. This, he thinks, secures both the contingency and the continuity or concern for existence' ('Challenge', pp. 8, 9. Italics mine).
28. AB, pp. 80–1.
29. WA 23, 157; quoted in AB, p. 81 n.
30. Cf. 'Challenge', pp. 8 f. This Christological argument with Barth is continued below, pp. 170–172.

Chapter 6: The New Christology

1. 'Challenge', pp. 14, 17.
2. GS III, pp. 166–242. Translated and published as *Christ the Centre*, New

York and London, 1966. In the form in which we have them, the lectures are reconstructed from the notes of students who participated in Bonhoeffer's seminar in 1933. 'Although any such reconstruction of a man's words from notes taken by his hearers and students must be used with caution,' J. Pelikan writes, '. . . the substantial authenticity of Bonhoeffer's *Christologie* is attested to both by the testimony of those who heard the lectures and by a comparison of the *Christologie* with other writings whose authenticity is incontestable' ('Bonhoeffer's *Christologie* of 1933', Marty, p. 147).

3. SC, pp. 22–37, 44–52.

4. Berger, in Marty, pp. 59 ff., develops Bonhoeffer's argument from the basis of his conception of person and corporate person. It would seem, however, that Bonhoeffer set this idea to one side in favour of 'objective spirit', and never really incorporated it into his theory.

5. SC, pp. 44–52.

6. AB, pp. 120–1. The concentration on the Christian concept of person demonstrates that Bonhoeffer has now set aside his attempted conversation with Seeberg (and the phrase 'objective spirit') and, following the publication of Karl Barth's *Die christliche Dogmatik*, has taken up a conversation with Barth. Barth's failing, as Bonhoeffer saw it, was a lack of a conception of God as Person. 'It is a fateful error on Barth's part,' he wrote, 'to replace the Lord and Creator with the concept of the Subject. . . . But the ultimate reason for the inadequacy of Barth's explanation lies in the fact that it fails to understand God as a person. From this failure arises a defective definition of the being of revelation, whence a defective concept of knowledge. . . . We must extract our answer from the result of defining the being of revelation as personal, accepting whatever consequences may follow for the concept of knowledge itself.' In Bonhoeffer's understanding of 'person', one is constantly free to give or withhold oneself from another person. By knowing another person, I do not thereby control him, as he remains 'Thou' for me and never becomes, from my perspective, an 'I'. Only I know my own 'I', which is not discoverable by another (SC, pp. 32 ff.). The problem of the person is, in one way, the problem of the revelation of God (SC, pp. 34–5). And because he is personal, God's giving of himself does not mean that his freedom is jeopardized. In the church, then, 'God gives himself in Christ to his communion, and to each individual as a member of that communion. This he does in such a way that the active subject in the communion, of both the annunciation and the believing of the Word, is Christ. It is in the personal communion, and only there, that the Gospel can truly be declared and believed. There, it follows, revelation is in some way secured and possessed. God's freedom has bound itself, woven itself into the personal communion, and it is precisely that which proves

it God's freedom – that he should bind himself to man' (AB, pp. 120–1. Cf. also pp. 125–6, 130, 137 ff.; especially important is the translator's remark, p. 138 n.). It is *personality*, not *entity* which Bonhoeffer sees to be the key to the solution of the problem of act vs. being in revelation.

7. AB, p. 121.
8. AB, p. 138 n.
9. SC, p. 221.
10. 'Concerning the Christian Idea of God', GS III, pp. 103–4.
11. GS III, p. 170. Bonhoeffer is careful first to establish Christ's 'otherness': 'Were this *logos* our *logos*, then Christology would be the reflection of the *logos* upon itself. But it is the *logos* of God. His transcendence is the *sine qua non* of Christology; his from-outside-into the centre of knowledge, his transcendence, authenticates its object, in so far as he is Person. The *logos* with which we have to do is a person. This man is the Transcendent' (*ibid.*, p. 167).
12. 'Christology . . . can offer no evidence as proof of the transcendence of her object. Her theme of transcendence – that is, that the *logos* is a person, man – is given and is not provable' (*ibid.*, p. 168).
13. *Ibid.*, pp. 169–70.
14. *Ibid.*, p. 170. At no place does Bonhoeffer develop the distinction between the transcendence possessed by *all men* as persons from the transcendence of *Christ*. One can point only to the 1931 essay on God: 'God as the absolutely free personality is therefore absolutely transcendent' (*ibid.*, p. 103). Without doubt, Bonhoeffer would insist that the distinction is qualitative.
15. *Ibid.*, p. 178.
16. *Ibid.*, pp. 180–1.
17. *Ibid.*, pp. 181, 233, and *passim*.
18. *Ibid.*, p. 227. Bonhoeffer does discuss historical issues in his lectures, but he sets out this section in parentheses, guided by what Pelikan deplores as an '*a priori* pattern' (Marty, p. 162). Some of this argument is relevant to our considerations, and may be summarized as follows:

The Lutheran interest in the *communicatio idiomatum* and the subsequent counter-arguments of the Calvinists were inspired by the forbidden question 'How?' Bonhoeffer felt obliged to defend the Lutheran development, because he saw Calvinist Christology primarily as the explication of a 'humiliated *logos*' which concerned itself with the pointless distinction between properties which belonged to Christ's divine nature and those which characterized his human nature. This view of the movement of the Incarnation (The Word becomes flesh by being humiliated) is false. The Lutheran view is the correct one: The Word which has become flesh then humiliates itself, choosing a particular form or status of man in which to reveal itself. Humiliation, not Incarnation, is the Christological problem. Bonhoeffer saw the problem inherent in the Lutheran *genus majestaticum* of turning Christ into a 'divinized man', but defended the insistent *hoc est corpus meum* of Luther's doctrine of the sacrament against the Calvinist *extra Calvinisticum* (pp. 221, 189–92).

Liberal Christology fell victim of the Docetic heresy in that it saw Jesus as the appearance of a divine 'quality' within history, a medium through which God speaks to man. This based Christology on an impossibly abstract view of God (p. 207). Thus (with Schleiermacher) Jesus becomes merely the historical representative of the idea of God, or (with Ritschl) Christ is the appearance of the value judgement of 'community' (p. 211), or Christ is a historical and dynamic power [Seeberg?] (p. 179). Herrmann's ideal picture of the "inner life" of Jesus, his personality, fell into the error of making Christology a synonym for soteriology. Against all these views, Bonhoeffer insists that Jesus is concretely a person, who includes his work in himself (pp. 179–80).

But there can be no going behind the Chalcedonian formula: 'The beginning is given: The man Jesus is the Christ, is God. This "is" cannot be set to one side. It is basic to all thinking and cannot be constructed *a posteriori*. From Chalcedon on, it can no longer be a question of how the natures can be different and the person one, but strictly: Who is this man of whom it is said that he is God?' (p. 277).

19. *Ibid.*, pp. 178 ff.
20. *Ibid.*, p. 180.
21. 'Here we stand before the first Christological problem: If Christ is contemporary not only as a power but also in his person, how is this presence to be conceived, if we are not to injure the integrity of his person?' (p. 180) Bonhoeffer's answer: 'The presence of the given God-Man Jesus Christ exist for us in the scandalous form of proclamation. The proclaimed Christ is the real Christ. The proclamation is not a second Incarnation. The scandal of Jesus is not his Incarnation – that is indeed the revelation! – but rather his humiliation. Jesus Christ is Man as the Humiliated and Exalted. . . . Christ as the Humiliated and Exalted is present only in proclamation, but that means in the form of renewed humiliation. In the proclamation, the Resurrected is present in the humiliation. This presence has a threefold form in the church: as Word, as Sacrament, and as the Church' (pp. 181–4).
22. *Ibid.*, pp. 187, 209, 232, 235, and *passim*.
23. *Ibid.*, p. 236.
24. *Ibid.*, p. 240.
25. Bonhoeffer concluded his introductory lectures at Berlin, *Die Frage nach dem Menschen in der gegenwartigen Philosophie und Theologie* (1931)

with these words: 'Christ exists among us as the church, the church in the hiddenness of the historical. The church is the hidden Christ among us.' (GS III, pp. 83–4.) Compare this passage from the 1933 lectures: 'With this humiliated one, the church goes its own way of humiliation. It cannot request the visible authorization of its way since he, at every point, refused this. As the humiliated church, it must neither look with vain complacency to itself, as if its humility were a visible proof that Christ is present. Humiliation is not a proof to which attention may be drawn. There is no law or principle which the church must follow. There is only this fact of humility, which is God's way with the church' (ibid., pp. 241–2).

26. Ibid., pp. 232–3.
27. The section is closest to the Christology of Sanctorum Communio in identifying the revelation with certain ecclesiastical forms, and for our purposes a brief summary will suffice:

As the Word, the full transcendent person of Christ confronts me as the 'personal address' (p. 186) of God. 'His presence is not any power of the church nor its objective spirit, out of which he is preached, but his being (Dasein) as the sermon'. (p. 186) (If we could be more certain of the exact wording here, this represents Bonhoeffer's last mention of the phrase 'objective spirit', which he used so widely in Sanctorum Communio.) 'At this man you shall point and say: That is God. We may modify that to read: At this word of man you shall point and say: That is God's Word. The sentences are basically alike' (p. 187).

As Sacrament, 'the whole person of the God-Man in his exaltation and humiliation is present. . . . Christ exists so that he is existentially present in the Sacrament. His being-as-the-Sacrament is not a peculiar possession, a quality among others; it exists thus in the church. The humiliation is not an accident of his God-Man substance but its existence' (p. 192).

As the Church, in the formulation which is already familiar to us from Bonhoeffer's earlier writings, the logos of God finds spatio-temporal extensity. 'The community is (not signifies) the Body of Christ' (p. 193).

28. Ibid., pp. 194 ff. It is difficult to trace the history of this idea in Bonhoeffer's early writings. I see the background of this section in the Christology lectures to be Bonhoeffer's remarks concerning 'conscience' in Act and Being and Sanctorum Communio. In the former, conscience is described as 'the last grasp of the self at the self' (AB, p. 160), 'the becoming aware of death and isolation' (AB, p. 168), the final limitation of man. But conscience may have a form appropriate to being in Christ, if it 'obscures my view of Christ, or shows him to be my judge from the cross, thus pointing constantly to my sin' (AB, p. 178). Bonhoeffer describes the conscience so conceived as rebellion

against Christ which, at the same time, is taken up in the act of belief. As this act (like theology) involves 'reflection upon one's limits' it must constantly be subject to the act of faith itself, the 'pure intentionality in looking only toward Christ' (AB, p. 175). This complicated and abstract argument emerges once more in *Creation and Fall* (1932–3), where Bonhoeffer develops the notion that 'man's limit is in the middle of his existence'; that the tree of life represents the Lord and Giver of life, who is 'at once the limit and the middle of our existence' (CF, p. 51). This middle/limit is connected closely with the knowledge of good and evil: when, in the Fall, man grasps knowledge for himself, he is cursed with the knowledge of good and evil and is thenceforth 'like God'. Knowing good and evil is man's death; for with this knowledge he can only strike out against the other person who is placed by his side to embody his limit, against the 'grace' of his limitation.

This argument next arises in the Christology lectures, where Christ is the gracious limit to the ego. In the *Ethics*, Christ overcomes the knowledge of good and evil (embodied in the Pharisee) and directs man solely towards himself as the 'limitation from the centre' (*Ethics*, pp. 142–61).

29. GS III, p. 194: 'The essence of the person of Christ is to be temporally and spatially in the centre. . . . Being in the centre belongs to the structure of his person. . . . Christ is the one who exists for me *(der pro-me Daseiende)*, the Mediator.'

Chapter 7 : Concrete Exegesis

1. Cf. Grunow, in MW I, p. 62, and Marty, pp. 120 f.
2. W. Harrelson, in 'Bonhoeffer and the Bible' (Marty, pp. 115–39), does not speak in a disparaging sense when he refers to *The Cost of Discipleship* as a collection of 'homilies'. Rather, and quite rightly, he wishes to point out that this book does not represent the kind of scientific historical-critical exegesis which has been developed in the course of the last hundred years of biblical study (*ibid.*, pp. 121 ff.).
3. Cf. MW I, p. 64; Godsey, pp. 20–2.
4. MW I, p. 64. Bonhoeffer recommended for the preparation of sermons Lietzmann's commentary, Calvin, Bengel's *Gnomon,* Kohlbrügge, Vilmar, and Schlatter (GS IV, p. 260).
5. CF, pp. 7–8. The idea of a 'theological interpretation' is rooted firmly in Bonhoeffer's earliest thought: Theology, the Bible, and the church are inseparable in the concept of revelation set out in *Act and Being*. 'Theological knowledge has its object in the remembered happenings of the Christian communion, the Bible, preaching; and the sacrament, prayer, confession: the Word of the Christ-person

which is stored as entity in the historical church." (AB, p. 143). In *Creation and Fall*, the relationship between Bible, Church, and Christ is more explicit: 'The Bible is nothing but the book upon which the church stands. This is its essential nature, or it is nothing. . . . Thus the creation story should be read in the first place only from Christ, and not until then as leading to Christ . . .' (*ibid.*, p. 8).

6. MW I, p. 69. On occasion in *Creation and Fall*, however, Bonhoeffer specifically acknowledges the importance of such questions, e.g. on pp. 41-3, 19, and 26. Discussing the Yahwist account of the creation of man, he writes: '. . . undoubtedly in this passage the biblical author stands exposed with all the limitations caused by the age in which he lives. The idea of verbal inspiration will not do. The heavens and the seas were not formed in the way he says: we would not escape a very bad conscience if we committed ourselves to any such statement' (CF, p. 26).

7. GS III, p. 204-5, italics mine.

8. CF, pp. 48-9.

9. GS III, p. 205.

10. In the introduction to *Creation and Fall*, Bonhoeffer writes: 'Theological interpretation accepts the Bible as the book of the church and interprets it as such. Its method is this assumption; it continually refers back from the text (which has to be ascertained with all the methods of philological and historical research) to this supposition. That is the objectivity of the method of theological interpretation. And in this objectivity alone is substantiated its claim to a scientific method. When Genesis says "Yahweh", historically or psychologically it means nothing but Yahweh. Theologically, however, i.e. from the church's point of view, it is speaking of God. God is the One God in the whole of Holy Scripture: the church and theological study stand and fall with this faith' (CF, p. 8). Whether or not Bonhoeffer recognizes what he has done, the fact remains that 'the method of theological interpretation' loses its 'objectivity' if 'all the methods of philological and historical research' cannot be allowed to affect the final outcome. God is One and reveals himself in Holy Scripture as One – but need this mean that the Bible is to be treated as though it had but one human author, and that each of its verses must be uncritically accepted and exposited with equal revelatory power given to each?

11. This marked Bonhoeffer's first personal encounter with Barth. He was amused by Barth's students who sniffed out theological deviation: 'No Negro passes for white (he wrote his friend, Sutz); they examine your fingernails and the soles of your feet' (GS I, p. 19). Bonhoeffer wondered how long his own 'bastardized theological heritage' would stand the test (p. 19). His delight with Barth's manner was, however, unconditional: 'Now one can breathe

regularly; one fears death by suffocation no longer. I believe that I regret nothing in my theological past so much as not having come sooner' (p. 19). Still, his joy did not make him uncritical. He reported to Sutz the events of an evening spent discussing ethics with Barth: 'We came very soon to the ethical problem and discussed it for a long time. He wouldn't give in to me, as I expected he must. There are (Barth said) many small lanterns apart from the great light in the night, even "relative ethical criteria" (whose meaning and essence and purpose he could not, however, make clear to me). It had to do with his approach to the Bible. He thought, finally, that I was making a principle out of grace and striking everything else dead. Naturally I contested the first point with him and wanted to know why everything else *shouldn't* be struck dead' (*ibid.*, p. 20).

Bonhoeffer found Barth's work terribly difficult to read and grasp, and confessed that he was far more impressed with him in action during his seminars and lectures (although he was not impressed in this way with Gogarten, who lectured in Berlin later in the Fall: Cf. *ibid.*, pp. 20, 22–3). During the following spring, Bonhoeffer again spoke with Barth about the problem of ethics: 'Barth doesn't stand by me in this matter – that is now clear to me. He spoke to me again about it and asked me whether I still think as I did, saying clearly enough that to him it had become even more suspect' (*ibid.*, p. 31). What exactly was the point at issue? It is at least certain that Bonhoeffer was disturbed by what he considered a central point in the whole of Barth's approach to theology. His perplexities were no doubt behind the exchange of letters with Barth concerning the writing of *The Cost of Discipleship* (GS II, pp. 283–91), in which Bonhoeffer reconsidered the doctrines of justification and sanctification, and the relationship between faith and obedience.

12. GS I, pp. 31, 32: 'At bottom it has to do with the problem of ethics, that is, with the question of the possibility of the proclamation of a concrete commandment through the church. And it seems to me to be a real gap in Brunner's ethics that he has not put this question in the centre . . .' (*ibid.*, p. 33). Later, shortly after Hitler became chancellor, Bonhoeffer wrote again: 'You know, I think that the whole matter comes to a critical point in the Sermon on the Mount. Perhaps you will wonder about that. I believe that the theology of Barth – and certainly that of Brunner – has only put off, even as it has made possible, the recognition of this fact" (*ibid.*, p. 40).

13. Bonhoeffer had just returned from an ecumenical Youth Peace Conference in Czechoslovakia, where he delivered a lecture on 'The Theological Basis of the World Alliance' (GS I, pp. 140–61, summarized in Godsey, pp. 97–104). Here he raised the question: 'How can the Gospel and the commandment be proclaimed with authority,

with full concretion? . . . Can the church proclaim the commandment of God with the same assurance as she preaches the Gospel?
. . . The Gospel, as the commandment, can publicly be proclaimed
with authority only when it is spoken in a wholly concrete fashion.
. . . Where does the principle of concretion reside with the Gospel
and where with the commandment?' (GS I, p. 145). Bonhoeffer was
especially concerned that the church give concrete and unconditional commands to the world in the name of Christ; that it say, for
example, 'we must have a socialist economic order' or 'do not go to
war' in the same way that it can say 'your sins are forgiven'. He
found the precedent for this action in the Sermon on the Mount and
the necessity for it in his own 'orders of preservation', but he warned
at the same time against the dangers of legalism: 'Recognition of
God's command is an act of God's revelation' (ibid., p. 148). Only
from Christ comes the Gospel, and only from Christ can the commandment come. It is therefore necessary to attain to 'the deepest
knowledge of reality' (ibid., p. 148). Bonhoeffer finally decided for
the formula: 'What the sacrament is for the proclamation of the Gospel, recognition of the concrete reality is for the proclamation of the
commandment. Reality is the sacrament of the ethical' (ibid., p. 147).

14. GS I, p. 41, italics mine. Bonhoeffer is thinking of St. Ignatius Loyola's
Exercitien, the 'Spiritual Exercises'. To complete the background of
Bonhoeffer's interest in the Sermon on the Mount, we must refer to
a very early lecture (1929) where he wrote: 'It is a great misunder-
standing if one makes the commandment of the Sermon on the
Mount into a law in itself; that one accepts it word for word in the
present day. That . . . goes against the free spirit of Christ, who
brings freedom from the law' (*Grundfragen einer christlichen Ethik*, GS
III, p. 54). Here, Bethge remarks, 'Bonhoeffer is still the traditional
Lutheran who has learned his lesson of how to escape the directness
of the Sermon on the Mount: the literal understanding makes it
Law, and the Law is abolished in Christ.' ('Challenge', p. 17).

15. GS III, pp. 24-5, italics mine.

16. *Ibid.*, pp. 26-7.

17. Although, in a section of his lectures on homiletics entitled 'The Pastor
and the Bible' (GS IV, pp. 255-6), Bonhoeffer speaks of three 'uses' of
the Bible: at prayer, on the desk and on the lectern. In all three
uses, however, it is clear that 'the Bible is the book which contains
the Word of God until the end of all things. Therefore it is different
from other books [Cf. the citation annotated n. 7!]. This axiom can
never be disregarded.'

18. GS III, pp. 28-9.

19. *Ibid.*, pp. 29-30.

20. *Vergegenwärtigung neutestamentlicher Texte*, GS III, pp. 304-5. It should be
noted that Bonhoeffer has taken the question of 'making the

biblical texts present' as one which is characteristic of the German–Christian adherents. He does not seem to have been able to converse fruitfully with conscientious Confessing Churchmen (among them, Bultmann) who were asking honestly and in a legitimate way the very same question.

21. *Ibid.*, pp. 306, 307, In 1931, Bonhoeffer could write: 'It is simply not enough, and therefore false to say: the principle of concretion can only be the Holy Ghost himself' (GS I, p. 31). It is interesting to compare this with the spirit of this essay in 1935: 'The *concretissimum* of the Christian message and exposition of the text is not a human act of actualization, but it is always God himself, the Holy Ghost' (*ibid.*, p. 307).

22. GS II, p. 238. After reading this statement, Hans Lietzmann, who had remained at the University of Berlin after Bonhoeffer had gone, wrote to a Swedish friend: 'Now our most gifted young teacher has turned into a fanatic . . .' ('Challenge', p. 3).

23. The story of the *Bruderhaus* is given in 'Challenge', pp. 21–4. That this movement towards a recovery of some aspects of monasticism was closely bound up with the questions which centred on the Sermon on the Mount is clear from a letter to Sutz of 1934: 'The training of young theologians belongs today in church-monastic schools, in which the pure doctrine, the Sermon on the Mount, and the cultus are all taken seriously – which for all three is not the case in the university and is, under present conditions, not possible' (GS I, p. 42). Bonhoeffer also wrote of *The Cost of Discipleship* and his difficulties with Confessing Church officials who suspected his experiment from the start, in a letter to Barth (September 1936, in GS II, pp. 283–7 and MW I, pp. 116–18). Barth's answer included the following: 'Now you tell me that you are occupied with the inexhaustible theme of justification and sanctification, both theoretically and practically. . . . You cannot expect otherwise than that I am looking forward with an open mind; yet with some uneasiness as well. . . . I can see already, especially among the young theologians of the Confessing Church, that there is approaching another wave of this kind, in which all of the past is revived. It might well be that you are the one who is called and able to be the speaker and leader in this field . . .' (GS II, pp. 288–9, MW I, pp. 119–20, 'Challenge', p. 19).

24. *Temptation* has been published separately in translation, the other studies are to be found in GS IV, pp. 294–320; 544–69.

Chapter 8: Christology and Discipleship

1. *Weimarer Ausgabe* (WA) 11.223.1 f; Ficker, Rom. 240, 10 f.; WA 10.1.567.12 f.; WA 8.236.

2. WA 3.11.33; quoted in Rupp, *op. cit.*, p. 134.

3. Reid, p. 72. 'Christ enters by the Gospel through a man's ear into his heart and dwells there; nor does he come empty-handed, but brings with him his life, Spirit, and all that he has and can' (Erl. A. 63.157). Reid is following Seeberg, among others, in his interpretation. He writes: 'The fact is . . . that for the understanding of Scripture and the recognition of its authority subject and object have to be held together. This coming together takes place in the stillness *(Stille-halten)* of the individual before the Word' (Reid, *op. cit.*, p. 71, following Köhler).

4. WA x.1; 160.22 ff.

5. Commentary on *Galatians*, Eng. tr. p. 110 (ii. 20).

6. Reid, *op. cit.*, pp. 70–1. The following references from Luther's works are important: 3.531.33; 3.532.12; Rupp, *op. cit.*, p. 135.

7. Rupp, following E. Vogelsang, sees decisive effects for Luther's development in the movement from Christological interpretation to purely tropological interpretation. He sees this as the background for Luther's discovery about *justitia Dei*, which possibly took place during Luther's work on the Psalms, in 1514 *(op. cit.*, p. 135).

8. GS IV, pp. 544–69. Cf. also R. H. Fuller, 'Liturgy and Devotion', in Marty, pp. 182 ff. We have here used Godsey's summary, *op. cit.*, pp. 190–1. Bonhoeffer made use of the topological method most radically in his biblical study, *Temptation*, which develops the theme of 'temptation in Christ' in the New Testament. Cf. especially pp. 23–4. Bonhoeffer made use in other biblical studies, especially in his *König David*, of another device of Luther and the Church Fathers: typology. He defended his use of the latter in his essay, *Vergegenwärti-gung neutestamentlicher Texte*, GS III, pp. 319–20. Cf. also MW I, pp. 70–1.

9. 'The Christ whom the scriptures proclaim is in every word he utters one who grants faith only to those who obey him. It is neither possible nor right for us to try to get behind the word of the scriptures to the events as they actually occurred. Rather, the whole Word of the scriptures summons us to follow Jesus' (CD, p. 73).

10. *Ibid.*, p. 73.

11. *Ibid.* p. 60.

12. *Ibid.*, p. 77.

13. *Ibid.*, p. 79.

14. Cf. GS III, pp. 195 ff.

15. CD, p. 274. Cf. the section in *Life Together* entitled 'The Day Alone: Meditation' (pp. 81–4). 'In our meditation we ponder the chosen text on the strength of the promise that it has something utterly personal to say to us for this day and for our Christian life, that it is not only God's Word for the church, but also God's Word for us individually. We expose ourselves to the specific word until it addresses us personally. . . . We do not ask what this text has to say to other people. For the preacher this means that he will not ask how

he is going to preach or teach on this text, but what it is saying quite directly to him. It is true that to do this we must first have understood the content of the verse, but here we are not expounding it or preparing a sermon or conducting Bible study of any kind; we are rather waiting for God's Word to us' (LT, p. 82).

16. 'Letter to P. W. Herrenbrück' (Appendix).

17. The following page references are to CD.

18. *Letters*, 30th April 1944 (p. 91).

19. Cf. 'The Suffering of the Messengers', CD, pp. 190 ff. Closely related is the question of the 'boundaries' of the Confessing Church (cf. MW I, pp. 123 ff.): 'But here it is not the church which sets the boundaries, but the world which arbitrarily shuts itself out of the church, in so far as it does not hear and believe. The church cannot ascertain where her boundaries must run; rather, they will always be already fixed, insofar as they are drawn from outside . . .' (GS III, p. 126).

20. CD, pp. 84–90.

21. GS III, pp. 194 ff.

22. CD, pp. 35–47; the quotation is from p. 42.

Chapter 9: Revelation and the Confessing Church

1. The diary is in the possession of Eberhard Bethge.

2. 'Challenge', pp. 4–6; Godsey, pp. 80–3.

3. GS III, pp. 48–58.

4. A considerable amount of material relating the church to the world was pruned from Bonhoeffer's dissertation when it was presented for publication. This has since been restored in the English editions and in the third (1960) German edition. See 'Community and Society' and 'The Church and the Proletariat'.

5. GS III, p. 286.

6. *Ibid.*, p. 270.

7. Godsey, p. 108.

8. GS III, p. 279.

9. CF, pp. 85–9.

10. Godsey, pp. 109–11; cf. Bethge, 'Challenge', pp. 12–13.

11. GS III, pp. 286–91; GS II, pp. 44–53.

12. Godsey, p. 110. Müller (pp. 175–8) cites this and other illustrations as evidence of Bonhoeffer's basic conservatism at the beginning of Hitler's persecution.

13. Hamilton notes that *The Cost of Discipleship* 'represented a deliberate attack on certain elements in traditional Lutheran theology' (p. 447). Curiously, Bonhoeffer was attempting to overcome the dangers of the Lutheran faith/justification-works/righteousness, which made these notions useless for confronting the issues of the church struggle. By so doing, he unwittingly fell victim to a sectarian mis-

interpretation of the Lutheran doctrine of the 'two kingdoms'. He overcame this in the *Ethics* with his essay on 'Thinking in Terms of Two Spheres'. Cf. below, pp. 191 ff. and Hamilton, pp. 445–6.

14. Godsey, p. 111.
15. 'Challenge', p. 18.
16. *Ibid.*, p. 14.
17. GS III, p. 182.
18. *Ibid.*, p. 189.
19. GS IV, pp. 240, 241, 242.
20. CD, p. 224.
21. *Ibid.*, p. 224.
22. *Sichtbare Kirche im neuen Testament,* GS III, pp. 325 ff.; Cf. GS II, p. 327.
23. CD, p. 228.
24. GS III, p. 326
25. CD, p. 226.
26. CD, p. 228.
27. 'Challenge', p. 17. Bonhoeffer's phrase 'Christ existing as the church' *('Christus als Gemeinde existierend')* could be translated 'Christ existing as community'. This would lend itself to Müller's thesis that in the course of Bonhoeffer's theological development, *Gemeinschaft* (also 'community') is replaced by *Gesellschaft* (society). But Bonhoeffer almost certainly had in mind Luther's notion of the church as a 'community', as opposed to an 'institution'. Therefore the phrase translates more properly as 'Christ exists as the church'.
28. AB, p. 131.
29. GS III, p. 193.
30. GS III, p. 326.
31. Cf. 'Challenge', pp. 14, 24.
32. CD, p. 233–5.
33. LT, pp. 94 f., 97–9, 99–100, 100–3, 103–8.
34. CD, p. 240.
35. *Ibid.*, p. 223.
36. GS I, pp. 232–3.
37. MW I, pp. 123–44; GS II, pp. 217–63.
38. Godsey, pp. 111–15.
39. GS II, pp. 245–63.
40. Müller, p. 195. Müller's analysis of the controversy between Bonhoeffer and his fellow Confessing Churchmen is very useful. He tends, however, to read Bonhoeffer's obstinacy as conservative stubbornness and fails to see that Bonhoeffer was trapped by his ecclesiological theory. To be true to himself, Bonhoeffer had no alternative but to affirm this position. Cf. Müller, pp. 181–96.
41. Cf. above, pp. 66 ff.
42. Müller, p. 181.
43. Cf. above, pp. 81 ff.

44. CD, pp. 251, 252.
45. CD, pp. 245, 243, 253, 230, 241, Cf. 'Thoughts on Baptism', *Letters*, p. 160.
46. GS I, 327 ff.

Chapter 10: The Disappearance of the Boundaries

1. GS II, p. 420.
2. 'Challenge', p. 27.
3. GS II, *Zeittafel*. Dohnanyi established contacts with Sack, Oster, Canaris and Beck. Cf. A. Leber, *Das Gewissen Steht Auf*, Berlin, 1960, pp. 111–12.
4. *Das Gewissen Steht Auf*, p. 190.
5. GS I, p. 325.
6. *Ibid.*, pp. 355–71.
7. 'Challenge', p. 30.
8. Bonhoeffer's reading included works by Immermann, Fontane, Keller, Gabriel von Bülow-Humboldt, and Tertullian, Cyprian, and the Church Fathers. Titles he mentions are Jean Paul's *Siebenkäs*, Kant's *Anthropology*, Ulhorn's *Geschichte der christliche Liebestätigkeit*, Reuter's *Kein Hüsung*, *Der grüne Heinrich*, *Die Mikrobenjäger*, Riehl's *Geschichte aus alten Zeiten*, Ortega y Gasset's *Nature of Historical Crises* and *History as a System*, H. Pfeffer's *Das britische Empire und die U.S.A.*, Thomas à Kempis's *Imitation of Christ*, Kindt's biography of Klopstock, and Dostoievsky's *House of the Dead*. He seems to have had more than a passing interest in Stifter and Gotthelf's *Berner Geist*, Hartmann, Dilthey, Harnack's *Prussian Academy* and Delbrück's *History of the World*; and he especially mentioned C. F. von Weizsäcker's *Geschichte der Natur* and W. H. Otto's book on the Greek gods in connection with his theological meditations.
9. Cf. Letter of 25th March 1942 (Appendix).
10. *Ethics*, preface, p. xi; letter of 18th November 1943. *Letters*, p. 40.
11. 'Challenge', pp. 29–30.
12. *Ethics*, pp. 142–82.
13. *Ibid.*, p. 180.
14. *Ibid.*, p. 162.
15. *Ibid.*, p. 8.
16. See above, pp. 158 f.
17. In Karl Barth, *The Humanity of God, op. cit.*, pp. 46–7.
18. *Ethics*, pp. 191–2.
19. *Ibid*, p. 33.
20. *Ethics*, p. 82.
21. *Ibid.*, pp. 66, 67.
22. Cf. especially *ibid.*, pp. 17, 23, 24.
23. *Ibid.*, p. 21.

24. *Ibid.*, p. 67.
25. *Ibid.*, pp. 68–9. Italics mine.
26. *Ibid.*, pp. 71–2.
27. *Ibid.*, p. 87.
28. *Ibid.*, pp. 85–6. Cf. below, pp. 219 ff.
29. *Ibid.*, p. 99.
30. *Ibid.*, pp. 73–8, 252–7. Quotation is from p. 73. It should be noted that this is the closest Bonhoeffer came to a reconstruction of his ecclesiology which would correct the exclusiveness of his equation of revelation with the Confessing Church. It appears that in his new formulation, revelation is not the sole possession of the church but is rather 'shared' through the interactions of the mandates, of which the church is but one. But Bonhoeffer did not continue elaborating his view in this direction.
31. *Ibid.*, pp. 254, 257.
32. Cf. *Church Dogmatics* III/4, pp. 21 f.
33. *Ethics*, pp. 256–7.
34. GS III, pp. 494–5.
35. 30th April 1944. *Letters*, p. 92.
36. Godsey would certainly be numbered among those whom this omission has upset, as would von Hase (cf. MW I, p. 46). Müller has, of course, based his thesis upon the assumption that Bonhoeffer's ecclesiology *has become* the non-religious Christianity of the prison letters.
37. 8th June 1944. *Letters*, p. 110.

Chapter 11: The Theme of the Secular

1. See above, pp. 154 f., 159 ff.
2. See above, pp. 60 ff.
3. See above, pp. 174–6.
4. See above, pp. 128–9 and Chapter 7, note 20.
5. *Ethics*, pp. 25–45.
6. *Ibid.*, p. 26.
7. *Ibid.*, pp. 27, 29.
8. *Ibid.*, p. 32.
9. *Ibid.*, pp. 32, 33, 37. That this statement is *not* the positive appreciation of the coming of age of the world which instructs the prison letters will become clear in what follows.
10. *Ibid.*, pp. 38–9.
11. *Ibid.*, p. 38.
12. At this point, Bonhoeffer seems willing, but not happy, to settle for the more or less traditional Christian response to Western history. It has become godless; the church finds herself opposed to this godlessness and she must bring the Western world back to the consciousness of the true unity in Christ she has forsaken. Even so,

he is more ready to describe rather than to prescribe. The prison letters are not after all far from such statements as: 'The world has known Christ and turned its back on him, and it is to this world that the church must now prove that Christ is the living Lord' (*ibid.*, p. 44). Although Müller is correct in seeing a great difference between the evaluation of secularism in the *Ethics* and that in the prison letters, his interpretation of the significance of this change is too heavy a burden for the evidence to bear (cf. MW IV, pp. 55 ff.).

13. *Ibid.*, pp. 62–72. The quotation is taken from p. 62.

14. *Ibid.*, p. 64.

15. CD, pp. 35–47. The dangers of 'cheap grace' seem to lie in the background of 'Inheritance and Decay', while the exclusiveness of 'costly grace' occupies Bonhoeffer's mind in 'Thinking in Terms of Two Spheres'.

16. *Ethics*, p. 45, 65. There are echoes here of the solution offered in '*dein Reich komme!*' (cf. above, pp. 15 ff.) in which the relationship of the kingdom of the sword to the kingdom of God is that of miracle to order, both preserving and serving the Gospel. Only the miracle ('the saving act of God which intervenes from above, from beyond whatever is historically attainable or probable, and creates new life out of the void') is the ultimate solution. But one cannot therefore turn away from the historically operating force of order which 'God makes use of . . . in order to preserve the world from destruction' (*ibid.*, p. 44).

17. *Ibid.*, pp. 39–40.

18. *Ibid.*, pp. 67, 262–3: 'The cross of atonement is the setting free for life before God in the midst of the godless world; it is the setting free for life in genuine worldliness.' Here is an anticipation of the concern of the *Letters and Papers from Prison*.

19. Hamilton, p. 465.

20. *Ethics*, pp. 70–1.

21. 30th April 1944. *Letters*, p. 91.

22. *Ibid.*, p. 91.

23. Of course, Bonhoeffer will have to affirm this 'better secularism' in another way as his thought develops, just as he will have to affirm a properly understood 'religion' as the inevitable partner of Christian theology before he completes his prison letters.

24. 30th April 1944. *Letters*, p. 91.

25. 8th June 1944. *Ibid.*, pp. 106–7. Bonhoeffer sees the beginning of this process in the Renaissance, but has no desire to be more specific. It began 'with the beginning of the discovery of the laws by which the world lives'. Later, he speaks of it as 'one great development' which 'leads to the idea of the autonomy of the world'. The names Bonhoeffer thinks important in this development are worth recording: In *theology*, beginning with Lord Herbert of Cherbury (d. 1648),

reason became the proper instrument for religious knowledge. Developments in *ethics* by Montaigne (d. 1592) and Bodin (d. 1596) saw moral principles supplant the Ten Commandments. In *politics,* Machiavelli (d. 1527) described statecraft as responsive to 'reasons of state' rather than to morality. Grotius (d. 1645) applied the phrase *etsi deus non daretur* ('as though God were not given') within the area of *law.* Descartes (d. 1650), then Kant and Spinoza, Fichte, and Hegel adapted the same principle to *philosophy*; Feuerbach carried it into religion. Finally, Nicholas of Cusa (d. 1464) and Bruno (d. 1600) discovered for *natural science* the idea of the infinity of space.

26. *Ibid.,* p. 107.

27. 30th April 1944 (*ibid.,* p. 91): 'We are proceeding towards a time of no religion at all', '. . . if we reach the stage of being radically without religion – and I think this is more or less the case already . . .'; 8th June 1944 (*ibid.,* p. 107); 16th July, 1944 (*ibid.,* pp. 120–2).

28. 16th July 1944. *Ibid.,* pp. 121–2.

29. Hamilton, p. 451.

30. Hamilton, p. 452: 'The new thing in Bonhoeffer's thought is neither the open acknowledgement of the inevitability of secularization, nor the particular Christology, but the combination of these two factors.'

Chapter 12: 'Positivism of Revelation'

1. Cf. 'Letter to Superintendent P. W. Herrenbrück' (Appendix).

2. Regin Prenter, *Dietrich Bonhoeffer und Karl Barths Offenbarungspositivismus,* MW III, p. 12.

3. 30th April 1944. *Letters,* pp. 91–2.

4. 5th May 1944. *Ibid.,* pp. 94–5.

5. 8th June 1944. *Ibid.,* p. 109.

6. MW III, pp. 21, 13.

7. *Ibid.,* p. 15.

8. *Ibid.,* p. 15.

9. Cf. *Church Dogmatics,* 1/2, pp. 280–361. This section, called 'The Revelation of God as the Abolition of Religion', is summarized and analysed in Daniel Jenkins, *Beyond Religion,* London, 1962, pp. 26–33. Cf. also above, pp. 282 ff.

10. 3rd August 1944. *Letters,* p. 128.

11. 8th June 1944. *Ibid.,* p. 109.

12. Cf. above, pp. 186 ff and 112 ff.

13. C. West, *op. cit.,* pp. 180–1, 352.

14. SC, p. 227. References are to *The Epistle to the Romans,* Eng. tr. *op. cit.*

15. Barth, *Epistle to the Romans,* p. 418. While preserving the dialectical basis for his ecclesiology which kept him from the extreme theological position Bonhoeffer was forced to take during the church

struggle, Barth arrived at a more positive evaluation of the nature of the church in the *Church Dogmatics*:

'At the same time as we describe the hearing of God by men as the mark of the church we at the same time stress: her humanity, her worldliness, her profanity. . . . The church takes in her existence in her form and message part in the darkness of men, whom God has forsaken and who are and remain forsaken if they are not found by God. She takes even more part in this darkness, she is more profane than the usual things of the world, because just the man listening to God – and he only in truth! – knows about his profanity. It is the real church which is not strange to men, which overall and above all is the church of men, the church of a particular time, people, speech, culture. But from this point is her sympathy, indeed solidarity with the world at the deepest point and where it appears clearest in the world – her politics, science, art – made most visible: in the church, the boundaries of mankind are drawn and guarded; in the church no ideology is served; in the church man must see and understand himself soberly: in his mortality, in his emptiness, in his solitude, in his loneliness. The world was not always thankful to the church for ignoring her gods. There was as you know a time when the church was followed for this reason. The church would perhaps be followed again if she were able to make it clearer to the world that she differs from the world in so far as she must ignore her gods. But one may not overlook: just in this differentiation is she more worldly than the world, more humanistic than the theologians, nearer than both to the real sense of the human tragicomedy of man's attempt to help himself, only then can she be genuine when she keeps all pomp and pretension outside of her natural boundaries' (IV/2, pp. 556–7).

This thinking lies behind Barth's lack of interest in any theological concern for 'a world come of age'. The proper response of the church to any efforts of the world to ignore her, attack her, isolate her, or secularize her because of any alteration in the world's self-understanding is and will always be the more careful description of the limits of mankind and the distinctiveness of her own self-understanding. Only in this way can she be *for* the world.

16. SC, p. 87.

17. AB, pp. 80–1.

18. WA 23.157, quoted in AB, p. 81 n.

19. AB, pp. 90–1.

20. In *Antwort: Karl Barth zum siebzigsten Geburtstag*, Zürich, 1956; quoted in Torrance, *Karl Barth, an Introduction to his Early Theology 1910–1931*, London, 1962, p. 835 f.

21. For the early development of Barth's theology from the *Epistle to the*

Romans to the *Church Dogmatics*, cf. Torrance, *op. cit.* and von Balthasar, *op. cit.*

22. Cf. C. G. Berkouwer, *The Triumph of Grace in the Theology of Karl Barth*, Eerdmans, 1956.

23. Cf. Emil Brunner, 'The New Barth', *Scottish Journal of Theology*, June 1951.

24. *The Humanity of God*, p. 37. Following references in the text are to this work.

25. Cf. below text, pp. 231 ff. Here, we should at least note the widespread disagreement at this point among commentators. Is Bonhoeffer interested primarily in the *language* of the faith (as, for example, William Hordern insists in *Speaking of God*, New York, 1964, p. 11) or is the *content* of the Christian faith itself being called into question (the position argued well by Gerhard Sauter in 'Zur Herkunft und Absicht der Formel "Nicht-religiöse Interpretation biblischer Begriffe" bei Dietrich Bonhoeffer', *Evangelische Theologie*, June 1965, pp. 283–97).

26. *Humanity of God*, p. 53.

27. Compare Barth's treatment of 'non-religious language' in *The Humanity of God* with his patronizing view of demythologizing, expressed in the preface to *Church Dogmatics* III/4: 'there must always be room in theology for this' (p. xi).

28. *Church Dogmatics* IV/3, part I, pp. 18–33.

29. *Ibid.*, p. 19.

30. *Ibid.*, pp. 19–20.

31. *Ethics*, p. 31. Italics mine.

32. A widespread misunderstanding, according to J. A. T. Robinson, *Honest to God*, London, 1963, p. 104. Barth used the phrase in a criticism of Liberal theology several years before Bonhoeffer spoke of a 'world come of age'. No doubt he has since identified Bonhoeffer's position with the one he criticized at that time. In any case, the argument of *Church Dogmatics* I/2 has been simply restated in IV/3:

'Western humanity has come of age, or thinks it has. It can now dispense with its teacher – and as such official Christianity had in fact felt and believed. . . . In the reconsideration of itself and its possibilities imposed by the new situation, [the church] did not attain again to the weakness in which alone it can always be strong. Instead it inwardly affirmed the new situation, as it had previously affirmed the old. That is to say, it accepted modern man with his energetic attitude to himself, asking how best Christianity could be commended to that man. It took up the role allotted to it, and was at pains to make itself indispensable in it, i.e. by pointing out or demonstrating that if there is a truth in the Christian religion which can profitably be heard and believed, especially in the modern age, it consists in this, that properly understood, the doctrine of Jesus Christ and the way of life which corresponds to it, has the secret power of giving to man the inward capacity to seek and attain the aims and purposes which he has independently chosen' (*Church Dogmatics* 1/2, p. 336).

33. *Ethics*, p. 32.

34. Cf. above, note 32; *Church Dogmatics* 1/1, pp. 166–7, 1/2, pp. 333–7.

35. As recently as his essay on 'The Humanity of God', Barth was reasserting his familiar position concerning the question of reopening conversation with Liberal theologians: 'Let one read the doctrine of Troeltsch! . . . the dogmatics of Seeberg! If all that wasn't a blind alley!' (p. 41). Barth simply cannot take the world with its history and secularity seriously, because the electing and justifying grace of God has already made the subject and all conversation about it unnecessary and uninteresting.

36. *Church Dogmatics* IV/2, p. 66.

37. *Ibid.*, pp. 66, 76.

38. *Ibid.*, pp. 81–2.

39. 'Challenge', p. 9. Bonhoeffer maintained this in spite of his acceptance of the theological direction Barth indicated in the nineteen twenties. In 1936, in a letter cited by Bethge (*ibid.*, p. 9), Bonhoeffer reiterated his fundamental belief in the correctness of this traditional Lutheran view which, as is well known, Barth has always regarded with suspicion.

40. 'Challenge', p. 10.

Chapter 13: Letting the World Be the World

1. Cf. above, pp. 50–1, 54–5.

2. Friedrich Gogarten, *Demythologizing and History*, Eng. tr. London, 1955, p. 32.

3. 8th June 1944. *Letters*, p. 108.

4. Troeltsch, *Protestantism and Progress*, p. 10.

5. Troeltsch, *Social Teachings* I, p. 42.

6. *Protestantism and Progress*, pp. 47–8.

7. *Ibid.*, p. 50. Italics mine.

8. *Ibid.*, p. 37.

9. *Ibid.*, p. 203.

10. *Social Teaching* I, p. 32.

11. *Ibid.*, II, p. 1006.

12. Troeltsch, *Der Historismus und seine Probleme*, p. 109, quoted in Gogarten, *op. cit.*, p. 32.

13. Dilthey, *Gesammelte Schriften* II, quoted in Gogarten, *op. cit.*, pp. 31–2. Dilthey was quite explicit as to the basis of the religious life in 'imperishable' metaphysics. In a characteristic statement, he wrote:

'This metaphysical consciousness is imperishable; as the plants prepare the roots for the next spring in the depths of the earth even as they bloom and fade, this metaphysical consciousness is in the depths of mankind. . . . It is the final business of all transcendence philosophy to approach this' (*Gesammelte Schriften* II, Leipzig and Berlin, 1914, p. 496).

14. Gogarten, *op. cit.*, p. 19.

15. *Ibid.*, p. 11. This is the central theme of what is to date the clearest and most persuasive presentation of Gogarten's position: Gogarten, *Verhängnis und Hoffnung der Neuzeit*, 2. Aufl., Stuttgart, 1958.

16. *Demythologizing and History*, pp. 21–4.

17. *Verhängnis und Hoffnung*, p. 12.

18. R. G. Smith and J. Corbett, 'The Disappearing God', in *The Listener*, 21st January 1960, p. 127. A good definition of the 'old gods' from which the world is freed by the incarnation – bringing to mind Paul's letter to the Galatians concerning the 'weak and beggarly elemental spirits' (4. 9) banished by Christ – might be that of the humanist Julian Huxley: 'Gods are creations of man, personalized representations of the forces of destiny, with their unity projected into them by human thought and imagination' (*Religion Without Revelation*, New York, 1957, p. 49).

19. *Verhängnis und Hoffnung*, p. 8.

20. Cf. *ibid.*, pp. 12 ff.

21. See above, pp. 151 ff.

22. It should be remembered that Bultmann's programme was not as clearly defined during the war (when Bonhoeffer learned of it) as it is at the present day. Certainly Bonhoeffer misunderstood Bultmann's intention, and probably this misunderstanding had its roots in a very common misconception. Gogarten writes:

'It is widely supposed – and indeed on both sides – that the object of the discussion is to achieve an understanding of Christian belief which is compatible with the thought of our day, that the controversy arose in the name of modern thought and is being carried on with modern thought in view. It is not indeed suggested that its purpose is to relieve modern thought of the necessity of making a difficult decision, without which there can be no Christian faith, or to make belief "easy" for it, but rather that it aims at enabling modern thought simply to know once again what Christian faith involves. . . . It is concerned with very much more than that. It is the Christian faith itself which demands its due, and it is for its sake that the controversy must be pursued' (*Demythologizing and History*, p. 10).

23. MW I, p. 47. Cf. Hamilton, p. 452, cited above in Chapter 11 note 30.

Chapter 14: Christ, the Worldly Man

1. Cf. above, pp. 210 ff.
2. 21st November 1943. *Letters*, p. 44; 29th–30th January 1944. *Ibid.*, p. 67; Advent II, 1943; 21st November 1943. *Ibid.*, pp. 50, 44.
3. Advent II, 1943. *Ibid.*, p. 50.
4. Hamilton, p. 447. Cf. above, Chapter 9, note 13.
5. 18th December 1943. *Letters*, pp. 56–7.
6. 20th May 1944. *Ibid.*, pp. 99–100.
7. 23rd January 1944. *Ibid.*, p. 63; 23rd January 1944. *Ibid.*, p. 64.
8. 30th April 1944. *Ibid.*, p. 93.
9. R. G. Smith, 'A Theological Perspective of the Secular', *The Christian Scholar*, March 1960, p. 21. Elsewhere, Smith has written:
    'God is not to be met primarily in some assertion about him. God is not to be found in an abstract belief about his omnipotence, or omniscience, or even in the idea of love. God is not any idea we have of him. He is not any idea. To attempt to elevate some idea to the place of God is to make an idol and worship that instead of God. When we set up some abstraction in place of God we are worshipping nothing more than an extension of the world' (*The New Man*, London, 1956, p. 98). Cf. J. A. T. Robinson, *Honest to God*, London, 1963, pp. 125–6.
10. 'Outline for a Book', *Letters*, p. 165.
11. Smith, *The New Man*, pp. 98–9.
12. 16th July 1944. *Letters*, pp. 121–2.
13. 21st August 1944. *Ibid.*, p. 130. Cf. Hammelsbeck: 'Nietzsche's saying is valid in a special way: "God is dead"; but in the Christian church the faith is nevertheless valid: Christ lives' (MW I, p. 47).
14. 21st August 1944. *Letters*, p. 130.
15. 8th June 1944. *Ibid.*, p. 130.
16. 5th May 1944. *Ibid.*, pp. 94–5.
17. Hamilton, pp. 444 ff.
18. 27th June 1944; 30th June 1944. *Letters*, pp. 112, 115.
19. Müller also analyses the *theologia crucis* of *The Cost of Discipleship* as one which, strangely, seems far more often a *theologia gloriae* because of the use Bonhoeffer made of it. Cf. MW IV, pp. 60–1.
20. 27th June 1944. *Ibid.*, p. 112; 25th May 1944. *Ibid.*, p. 104.
21. 21st July 1944. *Ibid.*, p. 124; 18th July 1944. *Ibid.*, p. 123; 21st August 1944. *Ibid*, p. 130.
22. 16th July 1944; 'Christians and Unbelievers'. *Ibid.*, pp. 122, 174.
23. GS III, p. 233.
24. Müller, p. 375.
25. 'Challenge', p. 34.
26. 21st July 1944. *Letters*, p. 125.
27. Cf. his 'Letter to P. W. Herrenbrück', MW I, pp. 121–2.

28. 28th July 1944. *Letters*, p. 127. Cf. Müller, pp. 384–7.
29. Müller, pp. 386–7, and above, note 19.
30. 'Outline for a Book'. *Letters*, pp. 164–5.
31. Cf. above, pp. 235 ff.
32. 21st August 1944. *Letters*, p. 130.
33. 'Christians and Unbelievers', *Letters*, p. 174.

Chapter 15: Religionless Christianity

  1. Daniel Jenkins, *Beyond Religion*, London, 1962, p. 9.
  2. Cf. above, pp. 208 ff., 213 f.
  3. 30th April 1944. *Letters*, pp. 91–2.
  4. Cf. above, Chapters 4 and 5.
  5. Cf. above, pp. 59 ff., 62 ff.
  6. Seeberg, *Chr. Dogmatik* I, p. 104. Quoted in AB, p. 46.
  7. GS III, p. 96; cf. pp. 91–2.
  8. GS III, p. 76.
  9. So Paul van Buren, *The Secular Meaning of the Gospel*, New York, 1963, p. 2. Van Buren's work, though it is in no way a study of Bonhoeffer, is a response to Bonhoeffer's challenge that theology 'make sense' to man in a world come of age. Van Buren sees the problem mainly as a *linguistic* one: *secularism* is a word which can be understood by examining the developments of British philosophy in linguistic analysis. His choice of conversational partners unfortunately places his interesting book outside of the considerations of this study.
 10. London, 1962, pp. 26–33.
 11. *Ibid.*, p. 29.
 12. *Ibid.*, p. 29.
 13. *Ibid.*, p. 33.
 14. 'Challenge', pp. 33–4; Jenkins, *op. cit.*, p. 35.
 15. Jenkins, *op. cit.*, p. 38.
 16. 30th April 1944. *Letters*, p. 91.
 17. MW I, p. 77.
 18. Of the five theologians Bonhoeffer mentioned in connection with his new thoughts in the prison letters, we have already dealt or will yet examine at length his relationship to Barth, Bultmann, and Tillich. We have not the space to develop a by no means passing conversation between Bonhoeffer and Paul Althaus. Althaus, like Gogarten, sided with the German Christians during the church struggle. His notion of the universality of the human religious situation as 'inescapable godlessness in inescapable relationship to God' (cf. *Die Letze Dinge*, 4th ed., 1933, p. 183) is the kind of eschatological-apologetic statement Bonhoeffer opposed as a 'last question', an improper one in the face of the coming of age of the world. Concerning Karl Heim, see the note immediately following.

19. Karl Heim's *Glauben und Denken*, which Bonhoeffer reviewed in 1932 (cf. GS III, pp. 138–59), attempted to mediate between theology and philosophy by means of a special understanding of the category of 'dimension' and a strong eschatology in the form of 'ultimate questions'. Bonhoeffer, following the arguments of Barth and Grisebach, termed Heim's theology 'religious titanism', believing that few men encounter such questions and that the Bible has more to say to those men who do not (GS III, pp. 158–9). Heim responded to other points of Bonhoeffer's argument in the third edition of his work (cf. *God Transcendent*, Eng. tr. of the above, London, 1935, pp. 235–9).

As with all of the theologians mentioned in his prison letters, Bonhoeffer learned much from Heim. In particular, a study of the relationship between 'this-worldly transcendence' and Heim's anti-metaphysical attempt to establish what he called a 'world-space' as the space of revelation, defined largely in terms of 'encounter' theology and heavily indebted to Buber's thinking, would prove interesting. But Heim also lent his support to the German Christians (so much so that he deleted all references to Buber, the Jewish philosopher, in the second and subsequent editions of *Glauben und Denken*), and Bonhoeffer turned away from still another conversation which might have proven fruitful.

20. D. Jenkins uses Tillich's notion of the 'God above God' to explain Bonhoeffer's attack upon religion, describing both as attempts to recover the principle of self-protest which must underly all protestant theology. J. A. T. Robinson has learned much from Tillich's use of such phrases as 'Ground of Being' and 'Depth of Existence' as substitutes for a concept of God. But cf. below, note 33.

21. AB, p. 73.

22. Berlin, 1929. The English translations of chapters 1, 2, 3, 7 and 8 appear, respectively, as XIII, XIV, V, VII and VIII in *The Protestant Era*, Chicago, 1948. Chapters 5 and 6 appeared in English as *The Interpretation of History*, New York and London, 1963.

23. *Ibid.*, p. 75.

24. Cf. *ibid.*, notes on pp. 87, 161.

25. GS III, pp. 71–2.

26. 8th June 1944. *Letters*, pp. 108–9.

27. 30th April 1944. *Ibid.*, p. 93.

28. 27th June 1944. *Ibid.*, p. 112. Cf. 25th May 1944. *Ibid.*, p. 104.

29. 8th June 1944. *Ibid.*, p. 107.

30. 30th June 1944. *Ibid.*, pp. 114–15.

31. 8th June 1944. *Ibid.*, p. 108.

32. Tillich, *Systematic Theology* II, Chicago, 1957, p. 9.

33. *Ibid.*, p. 10. Cf. Tillich's statement in his *Courage to Be* (Yale, 1952, p. 40): 'Man as man in every civilization is anxiously aware of the threat of non-being and needs the courage to affirm himself in spite

of it.' Only recently has there been a reaction against the use of Tillich's theology in order to fill the gaps in Bonhoeffer's prison meditations. F. G. Downing questions J. A. T. Robinson's interest in Tillich as the answer to Bonhoeffer's questions, believing that Tillich's apologetic is based upon the kind of religious *a priori* Bonhoeffer deplored (cf. *The Honest to God Debate*, London and Philadelphia, 1963, pp. 126–33). Another expression of scepticism has come from Grover Foley, a student of Barth, who asks whether an interpretation of God as 'the Ground of our Being' can possibly be at the same time a denial of 'religion' in Bonhoeffer's sense. He concludes: 'The fact is, Tillich is at heart a confessed religious *Philosoph*, a philosopher of religion *par excellence*, the very antithesis of one supporting Bonhoeffer's attack on religion' ('Religionless Religion', in *The Christian Century*, 11th September 1963, p. 1097).

This discussion is related closely to the argument of the present study which begins at this point. Perhaps the most useful bridge is a recent article which seriously questions the conviction of existentialist theologians that the experience of anxiety suggests, however distorted, a 'desire for God'. Kenneth Hamilton views the Christian doctrine of sin as more radical than the concept of anxiety which has sought to replace it; the latter seems to assume that 'man the sinner genuinely longs for God and actively struggles to attain to righteousness' ('Man: Anxious or Guilty? A Second Look at Kierkegaard's Concept of Dread,' *The Christian Scholar*, January 1964). Furthermore, Hamilton questions the widespread assumption that Paul, at least in the Letter to the Romans, is attempting to show that 'we all seek after God, desiring to be with him. The universal fact of religion proclaims as much, showing that none of us reaches out in love towards the Source of all the good' (*ibid.*, p. 294). Hamilton directs his counter-arguments against Tillich, but with the touchstone in Paul's doctrine of the Law, this same argument is useful for our analysis of Bonhoeffer's relationship to Bultmann's later theology. Cf. above, pp. 301 ff.

34. Tillich, *op. cit.*, p. 10.

35. W. Hamilton, 'A Theology for a World Come of Age', p. 458.

36. William Hamilton mentions the strangely attractive 'uncertainty' of Bonhoeffer's approach. R. G. Smith, accepting this posture *vis-à-vis* the secularist as a proper one, speaks of a 'defenselessness' which cannot but seem 'rather naïve and primitive and unsystematic to the theologians and rather arbitrary, and naïve as well, to the secularists' ('A Theological Perspective of the Secular', p. 11).

37. 30th April 1944. *Letters*, p. 91; 8th June 1944. *Ibid.*, p. 10.

38. *Theology of the New Testament* 1, New York, 1951, p. 269. Bultmann states that 'the ultimate purpose of the Law is to lead men to death and thereby to let God appear as God ...' (*ibid.*, p. 267). Bultmann

has recently reviewed and rejected contemporary theological interest in 'the death of God' and the disappearance of the religious *a priori* which began with the taking seriously of Bonhoeffer's questions in the prison letters. Cf. 'Der Gottesgedanke und der moderne Mensch', *Zeitschrift für Theologie und Kirche*, December 1963, pp. 335–48.

39. 'The "Non-Religious Interpretation of Biblical Concepts",' in G. Ebeling, *Word and Faith*, London and Philadelphia, 1963, pp. 98–161.

40. Krister Stendahl, 'The Apostle Paul and the Introspective Conscience of the West', *Harvard Theological Review*, July 1963, pp. 199–215.

41. Stendahl's argument, however, depends upon an understanding of the Law which differs somewhat from that of Ebeling and Bultmann. Stendahl claims that the Law became a theological problem for Paul simply because the Messiah had come, making the Law (which he understood always as the *Jewish* Law) invalid. Any suggestion in Paul's writings that the Law is universally apprehended and has the position of a 'schoolmaster' (a mistranslation, Stendahl points out) is incidental and secondary to the real problem. Paul is simply wrestling with the question of what possible meaning the Law can have for Jew and Gentile following the appearance of the One who supersedes and invalidates it.

42. Ebeling, *op. cit.* p. 142.

43. *Ibid.*, p. 147.

44. *Ibid.*, p. 147.

45. *Ibid.*, p. 147.

46. *Op. cit.*, p. 199.

47. Cf. above, note 41.

48. *Ibid.*, pp. 200–1. On the contrary, Stendahl argues, Paul's conscience was 'robust' and he gloried in his achievements as a righteous Jew (cf. Philip. 3).

49. *Ibid.*, p. 200.

50. *Ibid.*, p. 206; p. 207.

51. *Ibid.*, p. 215.

52. *Ibid.*, pp. 208–9. Cf. Bultmann, 'The Problem of Hermeneutics', in *Essays Philosophical and Theological*. London, 1955, pp. 234–61.

53. *Theology of the New Testament, op. cit.*, p. 269.

54. Cf. especially G. Harbsmeier, *Die nicht-religiöse Interpretation biblischer Begriffe bei Bonhoeffer und die Entmythologizierung*, MW II, pp. 74–91. In support of our argument, Harbsmeier states:

'It can very well be that [Bonhoeffer's] intention is indeed wholly at one with Bultmann's. Some utterances seem to me to strengthen this impression. But intention is one thing and carrying it through to a successful outcome is another. In any event, I understand Bonhoeffer's criticism of Bultmann in terms of the question of success. Bultmann doesn't want reduction and subtraction, but interpretation. He wants to conquer Liberal theology at this point. Is he successful in this? Bonhoeffer thinks: No. For Bultmann, as I think Bonhoeffer sees it, fundamentally misunderstands the *use* of mythological diction in the Bible' (*ibid.*, p. 82). Cf. also R. Prenter, MW III, p. 17 and our treatment of Bonhoeffer's relationship to the problem of hermeneutics (above, pp. 327 ff.).

55. 8th June 1944. *Letters*, p. 110.

56. *Ethische und mystische Religion in Urchristentum,* in *Die christliche Welt,* 1920, p. 740 (cited in J. M. Robinson and J. R. Cobb, eds., *The New Hermeneutic,* New York, 1964, pp. 29–30). Barth attempted to answer the charge in his preface to the second edition of the *Epistle to the Romans (op. cit.,* pp. 16–18).

57. *Karl Barths Römerbrief in zweiter Auflage,* in *Die christliche Welt,* 1922, p. 320 (cited in Robinson and Cobb, *op. cit.,* p. 30).

58. *Kerygma und Mythos* I, p. 26, cited in Ebeling, *op. cit.,* pp. 139–40.

59. Cf. the appendix to this study, where two letters from Bonhoeffer's hand give an indication of how he received and responded to Bultmann's essay.

60. 5th May 1944. *Letters*, p. 94; 8th June 1944. *Ibid.,* p. 110.

61. *Honest to God,* pp. 266, 7. Cf. R. Prenter, MW III, p. 17.

Chapter 16: Sharing in the Sufferings of God

1. Max Weber, *The Protestant Ethics and The Spirit of Capitalism,* New York, 1958, p. 154.

2. *Ibid. op. cit.,* p. 181. Weber describes this revolution as follows: 'Christian asceticism, at first fleeing from the world into solitude, had already ruled the world which it had renounced from the monastery and through the Church. But it had, on the whole, left the naturally spontaneous character of daily life in the world untouched. Now it strode into the market-place of life, slammed the door of the monastery behind it, and undertook to penetrate just that daily routine of life with its methodicalness, to fashion it into a life in the world, but neither of nor for this world' (*ibid.,* p. 154).

3. Cf. above, Chapter 8.

4. Smith, *The New Man, op. cit.,* p. 104.

5. 30th April 1944, 5th May 1944. *Letters*, pp. 92; 95.

6. MW I, pp. 55–7.

7. MW III, pp. 18–19.

8. 'Challenge', p. 35.

9. 'Thoughts on Baptism'. *Letters*, pp. 159–60.

10. Cf. CD. p. 45. On the historical foundation for Bonhoeffer's notion, cf. G. Meuss, MW III, pp. 70–1; Müller, p. 393; Hammelsbeck, MW I, p. 55; Bethge, MW I, p. 23.

Bonhoeffer's judgement of monasticism as a justification, in the last analysis, for the increased secularization of the church (CD, pp. 38-9) and his description of Luther's decision to leave the monastery as 'the worst blow the world had suffered since the days of early Christianity' (CD, p. 40; cf. *Ethics*, pp. 223-4) warn us against equating the 'secret discipline' with some sort of 'return to the cloister'. In this respect, Hammelsbeck's remark that 'the secret discipline' could serve as a subtitle for the work *Life Together* (cf. MW I, p. 56) is dangerously misleading, although not simply incorrect.

11. Cf. GS I, pp. 38-40.
12. 'Challenge', p. 24.
13. MW I, pp. 56-7.
14. R. Fuller, 'Liturgy and Devotion', in Marty, p. 179.
15. GS I, pp. 115; 133-9; 142, 143, 147.
16. Cf. letters of 30th April 1944 (*Letters*, p. 92); 8th June 1944 (pp. 109-10): 3rd August 1944 (p. 128).
17. 'Outline for a Book'. *Ibid.*, p. 166.
18. 18th July 1944. *Ibid.*, p. 125.
19. *Word and Faith*, London, 1962, p. 126. Hermeneutics embraces the whole theological enterprise as a movement of language: the confrontation, apprehension, preaching, hearing, and serving of the Word.
20. GS I, pp. 174, 178, 116 f.; *Ethics*, p. 204.
21. *Ethics*, pp. 232, 204 ff., 271, 283 ff.
22. *Ibid.*, p. 233. Bonhoeffer criticized Brunner for overlooking the question of whether and when ethic should become a topic of conversation at all. Cf. GS I, pp. 31, 33-5, 40.
23. *Ethics*, p. 234.
24. *Ibid.*, p. 84.
25. 30th April 1944. *Letters*, p. 92.
26. *Op. cit.*, pp. 112 ff.
27. *Soundings*, Cambridge, 1962, p. 247.
28. 'Retrospect upon the Effect of the Book in Post-War Theology', in *Christus und die Zeit*, Zurich, 1962, pp. 25 f. (tr. James M. Robinson). Bultmann, at least, is not unaware of these dangers, and has from time to time called for 'openness' rather than 'presuppositions' (cf. *Theology of the New Testament* II, New York, 1955, p. 241; cited in Robinson and Cobb, *op. cit.*, pp. 40-1).
29. *Zum Thema der urchristlichen Apokalyptik*, in *Zeitschrift für Theologie und Kirche*, February, 1963, pp. 259 n. (cited in Robinson and Cobb, *op. cit.*, pp. 42-3).
30. Ellul, *The Presence of the Kingdom*, Eng. tr. London, 1951, p. 45.
31. 20th May 1944. *Letters*, p. 129.
32. Smith, *The New Man*, pp. 104-5.

33. *Ibid.*, p. 106.
34. *Ibid.*, p. 107.
35. CD, p. 166.
36. *Müller*, pp. 395–6.
37. 'Vivendo, immo moriendo et damnando fit theologus, non intelligendo, legendo aut speculando' (WA 5.163.28).
38. Hamilton, p. 485. We must, however, remind ourselves that Bethge was forced to destroy the letters which passed during the following months, so that we have no way of knowing whether Bonhoeffer had finally arrived at a satisfactory solution.
39. *Letters*, pp. 122–5; cf. above, pp. 266–7.
40. Cf. 'The Bonhoeffer Revival', *The New York Review*, 26th August 1965, pp. 14 ff.
41. 28th July 1944. *Letters*, p. 127.
42. *The Meaning of Revelation*, Macmillan Paperbacks ed., New York, 1960, p. 122.
43. 21st August 1944. *Letters*, p. 130.
44. Cf. above, p. 197, annotated 31. It is important to recall that the *Cost of Discipleship* closed by referring to discipleship as an imitation of Christ (cf. CD, pp. 269–75) and the *Ethics* briefly sketched such a development (especially *Ethics*, p. 99).
45. Jenkins, *op. cit.*, pp. 81; 22.
46. Ellul, *op. cit.*, p. 122; 'Thoughts on the Baptism of D.W.R.' *Letters*, pp. 138, 136.
47. *Letters*, pp. 138–9.
48. Ellul, *op cit.*, p. 94.
49. *Ibid.*, pp. 12–13.
50. *Ibid.*, p. 60.
51. Alec Vidler's title for his excellent essay which owes its inspiration to Bonhoeffer. Cf. *Essays in Liberality*, London, 1957, pp. 95–112.
52. *Letters*, p. 157.
53. 'After Ten Years'. *Letters*, p. 144.
54. 'Outline for a Book.' *Ibid.*, p. 165.
55. 23rd February 1944, 20th February 1944. *Letters*, pp. 76, 38.

Abbreviations

I. Bonhoeffer's Works:

AB   *Act and Being*, London, 1962 and New York, 1961 (tr. of *Akt und Sein*, Gütersloh, 1931 and Munich, 1956).

CD   *The Cost of Discipleship*, 2nd ed., New York and London, 1959 (tr. of *Nachfolge*, Munich, 1937).

CF   *Creation and Fall*: A Theological Interpretation of Genesis 1–3, New York and London, 1959 (tr. of *Schöpfung und Fall*, Munich, 1937).

Ethics   *Ethics*, New York and London, 1955 (tr. of *Ethik*, Munich, 1949).

GS   *Gesammelte Schriften*, Vols. i–v, Munich, 1958–66.

Letters   *Letters and Papers from Prison*, Fontana ed., London, 1959 (tr. of *Widerstand und Ergebung*, Briefe und Aufzeichnungen aus der Haft, Munich, 1951. Translations have been altered by the author.) As there are several editions of this work in English (including one American edition entitled *Prisoner for God*), each letter is referred to by its date.

LT   *Life Together*, New York, 1954 and London, 1955 (tr. of *Gemeinsames Leben*, Munich, 1939).

SC   *The Communion of Saints*, New York and London (under the title *Sanctorum Communio*), 1963 (tr. of *Sanctorum Communio*: Eine dogmatische Untersuchung zur Soziologie der Kirche, Berlin, 1930; 3. Aufl., Munich, 1960).

II. Secondary Sources:

'Challenge'   Eberhard Bethge, 'The Challenge of Dietrich Bonhoeffer's Life and Theology', *The Chicago Theological Seminary Register*, February 1961.

Godsey   John D. Godsey, *The Theology of Dietrich Bonhoeffer*, New York and London, 1960.

Hamilton   William Hamilton, 'A Secular Theology for a World Come of Age', in *Theology Today*, January 1962, pp. 435–59.

Marty   Martin Marty, ed., *The Place of Bonhoeffer*, Problems and Possibilities in his Thought, New York, 1962.

Müller   Hanfreid Müller, *Von der Kirche zur Welt*, Leipzig, 1961.

MW (I, II, III, IV)   *Die mündige Welt*, Vols. i–iv, Munich, 1959–63.

WA   Weimarer Ausgabe.

Index of Names

(More important references are in italics)

INDEX OF NAMES

Subject Index